Studies in Social Policy

'Studies in Social Policy' is an important series of textbooks intended for students of social administration and social welfare at all levels. The books are directly related to the needs of undergraduate and postgraduate students in universities, polytechnics and similar institutions as well as vocational students preparing for careers in a variety of social and other public services. The series includes the following topics:

the roles of different public and private institutions such as social services departments and building societies in meeting social needs;

introductory guides to new technical and theoretical developments relevant to the analysis of social policy such as political theory and the newly emerging specialism of the economics of social care;

contemporary social policy issues such as the use of charges in the delivery of social welfare or the problem of determining priorities in the health and personal social services.

D1337605

Studies in Social Policy

Editor: Ken Judge

Published

The Building Societies
Martin Boddy

Access to Welfare
Peggy Foster

Health Policy in Britain
Christopher Ham

Policy-making in the National Health Service
Christopher Ham

Pricing the Social Services
Ken Judge (ed.)

The Economics of Social Care
Martin Knapp

Choices for Health Care
Gavin H. Mooney, Elizabeth M. Russell and Roy D. Weir

Power, Authority and Responsibility in Social Services
Malcolm Payne

Political Theory and Social Policy
Albert Weale

Forthcoming

Introducing Social Policy
Ken Judge and Roger Hampson

The Economics of Poverty
Alan Maynard

Health Care in the European Community
Alan Maynard and Anne Ludbrook

Power, Rationality and Social Planning
Adrian Webb and Gerald Wistow

The Economics of Social Care

Martin Knapp

MACMILLAN

First published 1984 by
Higher and Further Education Division
MACMILLAN PUBLISHERS LTD
Houndmills, Basingstoke, Hampshire RG21 2XS
and London
Companies and representatives
throughout the world

Printed in Hong Kong

British Library Cataloguing in Publication Data

Knapp, Martin
The economics of social care.—(Studies in
social policy)
1. Public welfare—Great Britain—Finance
2. Public welfare—Economic aspects—
Great Britain
I. Title   II. Series
338.4′7361941   HV245

ISBN 0-333-28938-2
ISBN 0-333-28939-0 Pbk

To Jane and Daniel

Contents

Preface

This book builds on research and teaching undertaken since I came to the University of Kent at Canterbury in 1975. The book is not a research manual or research report, although I hope it will be of value to researchers. It is written for anyone with an interest in social care services, or anyone who has to make a decision about the allocation of care resources at whatever level: from professional social workers to their directors and elected committees, from the administrators of small voluntary organisations to the Secretary of State. The book presupposes neither a knowledge of economics nor a familiarity with social care.

Since 1979 I have held a joint appointment as Research Fellow in the Personal Social Services Research Unit and Lecturer in Economics. This has had its drawbacks, but in preparing and writing *The Economics of Social Care* this intellectual schizophrenia has been unusually beneficial. It has given me space to develop ideas and perspectives and to test them in applied research, and subsequently to examine alternative modes of presentation whilst teaching. It has also allowed me to learn from two distinct groups of colleagues, and particularly to exploit both groups when seeking advice, assistance and comments on draft chapters. I am grateful to my colleagues on the Economics Board – especially Colin Cannon, Jim Hughes, David Metcalf and William Smith – for their comments and constructive suggestions on some of my earlier draft chapters. Peter Taylor-Gooby and Clare Ungerson, neither economists nor members of the PSSRU, also kindly gave up their time to comment on draft chapters. Within the PSSRU I have been especially fortunate to be able to call on the expertise and judgement of a number of colleagues and friends. Andrew Bebbington, David Challis, Ewan Ferlie and Robert Walker each made a number of extremely helpful points. Indeed, Ewan even drafted a couple of paragraphs on innovations lest I miss his point. I must also thank Robin Darton, Ken Judge, Spyros Missiakoulis and

Jillian Smith for allowing me to include details of jointly executed research in Chapters 9 and 10. Ken Wright, of the University of York, made a number of recommendations which greatly improved the earlier chapters.

My greatest debts of professional gratitude, however, are to Bleddyn Davies and Ken Judge. Bleddyn's unique style of leadership has benefitted me considerably. His desire always to lead from the front, his encyclopaedic knowledge, and even his back-handed compliments, have forced me to improve successive drafts of the book, if only in a futile attempt to catch up with him or to prove him wrong! His detailed comments at the penultimate stage ensured that some glaring inanities were removed. Ken's contribution has been all that an editor's should be, and more besides. Since signing the contract more years ago than I care to remember, he has cajoled and bullied me into writing and rewriting. Without his encouragement the book would not have been completed. His appreciation of the finer points of social care policy-making and research is surpassed, I suspect, only by his partiality for a couple of pints at the end of an evening's work. I have gained a great deal from both attributes. I must also express my appreciation to Bleddyn, Ken and David Challis for letting me see draft versions of their own books. I have been lucky to have the services of two excellent typists – Carole Phillips and Su Bellingham. Carole's typing of the very earliest of draft chapters helped secure the contract. Su's single-handed translation of manuscript into typescript in record time with a minimum of mistakes ensured that the latter was delivered to the publishers with rather less delay than would otherwise have been the case. Even when a whole chapter disappeared from the word processor, Su kept her smile and her efficiency. Steve Kennedy at Macmillan showed great patience and was even prepared to believe my claims that the manuscript would improve with age. Jack Barnes, for a number of years the PSSRU's liaison officer at the Department of Health and Social Security, provided encouragement – both official and personal – although the views expressed in this book are not necessarily those of the Department. This book is dedicated to my wife Jane, without whose support and encouragement it would certainly not have been completed, and to my son Daniel, without whose interventions it would have been completed much sooner.

Canterbury, Kent   MARTIN KNAPP
December 1983

List of Figures and Tables

Figures

Tables

1

Introduction: Social Care and the Economist

Economists, 'after taking strong oaths of ethical neutrality, perform as missionaries in the social welfare field and often give the impression of possessively owning a hot line to God'. (Titmuss, 1970, p. 199)

Introduction

This is not a book inspired by missionary zeal, nor a collection of celestial truths passed down heavenly hot lines. Nor is it one which rides roughshod over humanitarian concerns, nor one which places the minimisation of cost above the meeting of need. It is certainly not about monetarism or monopoly capitalism, unemployment or inflation, crises in the balance of payments or squeezes on the public sector borrowing requirement – or at least not directly. It is a book about economic analysis and its application in the area of social care. It is about scarcity, choice, resource allocation, effectiveness, efficiency and equity. It seeks definitions for these concepts and applications of them in the analysis of policy.

Social care provision ranges from residential provision, day care and domiciliary support to the variety of activities known collectively as fieldwork services and the even greater variety of 'informal' care activities. The principal focus of much of the book is upon *British* social care services although many of the arguments have been informed by experiences and research in other countries. Whilst the arrangement of social care can be very different in other countries, they do share one common characteristic: a dearth of economic research on the organisation, allocation and efficiency of the services they provide. If this book does nothing else, I hope that it will generate some appreciation of the economic research that has already been done. Naturally, I hope this book does rather more, and particularly that it will stimulate a more critical appraisal of decision-making in social care policy and practice.

In this introductory chapter I have two aims. I shall first describe what is meant by 'social care', although I am not keen to enter into discussions of semantics or social etymology. It is in the nature of current statistical collections that we know far more about products and activities which have an associated price or which are produced or provided by the public sector than we do about the range of activities and services provided by voluntary organisations and mutual aid groups and performed regularly and informally by families, neighbours and friends. There is also relatively little consistent information about the increasingly important *private* sector. The second section of this chapter describes the meaning and scope of economic analysis. The breadth of the subject known as economics, and no doubt also the inclinations of some of its practitioners, have been sources of both confusion and misrepresentation. I shall endeavour to dispel some of this confusion and to provide a fair and accurate description of economics. I should emphasise that this is a book about economics, not about the economy or about economies or even about economists. These last three get more than their fair share of attention already.

The meaning and scope of social care

It is helpful, I think, to temporarily dissect the term 'social care services'. We are concerned with *services* – activities that are difficult to measure and assess. *Care* is not only feeling concern for somebody else but actually doing something about it; it has both positive and normative connotations. We will therefore be considering what is done and what effect it has on the object of one's concern. The term *social* has two meanings: it can refer to the nature of some of the problems which give cause for concern, such as an inability to engage in normal social interactions, or social isolation; and it can also refer to the fact that such conern is felt widely in 'society', and not just by the individual with the problem. A second point concerns terminology. *Social care services* are not quite the same as other activities with similar labels, such as personal social services, welfare services, social work services or social services, or at least as these labels have come to be used in Britain. There is no real distinction between social care and *personal social services*, although the latter term is sometimes reserved for those services provided by local authority social services departments. *Welfare services* can either be taken to be the services provided by the old welfare departments prior to reorganisation in 1970 (a very narrow definition), or the whole system of public provision in a Welfare State (very broad), or something in between. There is also some likelihood of a colloquial confusion with 'being on the welfare', meaning to be in receipt of social security payments. I shall not use the term welfare to describe services, for, whilst evocative, it can be a source of unnecessary confusion. Nor will I use the term *social work services* unless I am referring to services which currently or usually are provided by social workers. Some social care services, such as home help or meals on wheels, do not involve social workers. Finally the most confusing term of all, *social services*, can be taken either to mean the housing, health, education, social security, employment, leisure and personal social services provided by central or local government, or all of these services provided by non-public as well as public agencies, or just the personal social services, or social care services themselves. It is best to avoid this shorthand term.

Social care services which are 'formally' provided are of four main types: *residential accommodation*, often taking the responsibility for each and every need of the residents; *day care* in centres or clubs; *domiciliary care* in the client's own home; and *fieldwork* which can take place in any setting and may focus on an individual, a group or a whole community. In principle, any member of the population can make use of the social care services if he or she has a need for them, and in practice we find that most services are provided in response to those needs most commonly displayed by the elderly, the physically handicapped, the mentally handicapped, the mentally ill, and children (and their families). Other clients of social care services may include expectant and nursing mothers, alcoholics and other drug abusers, and the homeless. Local authorities have a statutory obligation to provide social care for those deemed to be in need, but they have considerable autonomy and discretion in the way they interpret this obligation. Thus local authority social care services vary markedly across the country, some authorities favouring a residential emphasis, some organising social work on a 'community' basis, some innovating in community and day care services, some favouring highly selective rather than universal provision, some highly centralised and some decentralised into 'patches', and so on. Local authorities vary in their reliance on voluntary, private and informal carers. Some will 'contract out' a high proportion of their responsibilities to voluntary (non-profit) organisations or to private (for-profit) organisations or carers. Authorities make different uses of the informal care provided by relatives, friends and neighbours and the extent to which they encourage individual and community responsibilities.

The most recent expenditure figures for English and Welsh local authority social services departments are summarised in Table 1.1 and provide an indication of the scale and composition of *public* social care responsibilities. These include services purchased by local authorities from the voluntary and private sectors. Note that the apportionment between service types and client groups is only an approximation: most clients receive *packages* of care services and are not exclusively the responsibility of one care unit or carer. Of a total expenditure of £2412 million, nearly half is accounted for by residential care services and over half of this residential budget is spent on accommodation for those aged 65 and over. Fieldwork expenditure,which comprised 10 per cent of local authority spending, is mainly devoted to the salaries and expenses of social work staff and is difficult to apportion between clients or services without fairly detailed research.

Whilst these expenditure figures have their drawbacks they provide at least an approximate indication of the nature of publicly-funded social care. Activity indicators – headcounts of clients and staff – must also be hedged with caveats. Many clients of social services departments receive more than one service – for example, many elderly people receiving home help visits will also be attending day centres or clubs. In other cases the distinction between the helper and the helped is deliberately vague. Many clients of social care services are not actually 'in care' and therefore do not get recorded in local or central government statistics. A selection of activity indicators for three recent years is given in Table 1.2. Even over such a short period there have been many marked changes. Whilst the total number of elderly people in residential care grew at an annual rate of 2.2 per cent, the number in *private* homes grew by 8.3 per cent. Other high growth services were local authority day care for the elderly (7.3 per cent), residential accommodation for the mentally handicapped and ment- ally ill (both 7.1 per cent) and adult training centres (3.6 per cent). The

TABLE 1.1   *Local authority social services departments' expenditure, England, 1981–2*

Client Group and Service†	Gross expenditure* (£ million)	Total Gross expenditure (%)
Elderly		
residential homes	553.0	22.9
day centres and clubs	33.5	1.4
home help services‡	227.2	9.4
meals services‡	27.9	1.2
Children		
residential homes	360.5	14.9
boarding out services	59.1	2.5
day nurseries	73.7	3.1
pre-school playgroups	5.4	0.2
intermediate treatment	8.6	0.4
Physically handicapped		
residential homes	42.1	1.7
day centres and clubs	24.3	1.0
sheltered employment	26.0	1.1
Mentally handicapped adults		
residential homes	69.5	2.9
day centres and clubs	2.1	0.1
adult training centres	88.3	3.7
Mentally ill		
residential homes	18.1	0.8
day centres and clubs	8.5	0.4
Multi-purpose day centres and clubs	18.1	0.8
Aids and adaptations	10.6§	n.a.
Telephones	4.8§	n.a.
Holidays and recreation	4.9§	n.a.
Travel concessions	5.9§	n.a
Sheltered housing	7.9§	n.a.
Fieldwork services	251.9	10.4
Administration	281.8	11.7
Research and development	4.8	0.2
Total gross expenditure (all services)	2412.2	

*   Actual expenditure for 106 local authorities; estimates for the other two.
†   This is not an exhaustive listing of social services departments' activities.
‡   Elderly clients are the main but not the only recipients of this service.
§   These are not gross expenditures but are *net* of consumer charges.
SOURCES: Chartered Institute of Public Finance and Accountancy, *Personal Social Services Statistics 1981–82, Actuals* (CIPFA, London) December 1982.

number of children in residential homes declined at an annual rate of 4 per cent over the same period.

It is worth examining the growth of these services over a longer period, for this has had a noticeable impact on the attitude towards

TABLE 1.2   *Activity indicators, England, 1976–82**

Client group, service and sector	1976	1981	1982
Elderly			
local authority home residents	99.0	103.1	103.6
voluntary home residents	23.8	26.0	26.1
private home residents	21.2	31.8	35.8
local authority day care places	14.1	20.7	21.5
main meals served at home†	24.3†	27.0†	27.1‡
meals served elsewhere†	16.2†	14.4†	13.2‡
home help cases attended	570.4	659.4§	—
Children			
local authority home residents	35.2	27.9	—
voluntary home residents	4.9	3.7	—
boarded out with foster parents	33.1	37.4	—
supervised at home (etc)	18.0	18.2	—
local authority day nursery places	26.9	28.4	—
Mentally handicapped adults			
local authority home residents	8.7	12.7	13.1
voluntary home residents	1.9	—	2.3
private home residents	1.1	—	1.8
adult training centre places	36.6	43.6	45.2
Mentally ill			
local authority home residents	2.7	3.9	4.1
voluntary home residents	1.1	—	1.4
local authority day care places	3.4	4.9	5.0
Physically handicapped			
local authority home residents	6.1	5.2	5.0
voluntary home residents	4.8	5.9	—
private home residents	1.0	1.9	—
local authority day care places	9.2	9.6	9.4
home help cases attended	43.2	44.8§	—

*   All figures relate to years ended 31st March and are in thousands unless indicated
   to the contrary.
†   Elderly clients are the main but not the only recipients of this service.
†   Millions.
§   Figures relate to 1980. DHSS collections discontinued thereafter.
SOURCE: DHSS statistics (annual feedback returns and reports to Parliament).

and use of economic analysis. One of the most striking features of economic and social development in the twentieth century has been the steady growth in public expenditure. This has been true of most economies and has been particularly marked in Britain. In the thirty year period after 1945, public sector growth was especially fast. During this period the importance of military expenditure waned and the five principal social services (health, education, housing, social security and social care) took an increasingly large slice of the expanding cake. This period of expansion was abruptly halted during the 1970s. The 'oil crisis' of late 1973 prompted a careful reappraisal of public policies. Severe restraint was imposed upon virtually all categories of public spending, for many years real growth rates in component spending plummeted towards and then below zero, and current economic forecasts give little hope for a return to positive real growth in the immediate future.

Local authority personal social services expenditure followed the national trend during this period. Annual growth rates in total expenditure averaged 1.9 per cent between 1953 and 1960, 6.9 per cent during the 1960s, and were as high as 11.4 per cent between 1970 and 1976. The rate dropped dramatically to 2.1 per cent between 1976 and 1979. These are all *real* growth rates, calculated at constant volume prices for the current administrative definition of the local authority sector (Ferlie and Judge, 1981). As a proportion of gross national product, personal social services expenditure by local authorities grew from 0.2 per cent to 1.0 per cent between 1955 and 1976 (Gould and Roweth, 1980) and is slightly below that today. Of course, the publicly-financed social care sector grew from a very low base which tended to exaggerate the earlier growth rates. Equally, however, an annual expenditure growth rate of around 2 per cent is actually insufficient to provide a constant level of service, given the growing elderly population, the increases in the average costs of care, and the burden of joint finance (Webb and Wistow, 1982a and 1982b). The transition from a period of rapid growth to one of stagnation and recession is necessarily painful, requiring policy-makers at all levels of government to exercise skill and ingenuity to avoid the many pitfalls of false economy and drastic and indiscriminate pruning. Within the social care services, where the interface between agency and client is at its most sensitive, the need for skills, ingenuity and tact is crucial.

Growth has been such a soothing panacea for so many economic ills that recent constraints and cut-backs have revealed a number of glaring inadequacies in the repertoire of techniques and stock of experiences available to social care policy makers. Expenditure growth

has to some extent spared government the task of cutting low priority programmes in the social field, or indeed of having to decide which programmes should be given low priority. It has led to unrealistic expectations about the scope for improvements and extensions. It has also reduced the incentive to increase the

efficiency of existing policies and programmes. (Central Policy
Review Staff, 1975, paragraph 4)

Such characteristics were especially prevalent in the social care field,
in part because of the unusually high rates of growth and partly
because the input of economic analysis was not encouraged, indeed
was often actively discouraged. As growth rates fell and expectations
of continued growth gradually faded, so central and local government
departments, and also those voluntary and private care organisations
dependent on public money for their continued operation, looked
more carefully at their principles and procedures for allocating
resources between competing ends. Whilst giving many indications of
a wish to pursue rationality, the available evidence suggests that social
services departments have not been overwhelmingly successful in
achieving a more efficient or more equitable allocation of resources
(Ferlie and Judge, 1981; Glennerster, 1980; Webb and Wistow,
1982a).

Economics in a social care context

In discussions of the planning and organisation of social care services
the voice of the economist has been strangely muted. Care services for
the elderly, for children, for the physically and mentally handicapped,
and for other individuals have primarily been the day-to-day concern
of the social worker and the academic preserve of the social
administrator. Until fairly recently, for example, the economic
content of planning statements and policy documents has been almost
invariably limited to a tabulation of expenditure figures and occasional vague reference to such concepts as 'economies of scale', 'cost
effectiveness' and 'costs and benefits', none of which is defined. Only
in the last ten years or so have policy-makers felt the need to examine
carefully the economics of social care.

Economics shares with all of the social sciences two interrelated
features: it has its own seemingly impervious and impenetrable jargon
which serves to confuse the non-economist, but it also has a certain
intuitive appeal and an apparent simplicity which attracts the non-
economist. It is the tension between the attraction of economics and
the confusion it generates which has probably been at the heart of
much of the denigration and misrepresentation of the subject in social

policy contexts. One does not need a formal qualification in the subject to be able to talk with a fair amount of sense about cost effectiveness or efficiency. But at the same time, and as with most disciplines, a little knowledge can be dangerous. At the outset of this excursion into the economics of social care, therefore, it would be as well to set out precisely what the subject of economics covers and the range of principles and techniques which it can usefully bring to bear on the study and planning of social care.

Economics is a broad subject, although not as disparate or diverse as some students of the subject believe or fear when they are first exposed to its theories and applications. For most other people contact with the subject of economics is likely to come via media reports of the state of the national economy, the latest exhortations from government to work harder and expect less, and the purchase of goods and services and the daily handling of money. In all three ways we are exposed to economics as a *topic* and not as a discipline (Williams, 1979; Culyer, 1981). The media, for example, will provide us with the latest figures on inflation and unemployment, will keep us fully informed of the value of sterling on international exchange markets, and will enrich our lives with the latest doom-laden predictions from one of a number of economic forecasters. This is all *macroeconomics* – the study of *aggregate* economic concepts and relationships, and the examination of the behaviour of the whole economy (or major parts thereof). The state of the macroeconomy determines the economic well-being of the nation and its citizens. We are all affected one way or another by changes in taxation, fluctuations in the sterling exchange rate, increases in the percentage of the workforce unemployed, trends in the growth of productivity, and movements of leading interest rates. These macroeconomic changes also determine, indeed cannot be sensibly separated from, the *social* well-being of the nation and its citizens. At one level, the state of the economy determines how much money can be spent on the provision of social care and a whole host of other services aimed at improving the well-being of citizens. At the same time, fluctuations in national economic fortune have a direct impact on the *needs* of citizens for assistance, be it in cash or in kind, collective or individual. In other words, the study of social policy cannot be separated from the study of economic policy.[1]

This book is not concerned with the macroeconomy or its influence on social policy and social well-being, but with *microeconomics* – the study of individual consumers, producers and markets. I shall therefore have to assume initially that the total budget for social care provision is predetermined and temporarily immutable, even though this budget must itself be influenced by the analyses presented below. This is a book about the *discipline* of economics and not the topic of the same name. It 'is characterised not at all by *what* economists study but *by the way they study it*' (Culyer, 1981, p. 312; [author's italics]).

Economics as a discipline need not be confined in its application to economics as a topic. Nor should a dissatisfaction with the general direction or philosophy of macroeconomic policy provide reason for criticising the principles of microeconomic analysis. To study economics or to recommend its application in a social policy context does not necessarily involve the organisation and distribution of social care and other services under market conditions. Titmuss (1968) generated a deal of confusion with his false dichotomy between 'economic markets' and 'social markets', a view which now seems to have been largely dispelled (Reisman, 1977; Pinker, 1979). Furthermore, to adopt an economic perspective is not necessarily to focus only on the immediately quantifiable (which, nine times out of ten, means focussing on costs), nor to attempt to quantify everything, nor to indulge in the mathematical abstractions so beloved of some economic theorists, nor to cling to a set of archaic assumptions amounting to a simplistic restatement of hedonistic utilitarianism.

The discipline of economics has as its primary basis the observation that resources are *scarce*. There are not and there never will be enough resources to meet all of the wants and needs of all individuals. This is not to say that we are all greedy or excessive in our demands or selfish, but simply that the resources available to us as individuals and as a society are insufficient to provide for all of our material and non-material needs and wants. The scarcity of resources means that we have to make careful decisions in choosing how to employ them. The study of economics is the study of criteria for the allocation of scarce resources. One criterion has dominated the discipline of economics: that of efficiency.

The pursuit of *efficiency* is the pursuit of an allocation of our scarce resources which maximises the achievement of whatever objective we are setting. We may wish to maximise the output of a given production process, maximise our profits, maximise our income, maximise our cost savings, maximise the well-being of individuals, maximise 'social welfare'. Efficiency then, is the maximisation of 'ends' from given 'means'. The pursuit of efficiency in the longer run can also mean the search for increases in the 'means' that are available. Efficiency is not, of course, the only criterion for resource allocation. The criteria of equity and freedom will often be equally important, if not more so. *Equity* is concerned with the distribution of resources in accordance with certain well-specified value judgements as to the equal or unequal treatment of equal wants or needs. Thus, the scarcity of resources necessitates a choice which should be based at least on the twin criteria of efficiency and equity, although in practical circumstances one may dominate the other.

Of course, there are few circumstances in which the discipline of economics is alone sufficient to guide policy. There are, however, circumstances in which the discipline has a great deal to offer the policy-maker and in which the discipline and its attendant methodologies and techniques are uniquely well placed to provide answers to crucial policy questions. This may be because of the predictive power of the behavioural models established by economists, or because of the empirical techniques they have developed, or because of a clear conceptual framework, or simply because the normative criterion shared by the majority of people is one of efficiency (Culyer, 1981).

It is possible to distinguish a variety of policy questions to which economics can – generally in collaboration with other disciplines – provide useful answers. Indeed, for many kinds of question it can be argued that the particular conceptual bases, logical calculi and empirical traditions of the economics discipline suggest a dominant partnership in the collaboration. At this point, I shall do no more than list a set of illustrative questions (in no particular order) and return to them later, for the role of economics in providing answers cannot be fully appreciated until we have cleared a little more conceptual ground.

(1) What is the true cost of social care?
(2) What are the 'outputs' of social care and how do we measure them?
(3) What is the relationship between resources and outputs (between ends and means)?
(4) What are our staffing requirements?
(5) What are the relative costs and benefits of alternative courses of action?

(6)   What is the relationship between capital expenditure and current expenditure?

(7)   Why do the costs of ostensibly similar services vary so markedly?

(8)   What incentives are necessary to secure an efficient or equitable allocation of resources?

(9)   What do we mean by an 'optimal balance of care'?

(10) To what extent can we recoup some of the costs of care from charges to clients?

(11) Is 'allocation according to need' substantially different from 'allocation according to willingness to pay'?

(12) How can we sensibly allocate resources between different areas of the country?

(13) What do we mean by 'value for money'?

(14) Can privatisation benefit the social care sector?

(15) Is voluntary care cheaper than statutory care? Is it better?

(16) How can we effectively secure a greater supply of good quality community care?

Each of these sixteen questions will be addressed in this book, some in considerable detail, others only in passing. Some questions already have well researched empirical answers in some specific contexts or with certain client groups; others have been barely touched upon.

There is certainly a very pressing need for the application of economics to social care. As yet, however, this need had brought forth little empirical analysis, and the influence of economics on planning has been substantially less obvious than the influence of a number of other disciplines. There are a number of reasons for this very limited influence: a lack of economic expertise and interest among social care professionals and managers, a lack of interest among economists, a dearth of suitable and relevant data, and a lack of incentives to pursue efficiency. Alan Williams succinctly and entertainingly summarised the problems of integrating cost effectiveness analyses into social care decision making in terms of seven nested hypotheses. Altering these hypotheses slightly to fit the present discussion we might postulate:

(1)   Policy-makers do not believe (or recognise) these economic problems as being researchable.

(2) They do, but do not want to know.

(3) They would like to know, but cannot wait.

(4) They are willing to wait, but the research commissioning process is just not up to it.

(5) The commissioning process is fine, but the research community in general has better (i.e. more enjoyable) things to do than economic studies.

(6) The research community in general would be delighted to do economic studies, but cannot find any economists interested (or congenial) enough to take on board as colleagues to do such work.

(7) Economic studies, even when carried out, are written up so incomprehensibly that policy-makers could not respond sensibly to them even if they wanted to, so they have become disillusioned.[2]

An important objective of this book, therefore, is to provide the information and the persuasive arguments that are required to sequentially reject each of these hypotheses.

2

The Production of Welfare

Care objectives

Social care services in Britain today pursue a variety of objectives. Some are so general as to be denied by no one, for example, the enhancement of the well-being of the elderly population. Others are more specific and the subject of controversy, for example, the provision of family care for all children, or the extension of parental rights. Some objectives are focused on short term 'crisis' intervention, whilst others reflect long-term plans and hopes. Some care objectives have undergone long gestation periods before an explosive impact on practice. Two recent examples are the pursuit of 'permanence' in child care and the development of 'community' alternatives to residential care for the frail elderly. Some objectives are specified in terms of the extensiveness of intervention or coverage, such as the number of day care places per thousand population; others are statements of intensity and quality of intervention, as when services aim to reduce loneliness, raise morale, or compensate for disability. It is by reference to the objectives of care that we can define and measure *needs* and *outputs*, and thus examine the importance and influences of *inputs* and *costs*. The partial or complete achievement of care objectives and the conceptual and empirical manifestations of these elements are most usefully considered within a *production of welfare* framework, and it is this framework which provides the basis for the economic approach to social care.

A DHSS working party established in 1978 to consider future directions for social care research distinguished four stages in the process of social care (Goldberg *et al*, 1980, pp. 309–10). In slightly amended form these stages are:

(1) *Problems:* the processes by which the problems and difficulties of individuals are recognised, responded to and handled.

(2) *Becoming a client:* the process of referral and the assessment of needs.
(3) *Providing help:* the delivery of services in response to these assessed problems and difficulties.
(4) *Effects and outcomes:* the impact on the well-being of clients and the community and on budgets.

Most social care problems are recognised and tackled *informally*. The individual with the 'problem', or relatives or neighbours, will be able to take preventive or curative action without involving any of the formal care agencies in the public, voluntary or private sectors. Other problems will become the responsibility of the bureaucratic process and 'becoming a client' will follow naturally from their identification. In either case each of the four stages will have an associated set of objectives.

Consider, for example, the child care responsibilities and objectives of local authority social services departments. Broad guidelines are enshrined in the relevant legislation, particularly the Children and Young Persons Act 1969 and the Child Care Act 1980, but considerable local discretion remains. An immediate set of objectives, therefore, includes the development of the processes for defining criteria of 'need' and for recognising children and families which are liable to satisfy these criteria. At the second stage, authorities must assess the needs of children who have either been admitted into care (and their families), or are likely to be if preventive action is not taken. Two further objectives are therefore prevention and assessment. At the third stage services must be delivered in response to these assessed needs, and so authorities must seek to secure a sufficient supply of foster parents, field social workers and residential staff. Again, the objectives are numerous and might include the achievement of a permanent substitute home, the containment of delinquency, the removal of an exceptional burden from parents, and so on. Finally, the effects on children and on their families should relate to the 'final objectives' of child care services: the development of social skills and habits, the stimulation of emotional growth, the development of feelings of self-confidence and identity, and so on. In other words, objectives are set at a number of stages in the child care process, with different degrees of specificity, and (although it is perhaps not obvious from the foregoing) by a number of different people from a number of different perspectives.

Whilst these different objectives often have associated with them different sets of activities, they can be arranged in a hierarchy of importance. There is little sense in achieving some of the objectives corresponding to the early stages of care if some of the later objectives are aggravated. For example, the assessment of the needs of children should not be undertaken in a way which is liable to make it harder for a child to return to its family. Thus the 'final objectives' should dominate the discussion, evaluation and development of policy. The need for statements of objectives, therefore, does not seem to be in any doubt. As Shyne (1976, p. 8) remarks, with disarming simplicity, 'Clarity and specificity about programme and service objectives are central to evaluation. If you don't know where you're going, it's difficult to say whether you got there.' What *is* in doubt, at least in some minds, is the feasibility of specifying clear, agreed, operational and non-conflicting objectives.

Doubts about the utility of specifying objectives, and using them to guide policy and practice, have been expressed by a number of writers (see, particularly, Lindblom, 1963; Glennerster, 1975, Chapter 8). For some services it might be the absence of a clearly defined philosophy of care which makes the specification of objectives so difficult, whilst for others it could be the existence of a large number of objectives which conflict with one another. There will also be the problem that the goals set by one person may be rejected by another. Senior and middle management may well be able to reach some kind of agreement as to the objectives of, say, a residential children's home, but those same objectives may not be shared with field social workers, residential staff, or clients. Whose objectives do we accept? These are all reasonable reservations about the conduct of goal-related research or 'management by objectives', but their importance has been exaggerated and their relevance is always going to be context-specific. Within the social care sector there seems to be no over-riding argument for rejecting a goal-related approach, provided one recognises the variety of motives and interests (Davies, 1977).

For example, the most commonly cited and most important objectives of care of the elderly are the following:[1]

(1) Nurture, providing for comfort, security, warmth and general physical well-being.
(2) Maintenance or improvement of health.
(3) Compensation for disability.

(4) Maintenance or improvement of independence and identity.
(5) Social integration.
(6) Fostering family relationships, including relieving the burden of care.
(7) Improvement of morale.

These objectives have 'accumulated rather than . . . been deliberately planned' (Carstairs and Morrison, 1971, para. 7.51), and are neither independent, nor mutually exclusive, nor non-conflicting, but this has not been an insurmountable problem for either research or policy. Indeed, the methodologies and analyses that follow from the 'production of welfare approach' themselves provide the means for dealing with a multiplicity of possibly conflicting objectives (Davies and Knapp, 1981; Challis and Davies, in press).

Need[2]

Final objectives relate to the well-being of clients (and others) and are the 'ends' of policy. Intermediate objectives concern the services themselves and are strictly the 'means to these ends'. The distinction between them is crucial to an understanding of the philosophies, policies and practices of social care. It is also crucial to the definition of both outputs and needs. A *need* is said to exist when there is the potential for improving the well-being of an individual.[3] Further, need is a *normative* concept. For whatever reason, be it moral, ethical, religious or political, we are saying that an individual not only has some identifiable need which can be removed, but that it *should* be removed.

Needs are most reliably conceptualised in terms of final objectives ('the need to reduce loneliness or raise morale') and not intermediate objectives ('the need for home help or residential care'). Home help is needed only in so far as it helps an elderly person (say) to achieve a degree of independence, reasonable standards of diet, hygiene and safety, and enhanced morale. Home help services are not generally desired as end states in themselves. What is more, there will almost always be more than one way to achieve the final objective. In order for the elderly person to achieve independence, reasonable standards of diet, hygiene and safety, and enhanced psychological well-being, it is not essential that a regular home help service be provided. Within the present range of social care provision there are many ways to achieve those ends: day care, meals on wheels, volunteer visiting, residential care, and so on. There are also alternatives from outside the social care sector – health visitor and community nurse involvement, for example, and of course neighbourhood and family support. It is essential to avoid slipping into the 'monotechnic' way of thinking, the existence of but one technology to meet a specified set of needs. Indeed, the most interesting of present day innovations in social care are distinctly 'polytechnic'.

Whilst

> a need judgement often takes the form of an expression or description of an individual's state of welfare, [it] more usually combines this with an assertion about what form an intervention should take. Since interventions involve the deployment of resources, these assertions concern the allocation of resources. Indeed, a need judgement should have an essentially cost benefit nature (Bebbington and Davies, 1980, p. 434).

Given the range of formal and informal services which are capable, either singly or in combination, of meeting the needs of an individual, the need judgement is a statement about the most efficient use of resources. It combines information about the welfare consequences of services (the effect of home help services on client loneliness and morale, for example) as well as the resource consequences (the costs of providing home help services). Furthermore, it is a *social* and not a private judgement. The very nature of most of the objectives set for the social care services, and the consequent characteristics of those individuals with needs, make it highly unlikely that these individuals can act alone to make good the deficiencies. By definition, many of the social care services are concerned with needs which are of social concern and which require social action or intervention. Whether or not the adjective 'social' reflects the concern and requisite action of the whole nation, or the local community or immediate neighbourhood, or just a close group of relatives and friends, need not delay us at this stage.

Need is therefore a normative, social cost-benefit judgement about priorities in the allocation of resources. Its derivation in practice proceeds through four steps.

Step 1   A statement of objectives

We have already seen that the statement of objectives is not always straightforward. In particular the problem of conflicting objectives must be taken into account. The main protagonists in the conflict will be the set of *potential clients*, the *professionals* whose role it is to deal with the clients (either by helping them to avoid or identify welfare shortfalls or by providing the services to help remove those shortfalls), the *politicians* who take decisions on the allocation of resources, and the *electorate* (society at large) on whose behalf those decisions are taken. There can be little doubt that the social view of objectives is crucial here. Social care services essentially represent *social* interventions: moves by social or collective groups to meet some specified needs of an individual. The objectives of that intervention may be spelled out by the individual, but will need to be validated by the wider society before action will be taken to attempt to achieve them. That is, only socially legitimate objectives will be pursued, even if those objectives are idiosyncratically fashioned to individual members of society.

Step 2   A statement of welfare shortfalls

Having agreed upon some workable (but possibly temporary) set of objectives we require a statement of individual shortfalls from these objectives. But whose perception of deficiency is taken as our basis for defining need? If we rely on individuals' *felt or expressed shortfalls* we may miss a great deal of 'need', for individuals may be ignorant of their problems and lack the motivation or means to make them known. *Demands* are expressed shortfalls backed by the power to purchase the means to meet them. Individual demands are backed by individual ability and willingness to pay; social demands are really taking us closer to normative definitions of need – for they represent society's willingness to purchase (provide) the means to remove the shortfalls. An historically popular approach to the measurement of shortfall is to rely on certain *minimum standards* and hence measure 'absolute need'. Minimum standards can quickly become obsolete and can, by their apparent objectivity, become inflexible guidelines. They also tend to ride roughshod over the individual values and standards of members of society. We could thus arrive at a situation where rigorous guidelines for the allocation and delivery of the minimal amount of support would dominate social care planning. Another approach is to use what Bradshaw (1972) calls a measure of 'normative need', although it would avoid considerable confusion in the present context if we used the term *professionally-adduced shortfall*. This is the expert's or professional's assessment of the deficiency of the individual from somebody's set of objectives (presumably the professionals'). As Culyer (1980, p. 70) argues:

> Bradshaw's 'normative' need consists in technical judgements made by professionals that doubtless relate service inputs to end-state outcomes but it is not clear whence comes the moral imperative of the outcome or why it should be the professionals who should evaluate this.

The problem is that professionals are liable to associate a particular deficiency with a need for a particular set of social care *services*, that is to assume a one-to-one relationship between ends and means to ends, and such 'monotechnic' views ignore the essential substitutability of resources and the diversity of individual shortfalls. Secondly, the professionally-adduced shortfall assumes a very narrow degree of professional specialisation. Any set of welfare shortfalls can usually be met by a number of different public, non-public and informal care providers.

What all of these approaches have in common is the neglect of the 'social' dimension. Individuals with welfare shortfalls and professionals with responsibilities to deal with those shortfalls are clearly well-placed to assess those deficiencies, but this does not necessarily mean that their assessments will be flawless or socially acceptable. Social assessments are required not only because members of society will feel compassion for those suffering a shortfall (the so-called 'caring externality'), but also because the need judgement is in part a statement about the equitable allocation of resources and benefits, and society might reasonably expect that criterion of equity to reflect some general principles of justice (Culyer, 1980, p. 69). Thus need implies a social and not a private judgement and some representative(s) of society will be required to make the judgements. This is neither easy nor uncontroversial.

Step 3   A statement of the means to remove those shortfalls

Shortfalls can be removed by provision of social care services. As we have already seen, most types of shortfall can be met in any one of a number of ways. Each form of intervention will involve the suitable combination of care resources, such as staff and capital, with the personal (and often intangible) resources of clients and their relatives or neighbours. The removal of shortfalls is, as we have previously termed it, the *production of welfare*. Needs are then defined in terms of these means to remove (wholly or partially) the observed shortfalls in welfare. However, there is little point in expressing desired end-states which cannot conceivably be achieved.

Step 4   A statement of the most efficient means of removal

Among the set of all conceivable means to remove the welfare shortfalls identified for an individual (or, in aggregate, for the whole community or society) we need to identify the most efficient means in the given circumstances. The meaning of efficiency will be clearer once we have completed our account of all the major elements of the production of welfare process, but essentially an efficient technique, or service, or mode of intervention, is one which maximises the output (or benefit) achieved from given resources, or minimises the resources required to achieve a specified level of output. A definition of need is a judgement about the best use (or, in practice, the *better* use) of resources which weighs up both the expected consequences of alternative patterns of intervention and the expected costs. Once again, the question of *who* is involved and *whose* views are accepted is crucial. In this case, whose view of efficiency is to be accepted? Client's views cannot be ignored but may not be reliable. Social workers' views may not be sufficiently broadly based. The view of almost anyone else will probably not be based on a sufficiently deep appreciation of the case. The reconciliation of these difficulties in practice must inevitably involve value judgements. It is, however, important not to underplay or underemphasise the need judgements made by those whose role in this process is constitutionally established and accountable. It is also important to move from *views* of efficiency to *evidence* about the relationships between costs and benefits. We should note that the needs judgement implies that those interventions which do not generate benefits in excess of costs will not be undertaken.

Effectiveness and output

The success of a social care service is measured in terms of the extent to which its objectives are achieved, that is, the extent to which the needs of clients are met. For example, among the many objectives and criteria of 'success' that have been suggested and measured in studies of child care are improvements in physical, psychological, emotional and social well-being, improvements in attachment to peers and to family, the achievement of a 'permanent' placement, the containment of delinquency and so on. The success achieved in the pursuit of objectives has been variously labelled the effectiveness, outcome, output or benefit. I shall use the term *output* and it will denote both singular and multiple 'achievements'.

The performance of a social care agency in the attainment of its objectives is the production of output. The attainment of intermediate objectives (the production and delivery of services) is the *intermediate output*. The attainment of final objectives (the reduction of welfare shortfall) is the *final output*. Since the goal of social care is the improvement of the welfare of those in need, the measurement of the achievement of welfare or well-being should be the focus of attention. Final outputs can have both preventive and curative dimensions.

Outputs, needs and objectives are thus interlinked in both conceptual and empirical terms. Defining one will define the other two; overcoming measurement problems with respect to one will open the way for empirical advances along the dimensions spanned by the others.

Objectives of social care
↓
Deficiencies with respect to these objectives
are needs
↓
Removal or reduction of these needs
is the production of output

Outputs must clearly be related to objectives. Needs are also related to objectives, but the definition of a sensible and workable concept of need requires rather more than that. In particular, the definition of need requires us to take into account both the expected stream of outputs and the expected stream of costs.

It is helpful to introduce two other concepts at this stage: effectiveness and benefits. An intervention, activity or social care service is said to be *effective* if it results in an identifiable increase in output. The *benefits* of an activity are often defined as having virtually identical meaning to the effects, outcomes or outputs, but I shall use the term more narrowly to mean the *monetary value* of the outputs.

As a basis for evaluation and planning, final outputs will almost always be preferred to intermediate outputs. However, the practical problems of measurement are more severe for final than for intermediate outputs. This preference and these measurement issues are tackled in the next chapter.

The production of outputs

Care objectives are rarely discussed without explicit or implicit reference to a set of factors thought to have an impact on output. Indeed, a large proportion of the research studies commissioned in the social care field rightly has as one of its primary aims the identification of the factor or factors responsible for the observed differences in output. Some of these studies attempt to take account of these factors by adopting a research design in which 'experimental' and 'control' groups of clients are compared over a period of time. The range of characteristics believed to exert an influence upon the degree of success achieved with a particular form of care is clearly vast. The personal characteristics, experiences and circumstances of clients will be of particular importance not only in the understanding of care success, but also in its very definition at the outset. There is also the set of wider, broadly 'social' characteristics which will be of significance in the achievement or otherwise of objectives. Psychologists are quick to stress the importance of a 'good' social environment and supportive and stimulating staff attitudes and roles. A third group of influential factors would be the characteristics of the *physical* environment.

The discussion thus far has done little more than to draw out some of the underlying theoretical perspectives and empirical conclusions of a considerable body of research and writing on social care.

However, set out in this way the argument makes plain the similarity between a body of received opinion in the social welfare literature and the basic premises of what the economist calls the theory of production. The economist's basic assumption is that inputs (labour and capital) combine together to produce outputs (goods and services). This is not to suggest that social care, and the complex human relationships that go to define it, are to be perceived as a simple process which feeds in resources at one end and mechanically churns out well-being and happiness at the other. Rather, the production analogy that I would like to pursue helps us to be clear and precise about issues which, when they reach the desion-making stage, require clear and precise policies and directions. Nor is it to advocate taking the power of decision making away from the individual professional 'at the coal face'. Indeed, one of the most exciting innovations of recent years is explicitly based on this production analogy and has devolved considerable power to individual fieldworkers to respond to the individual needs of clients. The aim is clarity of thought, clarity of premise, and hence clarity of policy. Anything less is a recipe for confusion. The production analogy, or the *production of welfare* approach, underlies the arguments of this book. I hope that it will help to bury once and for all the myth that economics is concerned only with money, profit and markets.

The production of welfare model thus has five major components. Each has been mentioned already, but only two have been defined – the final and intermediate outputs. On the other side of the production relationship are the inputs. *Resource inputs* are the conventional factors of production. In the case of social care services the principal resource inputs include staff, physical capital (including buildings and vehicles), provisions and other consumable items. Associated with them are the *costs* of social care provision. In contrast, the *non-resource inputs* are those determinants of final and intermediate output which are neither physical nor tangible: they are embodied in the personalities, activities, attitudes and experiences of the principal actors in the social care process, particularly the care staff and the clients themselves. Obvious examples of non-resource inputs, therefore, are the characteristics of the social environment (the 'caring milieu') and the psychological make-up of clients.

The distinction between resource and non-resource inputs is an important one, both for causal argument and for policy formulation. The characteristics of the physical environment – the resource inputs – are often stressed in policy and planning documents, but it is a common assumption among professional and practitioner groups, and among some associated policy-makers, that non-resource factors are the more important. Certainly most of the social work and social care literature has focused upon the latter. However, to neglect the influences of the resource inputs is to severely limit the practical usefulness of any research concerning the association between non-resource factors and outputs. Differences in resource inputs will be partly responsible for observed differences in the extent to which care objectives are achieved, both because of their direct influence upon a client's welfare and because of their indirect influence through the configurations of social environments that they make possible. Equivalently, many of the influences of the resource inputs upon final outputs are mediated through and by the non-resource inputs. For example, the potentially detrimental effects of a poorly designed or inadequately staffed residential home may be ameliorated by a particularly supportive or stimulating caring environment. It is the resource inputs which enter the financial accounts of social care agencies and which, in the economist's terminology, have identifiable 'opportunity costs'. *Cost*, in fact, is the fifth component of the production model and can be seen as a shorthand term for (or summary measure of) the resource inputs entering the production relation.

Maintaining the distinction between these concepts allows us to state the basic premise of the production of welfare approach:

Final and intermediate outputs are determined by the level and modes of combination of the resource and non-resource inputs.

That the various inputs are highly intercorrelated should be no cause for difficulty or concern. The production relations approach is quite capable of disentangling these intercorrelations and, indeed, uses them to good effect in the development of care policies. Grossly simplified,[4] the production of welfare perspective is illustrated in Figure 2.1. Notice that I have assumed that the non-resource inputs do not exert an influence upon intermediate outputs. They do however exert a crucial influence on *final* outputs and should not be ignored if needs, costs and efficiency (for example) are to be properly specified.

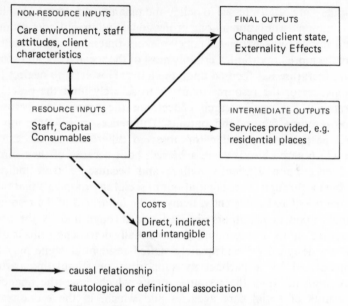

FIGURE 2.1   *The production of welfare*

The potential contribution of the production of welfare approach

The production relations or production of welfare approach was first *comprehensively* stated in the context of residential services for the elderly (Davies and Knapp, 1981), but has characteristics which are shared by other work in related literatures. This will become clear as we examine the main components of the approach and consider some of its applications.

The approach can contribute to our understanding of practice, and therefore to policy-making, in a number of ways. First, even the most cursory reading of the social work and social policy literatures reveals a whole host of theoretical and practical perspectives on care, but no coherent body of theory to explain them. It also reveals an even larger number of assumed and statistically corroborated causal relationships between aspects of care, carers and clients.

Recently, much of the literature has been critical of the vagueness with which providers specify ends, means and their interconnections. Goldberg posed the question thus:

Assuming that we are able to define some goals which permit the formulation of criteria of success or failure in relation to specific problems, and that we can describe the 'treatment' given in different cases, how can we be sure that the outcome – favourable or unfavourable – is due to the social work carried out, rather than to the myriad of events in the lives of our clients which have nothing to do with social work? (Goldberg, 1970, p. 26)

Whilst the production relations approach cannot hope to contain the multeity of alternative perspectives that have been put forward, it can nevertheless provide a coherent ideology and a coherent conceptual framework within which to examine the causal and non-causal relationships between characteristics. What is more, the production relations approach *suggests* which relationships should be examined and how these may be interpreted.

Many of the policy questions posed in the social welfare literature and by social care planners may be answered within this perspective. In application, the production relations perspective can yield the factual basis, for example, for providing answers to the illustrative questions listed on page 11 above. The production relations approach is essentially an evaluative technique, but one which builds explicitly and painstakingly on a body of received theory and empirical evidence, and so one which avoids the many pitfalls associated with many of the *ad hoc* evaluations which are all too common. The production relations approach provides a repertoire of tools – theoretically valid constructs with extensive supportive statistical techniques – whose primary aim is to answer these policy questions. Modelling techniques, such as the production function, cost function and factor demand or employment function, are purpose-built to test arguments about policy questions with statistical evidence. Other techniques, and particularly cost benefit and cost effectiveness analyses, often use rather less modelling but are equally dependent on the production of welfare framework for their validity and utility. Each of these techniques will be introduced or examined later in the book.

3
Outputs

The need for output measurement

There is no doubt that output measures are already used in the social care services, albeit in a form and with a purpose which might not readily identify them as such. A social worker writing up her case notes will invariably be attempting to record the outcomes of a placement or episode ('There has been a marked improvement in Jimmy's ability to cope with criticism and control from his foster parents . . .'), and often to relate these to particular interventive strategies and exogenous factors ('. . . in part due to his establishment of a close friendship with their son and in part because the visits of his rather authoritarian natural father, which still sometimes disturb Jimmy, have become much less frequent'). Output measures of this kind are necessarily informal, impressionistic and probably incomplete, but they are certainly useful. They do not range over the full set of objectives of a care episode or intervention, they do not necessarily attempt to compare what is happening with what might have happened if some alternative action (including 'no action') had been taken, nor do they necessarily package it all up neatly within conveniently specific time periods.

It is in the evaluation literature that we would expect to find comprehensive and carefully specified measures of output. However, the treatment and measurement of output in the vast majority of social care evaluations has been extremely poor. Output measurement is not simply the observation of whether or not an old person survives five years in a residential home, whether or not a foster care placement breaks down, or whether or not the WRVS can deliver meals to the housebound elderly which retain some semblance of warmth. These are all undoubtedly important aspects of social care, but they are not – except in very unusual circumstances – adequate measures of output. Output measurement needs to be comprehensive and to proceed carefully through a number of well-defined stages.

The need for the careful and controlled measurement of output is paramount, not only for evaluation and research, but also for care practice, planning, accountability, and regulation.

Outputs and practice

What social care 'package' is best suited to a client's needs? Given the resources that are available and given the wishes of the client and the social worker, what is the 'best' environment or service package? For an elderly client, will a 'package' of community services – home help visits, meals on wheels, attendance at a day centre – be most suitable, or would it be better to consider accommodation in a sheltered flatlet or residential home? How is the independence that may come from remaining in the community to be traded off against the increased risk of a fall or accident? How quickly will the client's health deteriorate if left in the community, and will this be worse than the shock of admission to a home and the cost of compliance in the residential setting? The social worker, in consultation with colleagues, with the client and with the client's relatives, must make a decision as to the 'best' placement. That decision simply cannot be reached without a comparison of the expected effects or outputs of each of the alternative environments. Output measurement is needed to aid practice. Indeed, the conscious consideration of these alternatives and their effects can *improve* practice (Whittaker, 1979).

A related question concerns the allocation of services between clients. How is a local authority home help organiser to allocate the limited home help resources at her disposal to the competing – and growing – claims of the elderly in the area? How is she to balance, for example, the competing claims of a housebound woman who is apt to get lonely and depressed and a gregarious old man who has no idea how to care for himself? Who has the greater need for the home help service? If we seem to be trying to compare chalk with cheese how then *in practice* do home help organisers allocate services? Output measurement can help to make explicit some otherwise implicit (and perhaps not entirely satisfactory) allocation procedures and to inform future allocations.

Outputs and planning

How does a local authority decide where to allocate any additional
resources that are made available, or (perhaps more realistically in
the 1980s) where to cut services next? What type of residential
provision is best suited to the needs of elderly people being admitted
to residential accommodation nowadays? Does group-living better
meet the objectives of these services than more conventional arrangements? Should a social services department be planning the expansion of its foster care programme and the running down of some of its
children's homes? How can it reach a sensible decision on planning
questions of this nature without some regard for the effects of the
decisions on the quality of care of the clients and the quality of their
lives; that is, without recourse to output measurement?

Outputs and accountability

Local authority social care services are probably the subject of as
much public and media criticism as any other area of local
government activity. It is easy for the media to highlight the apparent
failings of social services departments and the apparent misjudge-
ments of social workers. A child who dies as a result of non-accidental
injury in a foster placement and an old people's home which catches
fire make 'good press'. It is much harder to demonstrate what is a far
more common occurrence: a successful intervention. In part the
blame for this public image might rest with social care agencies
themselves, for it has been argued that the needs of clients and the
outcomes of services are the preserve of the trained social worker.
This is not convincing, for social care services address *social* needs in
response to *social* concern. It is granted that any assessment of needs
or outputs must inevitably be subjective, but this is all the more
reason to make these assessments overt and therefore accountable.
This is imperative even if only to demonstrate the non-violation of
basic human rights (Payne, 1981).[1]

Outputs and regulation

In some areas of social care responsibility the private and voluntary
sectors are becoming increasingly important. For example, the

number of residents in private old people's homes has increased by over 50 per cent in just four years (1978–82). In other areas it is the *role* rather than the extent of private and voluntary responsibility which is changing. This is quite obvious in child care, where local authorities are now much less likely to place children in private or voluntary homes unless those homes are providing very special care for children with very special needs. Whether it is the role or the extent of the non-statutory provision which is changing, public bodies have a need, and in some cases a statutory obligation, to monitor and regulate the quality of care. Output measurement is an integral part of the regulation of the private and voluntary sectors as well as the public sector: it is a form of 'quality control' (Davies and Knapp, 1981, pp. 193–200; Klein and Hall, 1974).

Outputs and evaluation

The evaluation of a policy or a service needs to include the assessment and comparison of effects. It is quite true, as Booth (1978) among others has argued, that the evaluative criteria by which many innovations are to be judged are usually more stringent than those used to assess existing services. It is equally true, however, that rigorous evaluation provides a 'safeguard against the new' (Goldberg and Connelly, 1982, p. 15). Output measures can tell us whether or not a new service will have a greater impact on the well-being of clients than do existing services. Output measurement should not be seen as yet another brake on progress; rather it is a necessary check that what we are doing or proposing to do is having the desired effect on the lives of clients.

Final and intermediate outputs

In the previous chapter, two levels of output were introduced. *Final outputs* measure the changes in individual well-being compared with the levels of well-being in the absence of a caring intervention. In other words, final outputs measure the degree of success of a care agency in meeting its final objectives, where due consideration is paid to the situation of the client had care not been available. Final output is a measure of the reduction of need.[2] In contrast, *intermediate outputs* are operationally defined in terms of the care services themselves, rather than the effects of these services on the clients. Intermediate outputs will thus be expressed in terms of levels of provision, throughput and quality of care. They are indicators of performance, service or activity rather than indicators of effect, influence or impact. The distinction between final and intermediate outputs is essentially one between achievement and provision, between ends and (some) means to those ends.

There are strong arguments for generally preferring final to intermediate outputs when monitoring, evaluating, planning or just discussing social care services. Final outputs are more flexible and ensure a greater flexibility of care, are less dangerous, and are really no more difficult to measure if measurement is undertaken properly.

Flexibility

Exactly identical resources, service configurations and caring environments will affect different people in different ways. One cannot assume that there exists a one-to-one association between the services rendered and the effects on recipients. There is more than one way to meet most kinds of need and it is this variety which is the very essence of dispute and innovation. To base one's policies entirely on intermediate outputs would run the danger of paralysing innovative practices which achieve favourable client-level effects by routes which appear to be unacceptable, immoral or unlawful. The symbolic value of buildings as edifices to the welfare state was one of the most powerful stumbling blocks in the way of community-based innovations in social care in the first twenty years after 1948. So long as outputs are measured in terms of services rather than impacts there may be little incentive to alter or improve practice. It is the flexibility of environments to respond to the needs of individual clients which holds the key to successful care.

Safety

Final outputs provide a less dangerous basis for the development of policy than do intermediate measures. One of the most common of intermediate measures – the quality of care – provides a good example of these dangers. We have little information on the relationship between quality of care and final output. In fact the hypothetical single concept 'quality of care' hides a number of other factors, each of which is quite possibly an important determinant of final output in its own right. To lump these factors together into a composite quality of care measure thus wastes information of value to the policy-maker. At first glance, quality of care has all the appearances and attributes of a good output indicator: it is concerned with social environment, with staff-client ratios, and so on. Because of this concern with something other than, and presumably beyond, the simple resources of care, and often because of its apparent complexity, it may appeal to the researcher and policy-maker. If so, the quest for information on the effects of care may cease prematurely. Quality of care, therefore, can only be an indicator of intermediate output (or perhaps only of input), and a wasteful composite one at that. There is also the danger that intermediate output indicators will be unthinkingly transposed from one context to another (Williams and Anderson, 1975). It is often argued, for example, that empty residential places are wasteful, and there are contexts in which this is undoubtedly true since staffing and other resources are generally fixed in relation to capacity rather than occupancy. But it would be wrong to argue that the maximisation of occupancy rates is the production of 'more' output, since an efficient care system must retain a certain amount of spare capacity to be able to cope with the varying demands made upon it. The more fragmented and specialised the individual units in the care system, the greater the need for spare capacity (Gianfrancesco, 1980).

Difficulty

The proper measurement and validation of intermediate outputs is no less difficult than the measurement of final outputs. The quality of care, level of provision or rate of throughput cannot sensibly be 'optimised' in the absence of information as to their relationship to final output.[3] They cannot provide a valid basis for policy formulation at least until they have demonstrated a purposive and significant correlation with final output. Thus we cannot use them until we have valid and reliable final output indicators. What is more, once care arrangements or client characteristics alter, even by just a little, the influences of these changes upon final outputs must once again be sought. This requires knowledge of the final output production relation. A good example is provided by the debate which gripped the attentions of social gerontologists twenty to thirty years ago. The so-called Activity Theory of ageing, which first appeared in the work of Havighurst and Albrecht (1953), asserted that the greater the role loss of elderly individuals the less activity they would engage in, which would eventually lead to lower life satisfaction or morale. That is, there is a positive association between activity (social participation) and psychological well-being. In 1961, Cumming and Henry proposed the Disengagement Theory that withdrawal or disengagement from social participation is actually advantageous to the elderly individual. In the planning of social environments in old people's homes, therefore, one perspective would imply the active stimulation of residents and the other a need to give residents the opportunity simply to do nothing. Clearly it is *not* possible to take both theories (and both with apparently supportive empirical evidence) as a basis for the development of a quality of care measure. Later research demonstrated that 'neither theory is sufficient by itself to explain all of the myriad patterns of ageing, many of which require further information of a sociological or social psychological nature to elaborate meaningfully' (Dowd, 1975, p. 585). Indeed, *both* theories can be supported if the components of psychological well-being of elderly individuals are adequately measured (Knapp, 1976, 1977). One cannot sensibly plan activity programmes for the elderly residents of homes without recourse to the assessment of the impacts of those programmes upon their well-being.

A complication arises in discussing the relative merits of final and intermediate outputs because of the presence of *externalities*. An externality exists if one person's well-being is in part influenced by another person's consumption of goods or services.[4] That externality may be negative (I suffer the smoke from your cigarette) or positive (I am relieved that you are getting the medical treatment you so obviously need). Social care services are very likely to generate positive externalities, but whilst we will generally derive some comfort from the knowledge that, say, children in need are receiving care, we are also likely to be concerned about the effects of these services on them. The externality is associated not only (if at all) with the services themselves but with the welfare of clients. Thus we are often concerned about the quality of care rendered to individuals only in so far as it enhances the quality of their lives, and there is, of course, every likelihood that our *perceptions* of the way that the former enhances the latter are awry. There may well be instances when intermediate outputs such as quality of care are valued in their own right, but the rationale for this requires careful scrutiny.

The most commonly revealed preference for *intermediate output* indicators stems from the apparent ease, directness and immediacy of measurement. The proper assessment of final outputs, as we shall see in the next section, usually requires a large sample of individuals, interviewed or observed at two points in time (at least), and enough scales to reflect the broad range of care objectives. The required information, furthermore, is not currently available in case files so that quite expensive purpose-built research would be needed. It is, of course, the apparent ease of intermediate measurement which has meant that the vast majority of planning statements and performance statistics have been couched in intermediate terms. Thus, improvements in residential care will be expressed in terms of increases in the number of residents accommodated or reductions in the under-occupancy of buildings. However, we have already seen that arguments as to the ease of measurement of intermediate outputs must be treated with caution. The configurations of resource and non-resource factors (and this of course, includes not only 'quality of care', but also a whole lot more) which determine acceptable levels of final output are far too complex and too variable to be able to rely solely on intermediate output indicators as useful guides to policy and practice. Of course, if one was able to so model variations in the resource and non-resource factors as to be able to predict variations in outputs with a sufficient degree of statistical significance, then it may be possible to use intermediate output indicators as useful short term predictors of the (unobserved) final outputs. However, this approach would need to be employed carefully and would need to be adopted only on the basis of indisputably reliable and comprehensive studies of the production of welfare process. This kind of approach would be particularly useful where the objectives are very long term and the progress towards those objectives is slow. For example, the monitoring of the outputs of services for delinquent juveniles is usually argued to require a follow-up study for two years from the end of treatment or incarceration. This is not only expensive on research resources but also of limited relevance to those practitioners who may need

guidance almost immediately as to the effectiveness of their programmes of treatment and care. In these circumstances intermediate
outputs with known association with final outputs have considerable
utility.

It is clear that the provision of one more place in a residential home
or day centre, or the recruitment of one more foster family for difficult
adolescents, or the delivery of one more midday meal *is* an output.
The additional place, family or meal has been made possible only by
the employment of further resources. Intermediate outputs may
therefore provide temporary indicators of performance. Provided
that the superiority of final outputs for the evaluation and formulation of policy is acknowledged, the careful and sensible use of
intermediate outputs will be a fruitful pursuit.

The principles of final output measurement

The arguments of the previous section emphasise the need to measure
final outputs if we are to evaluate, monitor and plan in a useful and
valid manner. Despite the central importance of changes in client
welfare for the practice of social care, the available literature is
remarkably cavalier about output measurement. Few studies make an
attempt to base their evaluative criteria on a suitable experimental
design, and few have employed scales of a sufficient degree of validity
and reliability.

Final output measurement proceeds through two stages: the
development of a scale of client well-being, and the assessment of the
impact of social care intervention upon it. At the first stage, therefore,
we need to identify and scale the relevant dimensions of client well-
being and perhaps combine them into a unidimensional well-being
indicator. At the second stage we seek measures of *changes* in well-
being.

Scaling states of well-being

In the scaling of well-being we have four tasks:

(1) Identify the dimensions of well-being or 'client state' which are
     to form the basis of our output measure.
(2) Scale or measure positions along each of these dimensions.

(3) Combine the various dimensions by placing relative valuations on the set of combinations of the characteristics.

(4) Obtain absolute valuations for these combinations.

By reference to the objectives of a particular service we can identify the dimensions of well-being over which our final output measure will range. We then seek ways of measuring client states or positions along each of these dimensions. This is generally equivalent to specifying a discrete set of descriptive statements which identify 'more' or 'less' of each characteristic of well-being. The third and fourth tasks are more controversial. They require us to place relative, and then absolute, valuations on *combinations* of characteristics in order to move to a unidimensional well-being scale. It could be argued that these last two tasks are not essential, or at least not at this stage. The alternative would be to carry the set of scales for the dimensions of well-being into the evaluation stage as an independent collection of measurement instruments, only seeking to combine them *after* measures of change have been obtained. This would have the advantage of retaining flexibility until the latest possible stage, but it cannot avoid the problem of synthesis altogether unless the different dimensions of well-being are always to be kept separate. Yet, we know in practice that they are *not* separate or independent, for trade-offs are made between, for example, keeping a family together and ensuring the adequate care and development of a child, or maintaining the independence of the frail elderly and reducing the risk of accidents. *Somebody* has to trade-off one against the other at some stage, and this can either be accomplished (overtly) by the researcher or left to the political process.[5]

None of these tasks can be undertaken in a purely objective, 'scientific', way; they each necessarily require us to make value judgements. The choice of dimensions, following as it does the choice of objectives, is clearly value-determined. The crucial questions are how great a degree of consensus can be achieved and how flexible is the specification of dimensions to the varying characteristics of clients and circumstances. The choice of weights or rankings in developing a scale will generally be value-laden, although in certain circumstances decisions as to the omission or inclusion of items and the ordering of circumstances could be value-free (Culyer, 1978). Generally, however, statements of 'higher morale', 'more independence', and 'better well-being' are all statements of value, and to treat them as if they were purely objective statements is to invite trouble. What we seek is a degree of 'controlled subjectivity' (Key, Hudson and Armstrong, 1976), not by basing our conclusions and recommendations on the phenomenological evidence gleaned from a non-random sample of one, but by making our assumptions and judgements fully explicit and by making it possible for the values of all concerned to be heard and, where necessary, counted. 'We thus find', argues Culyer (1978 p. 15)

> that choice of the dimensions of an index is partly a question of values, of interpreting the specific objects of policy, and partly a technical question, concerning valid, reliable, economical and reproducible methods of measuring the objects. Just as persons who may legitimately be thought to have a claim on the right to formulate objects of policy (e.g. the elderly, the representatives of those financing the programme) may have little competence in deciding those matters we have described as 'technical', so those with this latter competence are not necessarily those regarded as having a legitimate right to decide objectives, or dimensions of indexes.

It is not possible within the confines of this book to discuss the scaling of well-being in any detail. It would anyway be an inappropriate topic in an introductory account of the economics of social care, being better suited to a research manual or report. The first of the four tasks distinguished above – the choice of dimensions of well-being – has already been discussed in Chapter 2 and will be addressed again below. Scaling positions along these dimensions is a much more difficult task than the plethora of social care scales might suggest. All of the scales currently employed in social care research are either nominal (they simply classify individuals into groups) or ordinal (they rank individuals or states of well-being), and yet they are used as if they had the full cardinality properties of, say, a measure of height or weight. Few of the scales have yet been demonstrated to be *valid*, in the sense that they measure what they purport to measure, and *reliable* in that repeated uses of the scale in identical circumstances will produce identical results.[6] Nor is it clear that many of these scales are sufficiently *sensitive* to pick up the often very small changes in client well-being which occur during the period of assessment or evaluation. A fourth desideratum for any scale must be *manageability*. A morale scale of two hundred items may well be able to tap all of the many theoretical domains of subjective psychological well-being (from self-actualisation to positive self regard, and from ego-integrity to ego-transcendence), but it will also be likely to send most elderly respondents to sleep before it is even half completed. Thus, for example, Lawton's popular PGC morale scale was specifically designed to be 'of such length as to afford reasonable reliability, while at the same time not causing undue fatigue or inattention' (Lawton, 1972, p. 146).

The more contentious third and fourth tasks are undertaken when we are seeking a unidimensional and cardinal scale of client well-being. To the best of my knowledge they have not been attempted in social care contexts. However, a growing body of research on the measurement of health status and the outputs of health care services, particularly in Canada and the USA, clearly demonstrates the feasibility of performing these two difficult tasks. Culyer (1976, 1978) describes the principles of health status measurement, and Rosser (1983) has provided an excellent review of the more interesting applications.[7]

Scaling changes in well-being

Output is the movement towards care objectives so that a well-being scale is not enough on its own to measure output. It can only tell us the well-being of an individual or group at one point in time. Two developments are needed. We must first recognise that output is a *net* measure – it reflects the net effect of a care intervention. We thus need to make comparisons either between individuals or between time periods using a before-after design. Bare comparisons of values on the well-being scale are not enough, however, for relative positions on the scale (either for different individuals or for the same individual at two points in time) will be attributable to a great many factors other than differences in the amount and type of care received, as the production of welfare approach suggests. The second development is to introduce a *dynamic* component. Well-being is not a point measure (that is, a 'stock' concept), but a measure of 'flow' or trending. Most social care interventions are not occasioned by transient needs but by long-standing welfare shortfalls which require care over a period of time. Hit-and-run social care is rarely needed and rarely practised. Well-being thus has both *intensity* (measured, for example, by points on a scale) and *duration*. Related to this latter point is the complicating consideration that future levels of well-being will often be less important than present or immediate levels. We value the present more highly than the future. Thus in measuring well-being over a period of time we may need to weight (or 'discount', in the economist's terminology) future values on the scale to render them comparable with present values.[8]

Output measurement could be most reliably effected in practice if we were able to turn the clock back and examine the outcome of a different type of intervention (including no intervention) on the same individual. That is, we are interested in the effect of social care on an individual's well-being, over and above the level of well-being in the absence of care. On the horizontal axis of Figure 3.1 we measure the *duration* of well-being. On the vertical axis we measure *intensity* as reflected in the values of a well-being scale. At time t_0 the individual is referred to a social care agency or otherwise has his need assessed. At time t_1 the individual is placed, say in an old people's home. The impact of such a move is quite likely to be adverse: most new residents of old people's homes are vulnerable and disorientated, and the shock

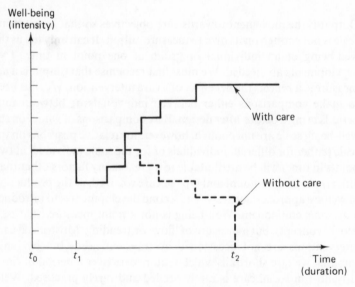

FIGURE 3.1　*Individual well-being – duration and intensity*

of 'relocation' can have very serious consequences, including mortality (Davies and Knapp, 1981, pp. 155–61). This initial adverse effect is illustrated by a dip in the solid line representing well-being in the event of care being received. The elderly resident will soon adjust to the new environment and well-being will improve, as illustrated by the gradual upward progress of the 'with care' line. This line traces the time path of well-being for the individual in care, but we cannot be certain that leaving the client in their own home might not have been a better option. We thus need to turn the clock back to time t_1 (the point of admission) and observe what happens in the event of no care. The well-being time-path in the 'without care' case is indicated by the dotted line. In this case a gradual decline in well-being is assumed until, at time t_2, the individual dies.

The two time paths have been drawn to represent deliberately contrasting well-being trends. The 'without care' line declines and the 'with care' line, after the initial adverse impact, rises. There will however be many circumstances in which both lines will move in the same direction. For example, any study of care services for the elderly must take into account the gradual process of biological ageing, which involves the deterioration of the major organs of the body, the nervous, circulatory and digestive systems, and the ability to resist disease. This may not be inevitable but it is very likely. As a result well-being may decline over time, both 'with' and 'without care'. This is illustrated in Figure 3.2 with an assumed slower rate of decline for the 'with care' alternative. Thus the intervention is, in some preliminary sense at least, effective. Similarly, there may be natural maturation effects which mean that both time-paths will rise. This will be the case, for example, in the assessment of the effects of care on a child's language acquisition or intellectual or emotional development (see Figure 3.3).

In all three illustrations there is no doubt that the effect of care has been favourable: well-being 'with care' is superior to well-being 'without care'. Consider now a further example (Figure 3.4). The initial impact of a placement (perhaps the admission to a home or removal of a child from the natural family) has such devastating effect that it takes a long time before overall well-being recovers to its pre-care level. How are we to judge on the basis of these trends in client well-being whether care is effective, for the time trends do not provide an immediately unambiguous result? Output is the differential effect of care – the 'additional well-being' that it generates. If we return to

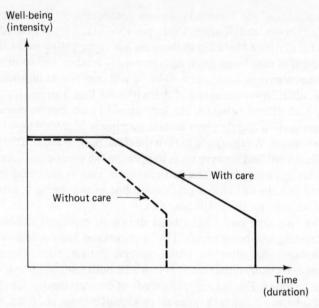

FIGURE 3.2 *Deteriorative trends in well-being*

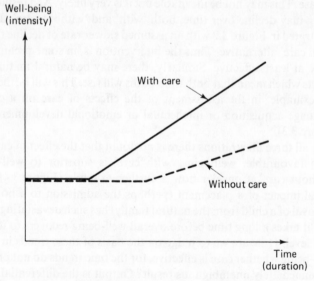

FIGURE 3.3 *Maturation trends in well-being*

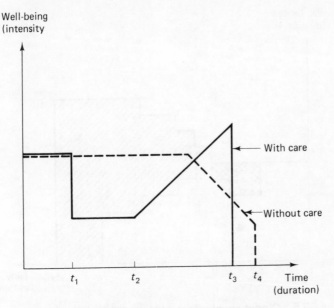

Figure 3.4 *Serious adverse effect of placement*

the somewhat simpler example that we started with (reproduced in Figure 3.5) we can define the *output*, as the single-shaded area *B* minus the double-shaded area *A*. Area *A* is the initial 'cost' of care to the individual (the adverse effect of the initial relocation) and area *B* is the enhanced well-being once the client has adjusted to the change. Four particular complications will arise when we attempt to translate these principles into practice:

(1) We have been drawing our diagrams on the assumption that after watching an individual progress through until (say) death we can then turn the clocks back and observe what happens without care. Obviously we cannot simultaneously observe a client in two completely different sets of circumstances.

(2) We cannot observe individuals continually but have to make do with discrete observations during the care period so as to obtain an approximation to the two time-paths.

(3) We cannot observe individuals for *ever* and yet many of the differential effects of care can only be observed over a very long period, perhaps seventy or eighty years. How do we assess

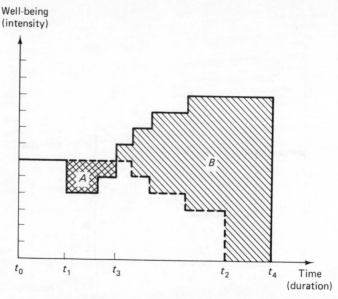

FIGURE 3.5 *Output equals differential impact on intensity and duration*

whether children brought up in a succession of different residential homes grow up to be 'well-adjusted' adults? We might only be able to tell by observing them throughout some, if not all, of their adult lives. A balance must be struck between allowing enough time to elapse for the full effects of care to be felt, and feeding findings back into the care system quickly enough to improve practice. This is not a trivial point. If we refer to Figure 3.5 we can see how the truncation date will influence the output measure. If we measured well-being until time t_4, area B would dominate area A and output would be positive and the intervention is effective. If, on the other hand, we truncated the measurement at time t_3, then area A would dominate and care is ineffective (output is negative).

(4) We will not be able to measure well-being without a certain amount of *error*. Some error will arise inevitably from random or chance fluctuations. Other errors will arise as a result of unreliable or invalid scaling techniques and because the data collection process will interfere in the lives of the individuals being observed.

Four corresponding decisions have to be taken. What *kind* of comparison should we make in order to measure the differential or net effect of care on a client? How *often* do we need to measure this differential effect? For *how long* do we need to monitor these effects? How do we minimise the *errors* and distortions associated with measurement? These are essentially all questions of research *design*. Do we compare individuals before, during and after care? Do we randomly assign referrals to 'experimental' and 'control' groups? Do we attempt to match individuals on the basis of certain prespecified criteria? Again, it is not my intention to dwell on these particular issues here. They are not straightforward or uncontroversial, and they can have very marked implications for the effectiveness of different research approaches.[9] They are considered at length in the evaluation and social statistics literatures, and a particularly useful discussion is given by Rossi and Freeman (1982).

Output measurement in practice

The requirements for a fully satisfactory output measure have now been set out. The measure must satisfy at least the following criteria:

(1) It covers the full range of care objectives.
(2) It measures individual well-being along each of the dimensions distinguished by the objectives, using valid, reliable, sensitive and manageable scales.
(3) Except in a limited number of cases,[10] it combines these scales into a unidimensional measure *or* is employed in an evaluative framework which later makes empirical or political trade-offs between them.
(4) It measures both the duration and intensity of well-being, observing clients over suitably long time periods.
(5) It employs a suitable research design in order to make valid comparisons between the 'with care' and 'without care' alternatives.

These are demanding criteria and it is perhaps not surprising that few (if any) attempts at output measurement for social care services have met them. Most progress has been made in relation to the first and second of these criteria – the identification and scaling of the dimensions of well-being – and the most comprehensive and coherent body of evidence concerns services for the elderly.

Research on residential environments for the elderly has identified and measured a large number of possible dimensions of output. Old people's homes are often almost self-contained communities so that all aspects of a resident's well-being are likely to be influenced by the experience of care. In principle, therefore, output measures need to range over almost every facet of resident quality of life. However, it has been argued that many aspects of quality of life are not valued for themselves but because of their contribution to a global well-being concept. This concept is usually operationalised as a measure (or a *set* of measures) of psychological well-being, life satisfaction or morale. Other outcomes of residential care, including mortality, morbidity and outputs enjoyed by residents' relatives, will generally need to be separately measured. These arguments are considered in detail by Davies and Knapp (1981). The consumer study of Willcocks *et al.* (1982) and the 'volunteer visiting' study of Power *et al.* (1983) provide useful insights into output measurement for British old people's homes, although neither is an output study *per se*. Power and his colleagues interviewed the residents of a small number of homes to assess their subjective life satisfaction. Interviews were conducted at two points in time. For the sample as a whole, no significant change in life satisfaction was found, although there was considerable inter-personal variation, and the authors expressed some doubts about the usefulness of the scales they employed. The consumer study of Willcocks and her colleagues was based on a much bigger data base. Stratified samples of ten residents from each of one hundred homes were included in the study, whose primary aim was to examine the effects of physical and social environments on the residents and staff of local authority homes. The residents were asked for their opinions about their physical and social environments. These were complemented by questions directed at a resident's happiness, health and a comprehensive indicator of general well-being. Unfortunately, these indicators of resident well-being apply to only one point in time so that it is not possible to examine the changes in well-being that are hypothesised to follow from residential care. Furthermore, only those residents able to answer questions were included, and the mentally infirm, deaf and blind (who comprised 21 per cent of the original sample) were excluded.

The most thorough of all output studies was that undertaken by

Challis and Davies (in press) for an innovative community care scheme for the elderly. Two dimensions of output were readily observable – mortality (a final output) and place of residence (an intermediate output) – and were examined over a three year period. However, the second of these was not a prime focus of the evaluation. Other dimensions required detailed assessments (nurturance, compensation for disability, independence, morale, social integration, family effects (psychological stress and coping difficulties) and community networks) and were measured twice during interviews, twelve months apart. In most cases it was possible to employ well-being scales which had proven validity and reliability properties (Challis, 1981). Comparative effectiveness was ensured by carefully matching clients receiving the new form of community care with a control group of clients receiving 'conventional' care packages in an adjacent area. The Challis and Davies study develops a tradition of evaluative research established in this country by Goldberg (1970) in her study of field social work services for the elderly.[11] However, it describes costs and outputs in greater detail, handles the interrelations in complex circumstances of joint supply and the dependence of costs and outcomes on client circumstances, and shows the connections between field arrangements, processes and techniques, and cost relations. These are essential developments in the methodology of evaluation research and output measurement.

Output measures for other client groups served by the social care services are less well established. For example, whilst there has been a lot of evaluative endeavour in the child care area, we still know relatively little about the comprehensive outputs of services. The objectives of child care include:

(1) Protection of the community and control of the child
(2) Reintegration with the family and the community
(3) Welfare support for families
(4) Development of socialisation skills and improvements in social behaviour
(5) Improvements in educational and intellectual performance
(6) Treatment of emotional disorders and improvements in emotional adjustment
(7) Improvements in or maintenance of children's physical health
(8) Development of independence and responsibility
(9) Development or maintenance of a sense of personal identity

These objectives are specified at a number of different levels, and very few child care studies examine more than one or two of them. Indeed, the majority of *foster care* studies in Britain employ just one indicator of output – placement breakdown – which is only an intermediate output, albeit an important one. There have been precious few methodological advances in this area since the work of Parker (1966) and George (1970). There have been some very detailed, small-scale studies of residential child care,[12] and a number of fairly narrow evaluations based on the longitudinal National Child Development Study.[13] Overall, however, 'very little study has been made of the effects of different types of care upon different types of children; research has not been concerned with evaluating methods of care and comparative studies of institutions and other types of care have been largely ignored' (Prosser 1976, p. 16).

Appropriately measured outputs have a number of important and urgent uses, but are difficult and expensive to obtain. We have seen that *in principle* there is an overwhelming preference for *final* output measurement, but that the exigencies of practice have often dictated the use of intermediate output indicators. This must be a cause for considerable concern. Virtually all social care services pursue *client-level* objectives and gauge their success (informally) in terms of client welfare. It is therefore both surprising and disappointing that output measurement in so many areas is still at such a primitive stage.

4

Costs and Inputs

But what does it cost?

In recent years it has been rare indeed to find a change or development of policy or practice that has not had to run the gauntlet of a long line of 'But what does it cost?' questions. The economic problems that beset Western economies in the mid 1970s forced upon public, private and voluntary providers of care a degree of cost consciousness hitherto unknown in the post-war period. As a consequence the cost constraint has been the subject of considerable criticism, and the short-sighted politician, the penny-pinching accountant, and the hard-headed economist have come to be viewed as the chief villains of the piece. Social care services, it has long been felt, are the preserve of the social worker or the student of social policy, and should not be the testing ground for economic theories or cannon fodder for central government fiscal policies. Costs, in short, are held to be anathema to social care.

The denigration, rather than applause, which greets many new attempts to impose a degree of 'cost effectiveness' upon care policies is a common feature of current trends. Criticism of the introduction of the economic element into policy-making stems in part from a feeling that services as indubitably and inherently 'desirable' as social care should be above the vicissitudes of national economic welfare. Nobody would deny the importance of social care services, but it would be dangerous and foolish to argue that they are beyond economic analysis. Few activities are costless. Resources are scarce and therefore have a positive value or cost to society. Allocating resources in one way immediately implies the rejection of an alternative allocation. The present economic climate has heightened our awareness of scarcity. If we want to make the best use of our scarce resources, if we want to deploy our available social care services in such a way as to maximise their effectiveness or their success, or to distribute them in accordance with agreed criteria of fairness or justice, then we need to take a long and careful look at the cost implications of our policy designs.

Unfortunately, social care administrators have only turned to a careful examination of costs at a time of economic adversity. Recession revealed a widespread ignorance of the basic principles of economic management and a distinct lack of both data and information for sensible policy-making, and the requisite expertise for gathering and applying it. Faced with a shrinking budget and a growing potential clientele, politicians and administrators have grasped unselectively the nettles of cost information readily available or readily collected. There has been little discrimination among available information sets, and little understanding of the problems of applying them in practice.[1] Higher staffing ratios have been criticised for wasting valuable skilled resources, community resources have often been exploited with little regard for their effectiveness, maintenance expenditure has been greatly reduced, and new capital projects have been pruned and/or postponed. The sad fact about a lot of this well-meant activity is that it is misplaced and misdirected.

Cost measurement is neither straightforward nor costless. In this chapter, therefore, I shall define and illustrate the concept of *cost* and demonstrate some of its many uses. This chapter is not, however, a 'manual of human service costing', although such practical guides build on the principles introduced here.[2] The *uses of cost information* are many and varied. Some of the most pressing and most interesting of these uses are illustrated later in the book: the examination of efficiency, the equitable allocation of resources, the development and application of pricing and other rationing mechanisms, and the evaluation of alternative strategies of care. Each of these uses applies equally at a number of levels – central government, local government, social work team, residential facility, individual client – although the details of application would need to be modified in accordance with particular circumstances.

Opportunity costs

'What does it cost to provide residential care for a mentally handicapped child?' This apparently straightforward and unambiguous question might be answered with an apparently straightforward and unambiguous answer, like '£200 per week'. But this and other similar questions deceive by their simplicity, for this answer is probably not the *real* cost of care.

To illustrate what is meant by the real cost, consider the tale of Robinson Crusoe. Suppose that Crusoe, on that eventful Friday when he first saw the footprints in the sand, had found not a fit, athletic man but instead a severely handicapped child. Crusoe would not have thanked us for giving him '£200 per week' to care for the unfortunate child, for money was of no use to him on his desert island. Much more useful would have been a gourd of goat's milk or a net of fish for, in caring for the mentally handicapped child, Crusoe would have to give up the time he would otherwise have spent milking or fishing. The *cost* to Crusoe of caring for the mentally handicapped child could not be reckoned in pounds sterling but in terms of what he had lost by not using his time and energy in an alternative pursuit (milking and fishing). Of course, Defoe's hero did not find a mentally handicapped child, but this distortion of a familiar story well illustrates the concept of *opportunity cost*. The cost of a resource or service cannot, in general, be reckoned merely by reference to its price, but must be gauged in terms of what is given up. Many care resources and services are not bought and sold in the market, and those that are have prices that are frequently influenced by market distortions. The concept of *opportunity cost* is intuitively appealing and indispensible in the study of efficiency and equity.

Robinson Crusoe had given up his milking and fishing in order to provide care, which had thus *cost* Crusoe the milk and fish he had not been able to collect. A little nearer home, we can imagine a social services department having to decide whether to build a new large multi-purpose family support centre or, using the same resources, to build two old people's homes. The cost to the department of the family centre is thus two old people's homes, and the cost of an old people's home is half a family centre. Alternatively, consider the case of the social worker who must sit in court for a whole morning awaiting a five minute hearing for a client. The cost of that court attendance is the value of the social worker's time spent in alternative pursuits — maybe arranging occupational therapy for an arthritic septuagenarian or visiting a prospective foster family. In each case we are expressing the cost in terms of the value of alternatives or opportunities that have been missed.

> *The cost of using a resource in a particular service or mode of care is not the money cost or price of the resource, but is the benefit forgone (or opportunity lost) by losing its best alternative use.*

Our need for cost information stems from our need to choose between alternatives. Resource inputs are scarce and we have to decide how best to employ them. Services are scarce, and we thus face the problem of choosing between alternative claims, wants or needs. Scarcity implies choice, and the act of choice gives us our definition of cost.

The social services department which chose to provide a family centre had not just rejected the old people's homes, but had rejected the *benefits* accruing from those homes. In principle, therefore, to measure costs we must be able to measure benefits or outputs. In practice, we will frequently use money to measure the opportunity cost, because money is a convenient yardstick against which to measure benefits. (It would be absurdly impractical to draw up a long list of alternative uses of a particular resource.) The money paid for a marketed resource will be a valid measure of opportunity cost if it reflects the value that the user places on it, and this will be the case if markets are 'perfect'. When market distortions are evident, the money price will need to be adjusted in order to give us an opportunity cost measure (see Chapter 7).

The cost to Robinson Crusoe in caring for a handicapped Man Friday could perhaps be reckoned in goat's milk and fish. Barring the total collapse of the British market economy, we would be unlikely to express the costs of care of the mentally handicapped today in such terms. Thus the cost of providing a particular service will depend on the alternative services that could be provided from the same resources, and there is no reason to suppose that those alternatives will remain unchanged over time or between locations.

It will be necessary to make the distinction between *private costs* and *social costs* for some of our subsequent discussions. Consider first the *expenditures* or *accounting costs* of social care. We might ask the matron of an old people's home to tell us the annual cost of running the home. Consulting the financial accounts, she would be able to list expenditures on staff, provisions, laundry, electricity, gas, and so on. The same question posed to the Director of Social Services might produce a larger figure with expenditure on field social workers, occupational therapy and chiropody services all added to the matron's list, even though it might not be easy to calculate the exact costs themselves. These services are financed by the social services department but do not appear in the accounts of the home. Asking the Secretary of State the same question could mean the addition of the cost of doctor's visits to the home. The Secretary of State's list of expenditures covers more of the services received by residents and is closest to the *social* accounting cost of care. Clearly when considering the *social* implications of a care policy we need to include a comprehensive listing of the costs to *all* agencies and individuals. We would thus need to include the costs borne by clients themselves and their relatives in this definition of social cost.

This same distinction between the private and social costs of care arises with the opportunity cost concept. *Whose* opportunity costs should we be monitoring? Ideally we need to be looking at the full range of resources employed in a care activity, whether or not directly costed to the providing agency, and to measure their opportunity costs to society as a whole. That is, we should be looking at the alternative uses of resources not just to their employers, but to society. There are likely to be constraints on the range of alternatives possible in any particular case, so that the opportunity cost in the short term may be different (presumably lower) than the opportunity cost over a longer period in which more alternatives may present themselves. This raises the related question of local autonomy and responsibility. In the short term there may be few incentives for social services departments to consider the wider, social, implications of their decisions. Indeed, they may be penalised for doing so, given the present context of local authority budgeting and allocation decisions and the arrangements for allocating central government grants.[3] In principle, all of the resources employed in social care need to be costed, whether or not they are provided by social services departments, and the method of costing should reflect the *social* nature of social care. The well-being of members of society is generally of *social* concern and many of the services or resources in this area are collectively financed. To ignore *social* opportunity costs could mean the misallocation of resources between, for example, the public and private sectors, between formal and informal carers, between the DHSS and the Department of Education and Science, between local authorities and the National Health Service, and between different local authorities. A situation in which it would be justifiable to measure the private opportunity cost to, say, a social services department rather than to society as a whole would be when the latter is difficult or impossible to value. A good *private* opportunity cost measure would be preferable to an uncertain or arbitrary social opportunity cost.

The adoption of an opportunity costing approach to social care thus has a number of implications:

(1)   We cannot measure the opportunity cost of employing a particular resource without knowing (or hypothesising) the alternative employments open to us.
(2)   Costs are forgone benefits.
(3)   Opportunity costs are context specific.
(4)   Opportunity costs and accounting costs (expenditures) are generally different.
(5)   Some apparently costly items or resources are actually costless.
(6)   Some apparently free items or resources have non-zero costs.
(7)   Administrative divisions in the planning and delivery of care should be ignored when reckoning the costs unless there are strong arguments to the contrary.
(8)   We should measure gross and not net costs. The incidence and scale of consumer charges, for example, varies widely (see Chapter 6).

Six examples of opportunity costing

Local authority accounts are designed for budgeting, financial probity and stewardship, and it is not therefore surprising that they provide an inadequate basis for opportunity costing.[4] The following six examples illustrate this problem and also emphasise the practical importance of the eight implications of an opportunity cost approach that are listed above.

Example 1: running an old people's home

The first two examples focus on residential care for the elderly. Consider a local authority home opened in 1970 and likely to remain in service for many years to come. Because the social services department already owns the building, the capital expenditure appears in the accounts as an estimated depreciation allowance or debt charge, the exact amount being a function of the original construction cost and the method of depreciation accounting employed. This is different from the *opportunity* cost of using the building as an old people's home. We need to place a value on the best *alternative* use of the building, which may be its social value as a hotel, or as pre-fostering unit, or as a home for severely mentally handicapped children. These alternative values may not be immediately obvious, but consider how much revenue could be attracted if the home was converted to a hotel. This forgone revenue is the opportunity cost of using the building as a residential home. Alternatively, consider the amount that the local authority would need to pay out to *rent* a building for use as a home. This too would provide a better indication of the opportunity cost of using the building as a residential home than would the depreciation costing. The opportunity cost of using the building, therefore, need bear no relationship to the annual depreciation allowance computed by the accountant, nor to the original cost of construction or purchase (see, for example, Sugden and Williams, 1978, p. 30).

The other resources employed in residential care similarly need to be costed in accordance with the principles of opportunity costing. It is helpful to distinguish staff costs and other running costs (call them 'living costs'). In many cases the (market) price paid for these resources will reflect their opportunity costs. For example, the social value of the provisions purchased for the home will be roughly the same as the price paid for them since, at the margin, members of society will not pay any more for these provisions than their value to them (cf. Williams and Anderson, 1975, p. 56). Thus, most living costs can be obtained with relative ease from the accounts of the home. Labour costs also appear in these accounts, but we have to be sure that the amount paid for individual staff members reflects the social valuation of their best alternative employment. This may be a reasonable assumption for regular, paid staff, but for volunteer staff, visiting general practitioners, field social workers and so on, the calculation of opportunity cost will be difficult. Personal consumption expenditure by residents should also be included. I shall consider these costs of old people's homes again in Chapters 8 and 9.

Example 2: building an old people's home

Consider now the costing of a *new* old people's home. This raises quite different practical issues. There are two immediate cost components and one more distant element: the cost of the land on which the home is to be built, the cost of design and construction, and the revenue consequences once the home is open. Again, it is important not to assume that publicly-owned land, or land already held freehold, is a free resource. Public land may not be on offer for private (commercial) use, but it will still usually have some alternative public use which bestows positive benefits upon society. A vacant plot of land may bestow social benefits simply by remaining vacant.

The second component, the cost of designing and actually constructing the home, raises the question of the alternative uses of the *funds* which would be allocated to construction. This is a complicated issue and it is not my intention to try to summarise the arguments here. Suffice it to say that we are interested in the social value of the next 'unit' of investment in the private sector, the so-called 'shadow price of capital' (see Sugden and Williams, 1978, pp. 215–17). Wager's (1972) study of alternative strategies of care for the elderly in Essex did not address this particular opportunity cost problem, but his study of *expenditure* on land and construction gives a good indication of its likely scale and variability. More recent figures are provided by Wright, Cairns and Snell (1981, p. 31) and Challis and Davies (in press, Chapter 10). Again the amount spent is not necessarily the same as the true social opportunity cost. The revenue consequence of capital investment should also be included at this stage. It has been estimated that: 'the amount of the additional revenue expenditure thus generated each year is about a fifth of the capital investment' (HM Treasury, 1973, p. 100). There are also consequences for other members of society, and for clients. New old people's homes outside built-up areas or on new estates may have lower land costs, but will impose higher visiting costs on relatives and higher social segregation costs on residents.

Example 3: recruiting new staff

Acting on the results of a recently completed survey, a social services department decides to establish two posts to consolidate and expand its foster care services for mentally handicapped and other 'hard-to-place' children. The senior fostering officer post is filled by the transfer of a senior social worker from one of the department's social work teams, who is paid the same amount as before. In this case we might make the reasonable assumption that opportunity cost and actual expenditure are the same. The second post is filled by a previously unemployed graduate holding a CQSW qualification. The alternative to employment in the fostering section is unemployment, and so the social opportunity cost is just the value of lost leisure.[5] Unemployment benefit should be disregarded as this is simply a 'transfer payment' – a redistribution or transfer of income from one part of society (national insurance contributors) to another (the unemployed) which is not payment for goods or services received.

Example 4: family care of disabled children

Recent changes in child care policy have laid much greater emphasis on family care rather than residential provision. For example, the establishment or expansion of specialist fostering sections can be observed in a great many local authorities and voluntary organisations. Consider the care of mentally or physically disabled children by their *natural* families. It is useful to distinguish those resources provided from the public purse and those provided by the family. In the former category are included the short stay residential (parental relief) provision, the incontinence service of the local health authority, the various household aids and adaptations, as well as social worker support, all provided by the social services department. Additionally some special education services may be provided in the home and financed by the local education authority and there will often be additional NHS services. The opportunity costing of these services presents no particular conceptual problem which has not already been discussed. However, the family services that constitute a crucial input into the care of the disabled child are more difficult to cost. One of the reasons for this is that we must decide to what extent the family services are voluntarily provided, in the sense that the satisfaction of caring for the child (partly) compensates the parents for the costs they incur, and to what extent the disability imposes a very real additional cost. This is not only difficult, but also controversial. That is, we have to decide how much additional burden is imposed on the family by the child's disability when compared with the usual 'burdens' of child-raising, for society may not wish to include the full burden in the opportunity cost calculation. Baldwin's recent study of this topic concluded that

> severe disablement in children has fundamental and far-reaching effects on family finances and the general management of money . . . The earnings of both men and women were lower . . . Men worked longer hours for smaller earnings and their long-term career and earnings were affected. The effect on women's earnings was widespread and substantial particularly as children grew up . . . Disability in a child led to a need for expenditure beyond what was normal for children of the same age (Baldwin, 1981, p. 477).

These substantial private costs should not be neglected in the calculation of the total costs of care.

Example 5: volunteers

The Conservative governments of 1979 and 1983 laid great stress on voluntary organisations and volunteers as alternatives to public services in the health, social care and other sectors. There are a number of reasons for this emphasis (Judge 1982b), including the arguments that this reliance reduces the burden on public expenditure and allows the more cost effective voluntary sector to expand. We will see in Chapter 10 that some of these cost effectiveness assumptions are simplistic and mistaken. For the moment, however, consider the opportunity cost of a volunteer. This cost will lie somewhere between zero, for a volunteer who forgoes no leisure of any value and who would not have been employed or actively engaged elsewhere, and the value of the wage that could have been obtained in normal, paid employment. Pollak (1976, p. 132) has argued that:

> The volunteer, by supplying his services for no remuneration is implicitly stating that the costs of voluntary participation (forgone leisure or alternative paid employment) may be equalled or exceeded by the personal benefits (enjoyment of the activity and/or satisfaction from benefits received by clients). The net cost of using

the volunteer, therefore, may be zero (or even negative!) since what the individual forgoes is compensated for by the benefits received.

What Pollak forgets, however, is the fact that some volunteers may be willing to work with more than one specific client or in more than one service, so that their use in care of the elderly means that benefits in the care of (say) the mentally handicapped have to be forgone. Research on the *motivations* and supply of volunteers provides some indication of the likely importance of this, particularly if – as now – there is an excess demand for voluntary support (see Qureshi *et al.* 1983, and the other contributions in Hatch, 1983). Philips (1981) costs volunteer time as forgone leisure time (valued at a lower amount than work time). However, Challis and Davies (in press, Chapter 10) report on a care scheme which included *paid* volunteers arguing that the negotiated payments might reflect not only the marginal valuations of volunteers' leisure, but also their perceptions of the 'psychic benefits and costs' of helping elderly people. For example, one in ten of the volunteers covered by this latter study were motivated by a desire to acquire the experience which could then be useful in getting a care job. The voluntary activity in these cases was a form of investment in human capital (Qureshi *et al.* 1983), so that a valuation based on forgone leisure would over-value the cost of voluntary activity.

Example 6: intermediate treatment

The final example of opportunity costing concerns the alternative treatments or 'disposals' currently used for juvenile offenders and clearly illustrates how relative costs will alter once one moves beyond the direct provision costs and beyond the 'monetary veil' of expenditure figures. The costs of a sentence to a youth custody centre or detention centre, or a period attending an intermediate treatment scheme, include the following:[6]

(1) *Direct provision costs* to the Home Office (custody), social services department or probation service (intermediate treatment).
(2) *Indirect public sector costs* falling, for example, to the education, housing and social services departments of local authorities, to schools and to the police.

(3) *Offender costs* associated with the deprivation of liberty (many or most of which should be ignored if they are viewed as part of the punishment or social retribution).
(4) *Family costs* incurred in visiting offenders in custody or supporting offenders attending community-based treatment programmes.
(5) *Society costs* from loss of output for those offenders in custody and offences committed during sentences.

This five-fold categorisation of costs provided the basis for a small-scale costing study of one intermediate treatment scheme in Kent in comparison with the costs of custodial sentences in borstals (now youth custody centres) and detention centres, and residential care in community homes with education. Expenditure figures for the direct providers were, respectively, £12.04, £27.07, £23.33 and £32.89 per trainee/resident week, suggesting that intermediate treatment was easily the cheapest alternative on a *per diem* basis.[7] Once the other elements of cost were included and once some of the apparently 'free' resources were costed (including prison officer housing, attendances at court, parental supervision, central and local government administration, and so on) the cost differentials narrowed considerably. For example the costs for intermediate treatment and detention centres became £17.33 and £23.25, halving the differential. These figures come from a small-scale study of a single intermediate treatment project using secondary data, and they should be treated with caution. However, they certainly suggest that the move from accounting to opportunity costs may substantially alter the picture.

Costs and outputs

We have already seen how unique 'point' estimates of cost are of limited value in the analysis of social care. We need to be aware of the likely variations in cost and the reasons for those variations. For example, the cost or expenditure per resident week in a children's home is higher in Inner London than it is in East Kent, is higher in a home accommodating older and more 'difficult' children, and will in part depend upon the proportion of available places occupied. The term 'the cost' is not, of course, the total amount expended but rather the *unit cost* or *average cost* per resident or per place. Ideally cost is measured as opportunity forgone. What then, is the relationship between cost and output? Because of the multiplicity, complexity and intangibility of final outputs I shall concentrate instead on an *intermediate* output – the number of clients. This is merely a convenient simplifying assumption which does not alter the general tenor of the argument. The cost-output relationship is fundamental to examinations of cost not only because of the obvious importance of the association between the two sides of the production equation, and therefore the care relationship, but also because it introduces a number of concepts which will be needed later in the book.

Fixed and variable costs

Fixed costs are those cost elements which exist no matter how much output we are producing, even if we produce nothing, whilst *variable costs* vary with output and disappear the moment we cease production. In terms of our opportunity cost definition, fixed costs are the *inescapable* benefits forgone, whilst variable costs are *escapable*. In the case of a children's home the fixed costs would be the benefits forgone by not using the building in an alternative way and these costs continue to arise no matter how many children are resident in the home and even after a home is closed (until the time that its function changes). The variable costs would be the opportunity costs of the staff, provisions, clothing and laundry. Of course, the adjectives 'fixed' and 'variable' are very much dependent on the time period under examination. For example, within a few months of closure, the home might be converted into a residence for old people and the building costs covered. The fixed costs have thus 'disappeared' or have become variable costs.

Time horizons

It is useful to distinguish three time horizons. The most immediate marks the limit to the *short-run* period within which decisions and plans are constrained by the fixity of certain resources. In the short run, certain (durable) inputs cannot be immediately added to or removed from the stock of employed resources. The dominant planning question in this short-run period is how best to employ existing fixed resources, particularly resources like land and capital, by applying varying amounts of the variable resources like labour and consumables. In the *long run*, the employment of any resources, no matter how durable or specialised, can be varied by the producer. If it was typically the case that children's homes could very easily be converted to old people's homes within two months of closure, then the long-run period in this conversion context might be two months away. As far as long-run planning is concerned, the producer must decide what new capital equipment and buildings to select and what existing 'fixed' resources to dispense with. Finally, we can distinguish a *very long-run* period within which the state of knowledge and technology, which were previously taken as parameters, can be improved or influenced. Current decisions pertinent to this third time period would thus cover the allocation of resources to research and development, and the search for improved or alternative services.

The short-run, long-run and very long-run time periods do not correspond to definite periods of calender time. Indeed they are really only theoretical constructions which correspond to sets of planning questions and decisions. However, the costs of providing a service will differ in character between the three periods. In the short run, we can distinguish components of cost which are attached to fixed inputs (the fixed costs) and components attached to variable inputs (the variable costs). In contrast, long-run costs are all variable, but only within the confines of existing knowledge. These differences between the short run and the long run are important in the examination of the cost-output relationship.[8] Very long-run costs must again all be variable, but in this case the extent of the variation is much greater and, by and large, unpredictable.

Total and average costs

The *total cost* of an activity is the sum of all expenditures incurred during some specified period, or – better still – the sum of all opportunity costs. The *average cost* or *unit cost* of an activity or production process is simply total cost divided by output. Returning to the distinction between fixed and variable resources we can further distinguish: total fixed cost, total variable cost, and their sum total cost. Corresponding to these are the average fixed costs, equal to total fixed cost divided by the level of output or scale of operation, average variable cost and their sum, average costs. These cost-output relationships are illustrated in Figures 4.1 and 4.2. When average costs are falling there exist *economies of scale*, and when they are rising there are *diseconomies of scale*. The initial economies are due to two factors: the sharply falling average fixed cost (as the fixed cost of running a building is shared between an increasing number of residents), and the falling average variable cost (due, for example, to economies in staffing). Diseconomies arise because beyond a certain occupancy level it becomes increasingly difficult for staff to cope with the larger numbers of children given the layout and scale of the home. In Chapter 9 I shall be examining the sources of economies and diseconomies with more rigour, and also looking at the realities of average cost curves in social care contexts.

Marginal costs

We have thus seen how the cost of providing residential care is a function of output. In this case we have focused on *intermediate*

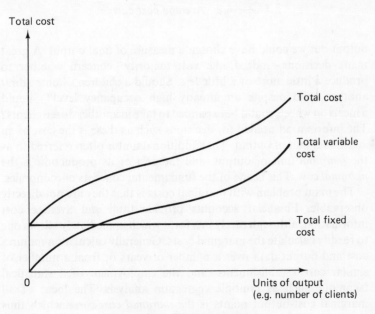

FIGURE 4.1 *Total cost curves*

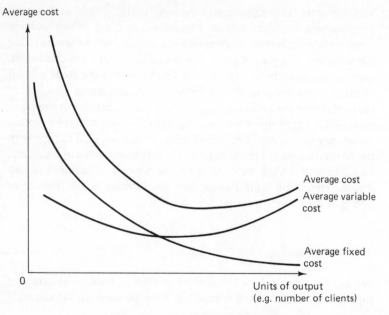

Average cost

Average cost

Average variable cost

Average fixed cost

0

Units of output
(e.g. number of clients)

FIGURE 4.2   *Average cost curves*

output but we could have chosen a measure of final output. A great many decisions – indeed, the vast majority – concern whether to produce a little more or a little less. Should a children's home admit another child despite an already high occupancy level? Should a meals on wheels round be expanded to take in another dozen clients? The information needed for decisions such as these is the cost of an additional unit of output. That additional unit is often referred to as the *marginal* unit of output, and the cost of its production is the *marginal cost*. This is one of the fundamental concepts of economics.

The main problem with marginal costs is that they are not directly observable. Financial accounts provide total and average cost information, although rarely in a form which immediately allows one to readily calculate the marginal costs. Generally calculation requires cost and output data over a number of years or from a number of similar care establishments, and the employment of a statistical technique such as multiple regression analysis. The locus of all marginal cost-output points is the *marginal cost curve* which thus shows how the cost of extra units of output varies with output (see

Figure 4.3). The point of intersection of the marginal and average cost curves is exactly at the cost-minimising level of output, for when average costs are falling, marginal cost must be *less* than average, or else costs would not fall. Contrariwise, when average costs are rising it must be the case that marginal is *greater* than average cost.

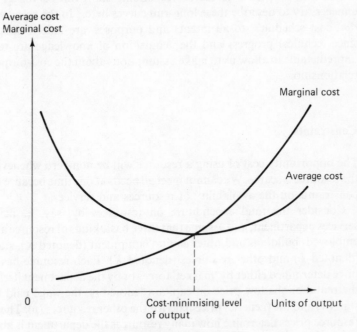

FIGURE **4.3** *Average and marginal costs*

Long-run cost curves

Each of the cost schedules described above was drawn on the assumption of a short-run planning horizon: at least one resource input was assumed fixed. In the long run all inputs are variable so that output can be expanded or contracted not only by altering the variable inputs (the amounts of the staff and other resources) but also by employing more or less of the previously fixed input. This could mean expanding the building or adding further buildings. The total, average and marginal cost curves previously derived are thus all *short-*

run cost curves which correspond to a particular quantity of the fixed input. They show how total, average and marginal costs vary as more or fewer staff and other resources are combined with the fixed amount of building capital. *Long-run* cost curves, which are plotted on the assumption that the quantities of all inputs can be varied, have similar shapes and properties to the corresponding short-run curves. It is unnecessary to describe these long-run curves here.[9] In the *very long run*, cost schedules, to all intents and purposes, are indeterminate since technical progress and the acquisition of knowledge are too unpredictable to allow us to make assumptions about the cost-output relationship.

Constraints

The opportunity cost of using a resource will be non-zero whenever the resource is scarce. We cannot meet all needs at one time because of constraints on the availability of resources and services.

Consider the total expenditure on resources by, say, a social services department, and assume that three basic kinds of resource are employed: buildings and other capital equipment (denoted K), staff (denoted L) and other resources (denoted X). Each resource has a price determined either by 'market' forces or by the department itself: the rental or shadow price on capital (denoted r), the wage paid to staff (w) and the (generic) price paid for the other resources (p). These resource prices determine how many resources the department is able to purchase from its budget (B):

$$B = rK + wL + pX$$

The amount spent is equal to the sum of the price of each input multiplied by the number of units of the input. This simple equation illustrates the nature of the constraints that the department faces. For example, the department can attempt to increase its budget allocation B so that more of some or all resources can be employed, or it can alter the *balance* of resources employed. In either case the aim will be to alter the quantity and composition of services that are provided; that is, to so change the inputs employed as to raise the level or alter the composition of outputs. However, the production technology will impose a limit on the extent to which input proportions can be varied.

The constraints faced by a producer at any level (from field social worker to government minister), are budgetary, technological, legal, distributional and supply-related. I shall only say a little about each of them here, for (where relevant) they have been or will be discussed in more detail elsewhere in the book.

Budgetary constraints

The social care budget is successively sliced and divided, starting at Cabinet level and ending with the allocation of services between clients.[10] Decisions about budgets in the public sector are taken by:

(1) *The Cabinet*, allocating resources between spending departments
(2) *Government departments*, allocating resources between services (the Department of Health and Social Security) and local authorities (the Department of the Environment)
(3) *Local authorities*, allocating resources between departments (education, social services, housing etc.)
(4) *Social services departments*, allocating resources between client groups (elderly, children, etc.), services (residential, day, domiciliary, etc.) social work teams, and administration (etc.)
(5) *Social workers*, allocating resources between clients

Technological constraints

This second constraint has also been encountered before: there is a physical limit to the amount of variation in the combinations of resource inputs employed. This limit is determined by the production technology. Some resources are essential for production; for example, staff are essential for virtually all forms of social care. However, different *types* of staff are substituted to a degree. For example, there is probably more scope for the substitution of highly qualified social work staff by unqualified welfare assistants than is generally acknowledged (Bebbington, Davies and Coles, 1979). Other resources can only be used in certain circumstances; for example, each meals on wheels van requires one and only one driver at a time. These technological or physical constraints are generally rather less obvious and predictable in social care contexts than in, say, manufacturing industry, but they are real constraints nonetheless. There will also be constraints on the administrative burden that can be borne, which can also be seen as a technological constraint.

Legal constraints

Some combinations of resources and services are ruled out by the existing legislation. Legal constraints may, for example, restrict inter-departmental or inter-service collaboration, or may restrict local authorities' use of the informal care sector.

Distributional constraints

Altering the total budget or the balance of component spending in order to increase output is not purely an efficiency consideration but also has implications for the distribution of services and, ultimately, of individual well-being. This distributional issue will be discussed in the next chapter.

Supply-related constraints

One of the most restrictive of constraints is the supply responsiveness of suitable skilled labour resources. This supply constraint exists whenever a social services department, for example, is unable to obtain as many units of a resource as it requires at the going price. That 'going price' may be exogenously determined (as are the salary ranges for social work staff), or laid down by a higher authority (the social service committee or government department, as in the case of, respectively, boarding out allowances and approved adoption allow-ances), or defined by convention (as with the zero wage paid to volunteers). However, there will generally always be some scope for altering the price offered so as to attract a greater supply of resources. We are thus interested in the *supply response*: the effects of changing prices and 'conditions of employment' (broadly defined) on the available supply of resources.

Cost considerations have always been important in the planning of the personal social services, and that importance can hardly have been more pressing or more widely acknowledged than it is today. Nevertheless, the 'cost of care' remains one of the most over-simplified and under-studied concepts in the lexicon of social care planning. A steadily growing demand for cost information in the last decade or so has not been matched by a stream of relevant or reliable cost research. Instead we can only observe a trickle of studies which are often peculiarly partial and misleadingly myopic, though nearly always undertaken with the very best of intentions. This is both unfortunate and dangerous at a time when so many choices between alternative policies (and practices) in the social care sector are so clearly influenced by perceived differences in cost. The scarcity of resources forces us to make choices, and it is to the criteria of choice that we now turn.

5
Efficiency in Social Care

Criteria of choice

It is scarcity which forces us to make choices, and not just in times of recession and cutback. The scarcity of *resource inputs* means that careful decisions need to be made as to their employment in the production of social care or their employment elsewhere. The scarcity of *intermediate outputs* means that the allocation of services to clients (or vice versa) must be purposive and acceptable. These scarcities imply, through the production of welfare process, the scarcity of *final outputs*. What, then, are these 'principles of allocation'?

This chapter focuses on the principal criterion of economic analysis for resolving competing claims – efficiency – although it will be important not to neglect another important criterion, that of equity.[1] Others, such as autonomy, liberty and diversity tend to appear but rarely, and are anyway not necessarily logically inconsistent with these other two. *Efficiency*, basically concerns the size of the social care 'cake' whilst *equity* concerns its allocation or distribution between individuals, although we shall see that this distinction is often a little too simplistic.

In this chapter I shall concentrate on the efficiency criterion and I shall have relatively little to say about the equally interesting criterion of equity. There are a number of good reasons and one bad one for this relative neglect. The bad reason is that there is more than enough work to do on the efficiency side for me to be able to devote time to detailed discussions of equity considerations. Of more pertinence is the fact that discussions of equity criteria are much more comfortably located in the domain of political philosophy than of economics. I am not suggesting that the often artificial divisions between the social sciences be rigorously upheld, but I am making a plea based on the principle of comparative advantage. In this case economists have a comparative advantage when it comes to the discussion of efficiency, and paramountly not when it comes to discussions of equity. I do not intend to ignore equity in what follows. In particular, I will be especially concerned to examine the efficiency implications of different equity criteria, as well as the efficiency with which principles of equity are put into practice.

Efficiency and equity

It is important to notice at the outset that efficiency and equity are neither independent nor mutually exclusive. A reallocation of available resources with a view to raising efficiency may well alter the distribution of benefits or burdens to clients. Similarly, redistributing available services and their benefits in order to achieve some new principle of equity or fairness could well mean a diminution of the total production of services because efficient working patterns are disturbed, or because resources are diverted away from production to distribution. In some circumstances, therefore, there is likely to be a direct conflict between efficiency and equity. Alternatively, of course, the pursuit of an equitable distribution may *improve* efficiency. Even if one or other criterion is clearly predominant it would be foolish to ignore the implications of a policy decision based on one criterion for the achievement of the other. Efficiency analyses cannot proceed in ignorance of equity.

Within the economics literature there are three approaches to the equity issue. There are a few economists who view efficiency and equity as independent criteria. Efficiency is argued to be the preserve of the economist and aspects of equity or distribution are either completely ignored or are left to the 'distributional branch' of government. As Culyer (1980, p. 60) writes:

One of the many ways in which economists have traditionally divided their analysis is into a box concerned with equity and social justice and another concerned with efficiency. There is a great deal more, one may note, in the efficiency box than the other.[2]

Some economists, therefore, have assumed that equity issues can be ignored – either out of ideological commitment, or from a desire for a quiet life, or because they are unhappy about the value judgements that equity discussions involve, even though these are more or less the same as those used in resource allocation decisions (Baumol, 1982). In doing so they often give the impression 'that if only the "problem" of income distribution could be solved, all else is merely a matter for efficiency analysis' (Culyer, 1976, p. 85).

A second approach to the dual criteria of efficiency and equity has been to recognise their interdependence and to assume that the economist is best positioned to integrate them. Classical utilitarianism regards utility maximisation as a criterion of both equity and efficiency, but more recent excursions by economists have tended to adopt a 'professionally arrogant' approach (Culyer, 1977, p. 152). Turvey (1963, p. 96) wrote that 'the value-judgements made by economists are, by and large, better than those made by non-economists'. More apposite is the problem that attempts to trade-off efficiency against equity run the risk of imposing the economist's *own* values on a social decision. The third approach, then, is to recognise the essential interdependence of efficiency and equity, and either to examine the efficiency implications of alternative equity criteria and to leave the trade-off to others (the 'decision-maker') or attempt to obtain some consensus values for use in the analysis. This third approach is probably the most popular and useful today and will be illustrated in Chapter 7 in the context of cost benefit analysis.

Equity is not the same as equality: the latter would imply equal shares and the former fair shares. An egalitarian distribution, therefore, would give everyone an exactly equal amount of a particular service (say) whilst an equitable distribution would, perhaps, give rather more of the service to the more needy. Egalitarian and equitable distributions will only coincide if everyone's needs are the same, or in the case of equity defined as outcome equality. The pursuit of an equitable distribution is thus the pursuit of fairness or justice, and each individual is likely to have his own view as to what does and does not constitute fairness.

The unifying objective of the various social care services is to meet the social needs of the population. Allocating resources or services according to need, however, is *not* in itself an equity criterion as the term 'need' is conventionally (and loosely) employed. As Weale (1978, p. 70) explains:

the satisfaction of needs is itself a benefit to be distributed in accordance with some principle . . . It is therefore wrong to assert that social justice is distribution according to need, since the benefit to be distributed, i.e., the satisfaction of needs, is being confused with the rule under which the benefit is distributed.

The question of equity arises when we decide *how* to allocate according to need. Furthermore, need is 'invariably instrumental' (Culyer, 1980, p. 63): an individual needs care in order to improve (say), self-care capabilities, but there are various ways in which that improvement can be achieved. What in fact has happened is that the equity criterion is itself embodied in the particular definition of need. For example, to say that day nursery provision should be available for *all* children under the age of five is to define equity in terms of basic *rights* and to imply a definition of need which has but one criterion: the individual must be under five. In contrast, a more selectivist view of equity would give priority in the allocation of day nursery provision to children at risk of (say) physical abuse or neglect and this would give a much narrower definition of need.

It is helpful to make the distinction between horizontal and vertical equity. *Horizontal equity* is the equal treatment of equals: individuals with the same 'needs' should receive an equivalent amount of care or service. There are two immediate complications here. Firstly, we should take care in our use of the term 'needs' since we have already given that term a very precise meaning in contrast to the rather loose usage in most of the social care legislation which advocates allocation according to need. Horizontal equity could thus mean the equal treatment (in a sense to be discussed below) of individuals with identical 'welfare shortfalls' (along separate dimensions or aggregated in a weighted sum to a single dimension) or it could mean the equal treatment of individuals with welfare shortfalls whose removal by the most efficient means would cost an identical amount. Secondly, we face a number of alternative meanings for 'an equivalent amount of care'. Do we take it to mean that individuals with equal shortfalls receive exactly the same type and amount of service? No, because this denies the opportunity to exploit variations in technology and variations in input prices, as we saw in Chapter 2. Does it mean, therefore, that 'equivalent individuals' receive services (possibly different services) which *cost* exactly the same amount? It could do, but it must be remembered that allocating services to equalise costs could mean that individuals with identical shortfalls end up at different levels of welfare. This is because the scarcity of resources means that only *part* of the shortfall is likely to be removed, because different care technologies will be appropriate (and efficient) in different areas, and because different services will produce outputs (i.e., remove shortfalls) at different rates. An alternative definition of 'equivalent treatment' would be to ensure that similar individuals end up (after a social care intervention) with similar levels of welfare, that is individual outputs are the same across like individuals. Ultimately, of course, the resolution of these alternative approaches can only be achieved by value judgement.[3] There are other complications concerning the concept of horizontal equity which will not be discussed here (see Feldstein, 1976; Plotnick, 1982).

In contrast, *vertical equity* is the unequal treatment of unequals. In most social care discussions the vertical equity concept is discussed in terms of the differential allocation of services or outcomes to individuals with different needs. However, we must again guard against the inappropriate use of the term 'need'. Need is a relative, normative, cost benefit-type concept and embodies in it a particular principle of equity. To talk about the differential allocation of services in accordance with different needs, then, is simply to state a tautology, and we would be better advised to define it as the appropriately different treatment of individuals with different welfare shortfalls. The question of vertical equity, then, is to rigorously define what 'appropriately different treatment' means in practice, that is to arrive at a particular set of need judgements, or, to anticipate a later discussion, to define target groups and to allocate resources to them. The *principles* of deciding 'appropriately different treatments' have rather been dodged in *empirical* forays into the allocation of services. Bebbington and Davies (1980) and West (1981) use as their working criterion of vertical equity the *present* allocation of services to clients by service professionals. The unequal treatment of unequals is thus left in the hands of (informed) professionals. In the empirical workings of the Bebbington and Davies study these professional judgements are taken from a deep trawl of the relevant literature on care of the elderly. That these authors have side-stepped the issue of vertical equity should not be taken as too serious a criticism, for Bebbington and Davies assume a number of different allocations to reflect different allocation criteria. Starting from the other end (with clear philosophical intent) would certainly be most interesting, but would not necessarily be helpful in the search for a set of widely approved need indicators for the allocation of central government grants.

What then are the principles of equity espoused by political philosophers? The most commonly discussed principles in general discussions of equity or distributive (or social) justice are distribution according to desert, distribution according to the maxims of utilitarianism, and distribution according to some contractarian principle, the best known being that of Rawls.[4] Distribution according to *desert*, however, is unlikely to find many supporters in the social care field, although its attractiveness in discussions of, for example, earnings has been noted by both the entrenched supporters of a capitalist economy and its opponents. Certainly some of the better known characteristics of the Poor Law, with its distinctions between the deserving and undeserving poor, rested on the criterion of desert, and Smith (1980) uncovered some allocative procedures in his work which could be interpreted in this way.

Distribution according to *utilitarian* principles follows from the maximisation of the total net satisfaction of the members of society. Accordingly an individual's level of satisfaction or welfare is to be weighted by something called the 'marginal utility of his income', a concept familiar to many readers, but one which no reader will ever have actually seen measured. Estimation of such marginal utilities is left to some 'mythical omniscient observer who, somehow, makes the necessary interpersonal comparison' (Culyer, 1976, p. 82). Utilitarianism has been criticised on this and other grounds, and particularly because of its neglect of the basic rights and liberties of individuals (Rawls, 1972; Weale, 1983).

Rawls is one of a number of political theorists who have proposed a *contractarian* alternative to utilitarianism as a principle of distributive justice. Within the contractarian approach members of society are assumed to enter into a social contract which governs various aspects of social choice (including distributive justice), but in entering into the contract they are ignorant of their own future positions in society. This 'veil of ignorance' will lead, Rawls argues, to an equity criterion which seeks to maximise the satisfaction or welfare of the least advantaged member of society. In social care terms this so-called *maximin* rule would mean achieving the highest possible level of well-being for the person with the *lowest* level. The strength of the Rawlsian approach lies in its development of a principle of distributive justice from a set of purely *rational* premises. As a practical guide to the use of scarce social care services, however, its strict allocative mechanism could lead to the absorption of all or most care resources by just a small number of very needy individuals. Furthermore, Rawls' argument that distributive justice must always dominate efficiency is unnecessarily restrictive and the suggestion of a utilitarian trade-off between the two might be more valuable. In other words the Rawlsian maximin procedure, whilst undoubtedly useful for general social policy purposes (such as the distribution of income or opportunities) is of relatively limited value in our narrower social care context.[5]

Before moving on to consider efficiency, it should be noted that the equity criterion must be distinguished from the 'caring externality'. The latter arises because of our concern or compassion for others and generally will be rather more specific in focus than the general principle of equity to which one might alternatively wish to make appeal. Both concepts, externality and equity, will therefore arise again in the next chapter.

Definitions of efficiency

Efficiency is achieved by allocating resources to generate the maximum possible output. Inefficiency in the use of inputs thus means that they could be reallocated in a way which would increase the amount of output produced. An alternative way to view efficiency is that it is the minimisation of the cost of producing a given level of output. The concept of efficiency is thus straightforward, although there are a large number of alternative basic definitions and conceptualisations both within economics and elsewhere.[6] I make no attempt to provide a comprehensive review of these various efficiency concepts, but I shall introduce a number of the most important varieties, particularly those which are needed in the study of social care.

Allocative efficiency

Efficiency can be studied at so many different levels of generality and specificity that no single concept can be sufficient. The most general or global concept is *allocative efficiency* which takes account not only of the productive efficiency with which inputs are transformed into outputs, but also includes the efficiency with which outputs (goods and services) are distributed among consumers (so as to maximise their well-being) and the efficiency with which production is adjusted to consumer preferences. The concept of allocative efficiency is closely related to *Pareto optimality* which pertains when no input or output can be reallocated to make someone or some group better off without simultaneously making some other person or group worse off. The use of Pareto optimality as a criterion for comparing alternative social states arose out of a desire to avoid making interpersonal comparisons of well-being, a desire which was not to be fulfilled. Today, whilst many economists adhere to the concept of Pareto optimality it has also attracted a lot of criticism (see Lutz and Lux, 1979; Nath, 1969; Ng, 1979; Weale, 1983; and Wilson and Wilson, 1982). I shall say no more about allocative or Pareto efficiency, for it is of limited value at the level which interests us here. Instead I confine my attention to efficiency in production where we can distinguish a number of useful constructs: effectiveness, technical efficiency, price efficiency, and social efficiency.

Effectiveness, productivity and X-efficiency

Effectiveness refers to a simple increase in output following the introduction of an additional unit of input. An effective production process is simply a process which produces something. A necessary but not sufficient condition for efficiency is effectiveness in production. A social care service or activity cannot be efficient if it is not effective, and the effectiveness has sometimes been doubted (Goldberg and Connelly, 1982, pp. 86–9). A closely related concept is *productivity*, the capacity to produce, which can be simply defined as the ratio of output to input.[7] Problems have arisen with productivity measurement in the past, mainly because of the undue reliance placed on single outputs or single inputs. In many studies, productivity is measured simply as labour productivity, and this immediately gives rise to problems if capital inputs are not equally distributed or of equal quality in the different firms or plants under consideration. When more than one output is used, and when more than one input is considered, there are considerable difficulties of aggregation. Of course, productivity measures which take account of all inputs (and possibly, too, all outputs) are little different from measures of technical efficiency (see below). It is useful to distinguish productivity as a separate concept for a number of reasons, one of which is the relationship between labour productivity and the concept of *X-efficiency*. 'When an input is not used effectively, the difference between the actual output and the maximum output attributable to that input is a measure of the degree of X-efficiency' (Leibenstein, 1978, p. 17; see also Leibenstein, 1979; and Hampson, 1979). X-efficiency is not discussed in any great detail here, although it will appear again in Chapter 9 as one reason for diseconomies of scale. Effectiveness, productivity and X-efficiency are really concerned with the performance of individual inputs, and particularly individual staff members, employed by a firm or plant (at least when measured in practice). We are generally concerned with more than just one or two inputs, and efficiency is more usefully discussed as a firm-level or plant-level concept.

Technical and price efficiency

It is useful to make the distinction between technical efficiency and price efficiency, although it is well known that in some respects the distinction is arbitrary and made only for computational convenience. A firm or plant is fully *technically efficient* when it produces the maximum set of outputs from a given amount of inputs. With a number of alternative production processes for a single output, or for a production unit producing a number of distinct outputs, inputs should be transferred to alternative uses in such a way as to equalise their marginal productivities in alternative uses. *Price efficiency*, as its name suggests, is attained by a production unit when it employs the various inputs in such proportions as to produce a given level of output at minimum cost. Under certain assumptions as to production behaviour, such as cost-minimisation or profit-maximisation, price efficiency is attained when the ratio of input marginal productivities equals the corresponding ratio of input prices. A technically efficient production process which is also price efficient can be called *cost effective*, since it produces the given output at minimum cost. The concept of *organisational slack* (or *budgetary slack*) is a form of price inefficiency. Cyert and March (1963) introduced the concept, defining it as the set of 'payments to members of the coalition (or firm) in excess of what is required to maintain the organisation'. Thus, wage levels may be set above the level required to keep employees working for the organisation, and managers' conditions of service (their salaries, office accommodation, expense accounts, mileage allowances, and so on) are also more generous than needed. It may also be characterised – in social care organisations – by over-spending per client, and is most likely to occur in periods of growth. It is the presence of budgetary slack which may help to explain patterns of local authority spending on social care. We will be particularly concerned with technical and price efficiency in the discussion of cost variations in Chapter 9.

Social efficiency

It should be noted immediately that a cost effective technique or process need not be 'socially efficient'. Cost effectiveness indicates only the most sensible among different ways of doing something; it does not tell us whether we should be doing the thing in the first place. Full *social efficiency* is achieved when net social benefits (social benefits less social costs) are maximised. By considering social benefits and costs we immediately concentrate attention on the full ramifications of the care services under consideration. Social costs are defined in the normal way as the benefits that could have been derived from the consumed resources had they been employed in their next best alternative use, that is, they are opportunity costs. The social benefits, preferably measured in units commensurate with the units of social costs, should cover each and every output of the service including, of course, the direct private benefits to the client. One thus faces

a formulation of the efficiency test in which the unit to be costed is a true unit of output or achievement, and in which the measurement of costs ranges over all resources or inputs, and not just one 'key' one, nor even just those which have to be paid for out of the agency's own budget. The main conceptual blockage in the way of sensible and relevant efficiency analysis in the social services is the failure to realise this simple truth (Williams and Anderson, 1975, p. 5).

The concept of social efficiency is illustrated in Figure 5.1. The total social cost curve was encountered in Chapter 4. It is drawn concave to the horizontal axis in the upper part of the figure to represent that part of the marginal cost curve which is rising. In the lower part the marginal social cost curve is plotted against output (Q). The total and

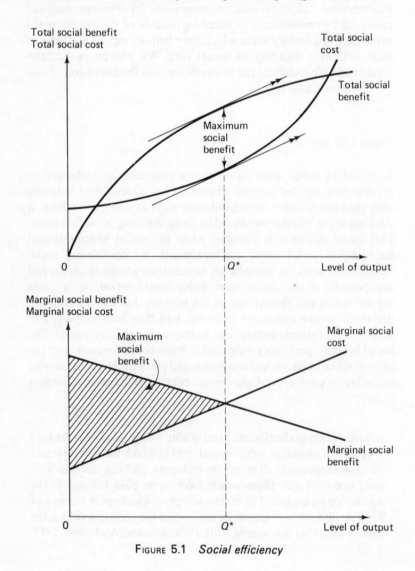

FIGURE 5.1 *Social efficiency*

marginal social *benefit* schedules are logical developments of the output concepts discussed in Chapter 3. Purely for expositional purposes I am assuming that the costs and benefits of a particular activity can be measured in identical (monetary) units, although in moving from exposition to application we will clearly encounter difficulties in trying to find a common unit of measurement. (In practice we should be able to obtain monetary measures of cost but we might prefer to leave the (implicit) imputing of the monetary values of the outputs to the decision-maker. Also in practical circumstances we would not need to derive the *full* benefit and cost schedules, but only those parts of the schedules around the hypothesised intersection point, or around the current or proposed levels of activity.)

What is the justification for the particular shape of the marginal and total social benefit schedules illustrated in Figure 5.1? To make the discussion rather less abstract, assume that Q denotes the number of home help hours received by a client each week. It is clear that the *total* value of the home help to a client should increase as the number of hours is increased. In each hour a little more assistance is provided, thus raising the physical and psychological well-being of the client. The total social benefit schedule should therefore rise as Q rises. The marginal benefit (or marginal value) is likely to *fall* because each successive hour of home help will be of *less* value than the previous hour. (Alternatively the concept of diminishing marginal value or marginal benefit can be illustrated with the help of consumption of a more familiar kind, such as tea-drinking. The benefit or value to the consumer of a second cup of tea will generally be rather less than the benefit derived from the first cup.) With a falling marginal benefit curve the total benefit curve will be convex to the horizontal axis (as illustrated).[8] The aggregate of a set of individual marginal benefit curves will also be of this general shape. Note that the marginal private benefit schedule (the incremental benefits to the client alone, ignoring the effects on other people) is generally the same as the client's *demand* schedule, and that the marginal private cost schedule (the incremental costs of production incurred by the producer alone) is the producer's *supply* schedule. In this discussion of efficiency we are thus very close to the conventional demand and supply analysis.

The total benefit and cost schedules both rise as the number of home help hours increases. What is crucial is not the point at which total cost exceeds total benefit (if such a point even exists), but the point at which the difference between them is maximised. This is point Q^* on the upper part of figure 5.1. This point is most easily found, not by studying the total curves but by considering the *marginal* schedules. Because a marginal curve is derived as the differential of the corresponding total curve the point of *maximum net social benefit* will occur at the point of intersection of the marginal benefit and cost schedules. If more than Q^* hours of home help are provided, the cost of the last hour will exceed the benefits it generates and is thus *inefficient*. If less than Q^* hours are supplied the marginal benefit of the last hour will exceed the marginal cost. There thus remain unrealised net benefits.

At this socially efficient level of provision (Q^*) there remain unrealised (gross) benefits. Beyond Q^* it is not 'socially worthwhile' to provide home help to this particular client. But from where does this criterion of 'social worth' derive? The social cost curve which imposes this constraint on the realisation of all known benefits is based on opportunity cost considerations. The opportunity cost of one more hour of home help beyond Q^*, which is most likely (conceptually) to be measured in terms of the *benefits forgone* by not supplying this hour of help to a different client, is greater than the benefit generated by providing to the present client. If benefits forgone exceed benefits generated, then a social resource (one hour of home help) has been inefficiently employed. Thus the limiting cost constraint is not something arbitrarily imposed by an uncaring accountant (or even a caring economist), but is an inevitable consequence of the scarcity of resources relative to welfare shortfalls or needs.

The move from effectiveness through to social efficiency thus proceeds logically: effectiveness is a necessary prerequisite for technical efficiency; cost effectiveness is defined with reference to the set of all technically efficient activities or techniques; and social efficiency builds on these lower level concepts.

Target efficiency

One further concept which has attracted attention is *target efficiency*, defined as 'the efficiency with which resources are allocated to and among those for whom receipt has been judged the most cost effective method of intervention' (Bebbington and Davies, 1983b, p. 311).

Target efficiency is a measure of the extent to which a particular principle of equity (embodied, as we have seen, in allocation according to need or allocation according to some individually-based measure of cost effectiveness) is met in practice by the distribution of care resources. Equally, it could be seen as one aspect of the degree of efficiency given an equity criterion. Thus equity and efficiency are of equal importance and are simultaneously prescribed in defining target efficiency. It assumes, not unreasonably, that one can first (loosely) order all potential clients with respect to the net benefit to be received from a particular service (a question of efficiency), having previously decided that this is the most cost-effective means for producing the output. One then compares the actual allocation of services with that allocation which distributes services to clients in decreasing order of expected net benefits (a question of equity).

The Bebbington and Davies study of target efficiency is timely, for an earlier commentator found 'no statistical evidence concerning the distributional impact of the (personal) social services' (Le Grand, 1982, p. 18). Focusing on the home help service and its distribution between areas and sexes, they employ two measures of target efficiency:

(1) *Horizontal target efficiency* – the extent to which those deemed to be in need of a particular service actually receive it.
(2) *Vertical target efficiency* – the extent to which the available social care resources are received by those deemed to be in need.

These can both be illustrated with the help of Figure 5.2. The circle $(A + B)$ denotes the currently available home help services and the larger circle $(B + C)$ denotes the set of 'needy' clients. Only B of these $(B + C)$ clients receive home help so that the degree of vertical target efficiency is $B/(B + C)$, and only B of the currently available services go to 'needy' clients so that the degree of horizontal target efficiency is $B/(A + B)$. The vertical measure thus indicates the concentration of resources on the 'target group' and the horizontal measure indicates the rate of uptake.[9]

These two measures of distributional impact allowed Bebbington and Davies to examine both territorial justice and sex discrimination in the allocation of home help services. They find evidence of inequity. The elderly in metropolitan areas are favoured relative to those living in rural areas and this may not be fully compensated for by the availability of other services. They found no distributional bias by sex

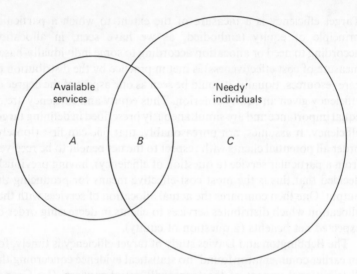

FIGURE 5.2   *Horizontal and target efficiency*

for those living alone, but a man caring for a dependent wife was more likely to receive home help than a woman caring for a dependent husband. These are important findings and methodologies which deserve further investigation (cf. Fuller and Bebbington, 1984) and application in other areas.

Non-resource inputs and efficiency

There has been no mention yet of the non-resource inputs into the production of welfare process in this discussion of efficiency, and it is all too easy to forget them. By this token, unexplained differences in output (that is, after the 'explanation' by the resource inputs) would be erroneously interpreted as reflecting inefficiency. However, two residential homes with identical resource inputs may produce quite different final outputs, the difference not being due to the efficiency of production but to the incidence and influence of those non-resource characteristics beyond the control of the producer, such as resident characteristics at the point of entry. Because residents are not randomly assigned to homes, and because the incidence of other exogenous non-resource inputs will similarly be non-random, the omission of these non-resource influences upon output will bias both the observed production relationship and the efficiency measures. The production of welfare approach not only emphasises the need for non-resource factors to be included but also demonstrates how this might be achieved. Obviously, then, it is necessary to supplement the conventional measures of efficiency with information on non-resource factors, and this is undertaken wherever possible in the chapters which follow.

Some mistakes and fallacies in previous social care evaluations

Each of the definitions of efficiency discussed in this chapter includes *both* sides of the production relationship. Information or commentaries on, and analyses of, either costs or outcomes are of limited utility without a consideration of the other. Previous evaluative excursions into the social care field have nearly all been deficient in this respect. They have either disregarded one side of the production relationship or they have contemplated both, but inadequately. Armed with these definitions of efficiency, I will conclude this chapter by briefly summarising some of these earlier inadequacies, most of which are still perpetrated today. They will each have important implications for the conduct of applied evaluative work and for the interpretation of the policy recommendations that they generate.

The dark side of the moon

It is much too easy for the finance officer or accountant to compare only the costs of two or more services and make policy recommendations on that basis. It is similarly too easy for senior management in a social services department and for the social work researcher to compare only the benefits for clients of these same services and to make quite different policy recommendations. Too often the dark side of the moon is ignored as we do only what comes easily and naturally. Clearly it is imperative to take into account *both* the costs and the outputs (or benefits) of alternative services or systems of care.

Good examples are provided by three studies of local authority services (child care, care of the elderly and care of the mentally handicapped). These were all conducted on behalf of District

Auditors by a firm of management consultants (District Auditors, 1981; Audit Inspectorate, 1983a, 1983b). The studies make no attempt to examine the effects of alternative services on clients and their families. The total neglect of the output side of the production relation means that they are able to throw no light on 'value for money' despite their many claims. On the other dark side we find virtually all social care evaluations conducted in the last thirty years, for they all focus exclusively on the effects on clients to the neglect of the costs. Unless there is an excess of resources over needs such an approach to evaluation is no less indefensible, although historically less likely to attract criticism.

The Roman emperor

The 1982 Nobel Prize winner in economics, George Stigler, tells the story of the Roman emperor who was called upon to judge a contest between two musicians. After hearing only the first musician play he duly awarded the prize to the second (Stigler, 1975). It is not uncommon, for example, to find vociferous support for domiciliary care based solely on an examination of residential care. Some of the arguments against residential care voiced in the 1950s and 1960s were of this kind. We need to look carefully at the *full* range of care services for clients before making any such judgements.

The free lunch

Some other comparisons between services make the mistake of neglecting all expenditures which do not fall directly to social services departments. Thus, for example, expenditure incurred by the NHS, by housing or education departments, by voluntary organisations, by informal carers and, of course, by clients are omitted from most calculations of the cost of providing a service, even though these may be considerable. Few elderly people living in the community would receive domiciliary care services (home help, attendance at day centres, meals services, etc.) which total more than 24 hours a week. Yet the costs of these services are often compared with the costs of residential care which covers 24 hours a *day*. The remaining 144 hours in the week are ignored (cf. Armitage, 1979; Shenfield, 1957, p. 168).

Part of the problem (as we saw in the last chapter) is that there is little incentive for a social services department, for example, to include these figures in its calculations. Worse still, we find cost comparisons which are incomplete even by the criteria of internal financial management. For example, the children in care statistics laid before Parliament each year by the DHSS are most peculiar in their coverage. The figures for 1979–80, for example, quote an average cost per child week of £20 for those boarded out and £132 for those in community homes. The former neglects, *inter alia*, the costs of social worker support for foster families and the cost of finding a suitable foster placement in the first place. There is no such thing as a free lunch: resources which do not appear in the 'direct provider' accounts should not be taken to be free resources. As the Barclay Report (1982) stated:

> The bulk of social care in England and Wales is provided, not by the statutory or voluntary social care agencies, but by ordinary people (acting individually or as members of spontaneously formed groups) who may be linked into informal caring networks in their communities (paragraph 13.8).

The average client

Reliance on averages is almost inevitable when the time and resources available for policy planning is constrained. It should not, however, be forgotten that an 'average cost per client' figure or a measure of 'average output' hides a great deal of variation. There is no such thing as an 'average client'. Individualised care programmes and decisions surely require individualised costings. Whenever possible, account should be taken of the considerable differences between clients and their implications for costs (see Chapter 9). *Marginal* cost and benefit measures are needed for the assessment of efficiency and these will often be markedly different from *average* cost and benefit.

Smash and grab

As expenditure constraints have tightened, so planning and budgeting horizons have shortened. However, the majority of social care policies and practices have implications over very long periods, and certainly periods longer than one financial year. Very few social care interventions can be seen as forms of short-term crisis control. It is not enough, therefore, merely to conduct one-off, 'smash and grab' research studies which ignore the longitudinal implications for clients, for their families, and for the budgets of social care agencies.

6
Social Care and the Market

Rationing care resources

The rationing of services between clients is an inevitable consequence of the excess of needs and demands over supplies. It may be achieved formally, through official waiting lists or consumer charges, or informally through the independent working procedures of care staff. Almost always it will be a combination of devices that will ration the available supply.[1]

Waiting lists or *queues* are widely used in the social care services for the allocation of non-emergency services. Usually a set of official queue–jumping procedures will be introduced to take account of differences in the perceived need for care. *Consumer charges* are utilised in the hope that they will promote both efficiency and consumer choice. *Means tests* and *insurance* schemes will often be logical corollaries of the introduction of charging, because willingness-to-pay and ability-to-pay will not always coincide. A third rationing device is the *eligibility rule* which has both formal and informal manifestations. Some services are strictly limited to clients with particular characteristics (say within an age band); others have eligibility criteria determined by social workers or office managers. There are many informal rationing procedures: *delaying* the delivery of care, *diluting* the amount of care received, *deterring* clients perhaps by stigmatising them, *withholding information* from them, and introducing *unauthorised* eligibility criteria.

It is difficult to justify the use of some of these rationing devices. Their lack of uniformity and consistency will mean the unequal treatment of equal needs, that is both horizontal and vertical inequity, and their arbitrariness will mean a waste of resources, that is inefficiency. Furthermore, they are not procedurally fair: 'services should not be rationed by the personal predilections of providers, by ignorance, complexity, stigma or physical barriers to access' (Weale, 1983, p. 144). Formal eligibility rules, when used alone, need to be very detailed and based on comprehensive data collections if decision-makers are to legislate for all possible needs and need-generating characteristics. When used alone they allow no room for either consumer choice or the professional autonomy of care agencies and staff. They are therefore most valuable when they are used in combination with allocation by time (the waiting list or queue) and allocation by price (consumer charges).

Allocation by time is probably the most commonly employed of *formal* rationing devices in the social care sector. Potential clients will wait at their local social services office to see the duty social worker or wait at home for a social worker to call. Elderly people will wait to be assessed for a home help, for meals on wheels services, for day care and for residential care. Once their eligibility has been established they generally join the waiting list for a vacancy. Children in care will have to wait for a suitable foster or adoptive placement to be found. Families with a mentally or physically handicapped dependent will wait before the social services committee authorises placement in a specialist voluntary or private home. In each case, time is used to deter users. Time, of course, is distributed in equal amounts to all individuals but its perceived value to these individuals will vary considerably. Those whose time is more valuable will find waiting a more costly activity and are more likely to be deterred.

If the value of time is highly negatively correlated with need the simple waiting list (without queue-jumping) will be a useful allocative device. Unfortunately, the cost of waiting is likely to be *higher* for those with greater needs.[2] In these circumstances the waiting list will be both inequitable and inefficient. Officially-sanctioned queue-jumping can help to ensure that individuals in most need receive priority on the waiting list. This will require fairly detailed eligibility rules, where eligibility is defined in terms of need. There will also be a problem of fairness if a private care sector exists, since the more affluent can buy their way off the waiting list.

The advantage that allocation by price might enjoy over allocation by time is that it is unnecessary to specify such detailed eligibility rules. Under a system of pricing an individual would not purchase a service unless it generated benefits to him or her which were at least as valuable as the price paid. To what extent, therefore, can we rely on rationing by price – that is, the market mechanism – to generate an efficient allocation of resources?

Efficiency and the market mechanism

It is sometimes argued that the attainment of an efficient allocation of resources can best be achieved through a market system. The price mechanism will efficiently match the demands of consumers with the supplies of producers, allowing individuals on both sides of the exchange relationship to make their wants known. It is also argued that, subject to the partial or complete removal of certain inequalities of access and opportunity, the market mechanism allows the expression of choice and so promotes freedom and autonomy (Friedman and Friedman, 1980; Hayek, 1960). Market forces may also help to remove bureaucratic inefficiencies, generate greater consumer and producer responsibilities, and stimulate a higher level of social welfare expenditure (Seldon, 1977). The crucial questions for social care, therefore, concern the validity of the assumptions necessary for markets to generate efficiency, the extent to which the preconditions for genuine freedom of choice and action have been met, and the implications for the distribution of burdens and benefits.

There are four reasons for doubting the ability of the market mechanism to generate an efficient and equitable allocation of social care resources: the presence of externalities, a lack of consumer information, distortions arising from market power, and the unequal distribution of welfare shortfalls. Additionally, doubts have been expressed about the ability of a market for *insurance* to overcome some of these problems. Surprisingly, perhaps, these sources of 'market failure' have received little attention in discussions of the organisation and allocation of social care services. Whilst some might be taken as self-evident it would be wrong not to consider them in a little more detail, for the precise *nature* of market failure is obviously going to be crucially important in deciding whether and what kind of collective action is required.

Externalities

An externality is a side-effect of either consumption or production which is not traded on the market or taken into account in setting a price. Some externalities are desirable, such as the pleasure I derive from my neighbour's garden or the relief you feel when a friend or relative receives the medical treatment he or she so clearly needs. These are *external benefits*. Others, the *external costs*, are rather less desirable and include the smoke from my neighbour's bonfire, other forms of environmental pollution, and the congestion experienced in a traffic jam. Externalities, therefore, are either benefits which one can enjoy for free, or costs which one suffers without compensation. Some external effects were discussed in the chapters on output and cost. The outputs of residential care range over the effects on clients' principal carers and include the relief from strain and responsibility. Indeed, these latter individuals are often recognised as *clients* because of this interdependence of welfare. If residents are responsible for purchasing their care within the market, these principal carer effects are external benefits. External costs were implicitly included in our definition of social costs, although many of them are difficult to measure. There are four sources of social care externality.

(1)   Production externalities. The worries and complaints expressed by people living close to some social care 'production units', particularly provision for the mentally handicapped or delinquents, are external costs of production. They are localised, often temporary, and can probably be 'internalised' by some form of compensation without undue difficulty.

(2)   Caring externalities. Of considerably more interest and pervasiveness are the effects of one individual's receipt or *consumption* of social care upon another's well-being. Following Culyer (1980), we can distinguish four 'types' of consumption externality depending on whether the 'non-consumer's' well-being is influenced by knowledge of services consumed (in our terminology, intermediate outputs) or characteristics to be changed (final outputs), and by absolute or relative levels of receipt. You may derive psychic benefits from the observation that old people receive residential care (a type I consumption externality), from their receipt of an acceptable standard of residential care relative to the average standard of living elsewhere in society (type II), from the observation that such care has an effect on the well-being of residents (type III), or from the belief that the welfare shortfalls of residents *relative* to others have been

reduced (type IV). These psychic benefits arise because you *care* about elderly people, and one great benefit of Culyer's typology is that it emphasises how these caring externalities raise both efficiency and distributional issues. If the caring externality is important but service allocation is left to the market, then residential care will be under provided, since the consumer (the resident) will take into account only the *personal* benefits of care. When external effects are also taken into account an efficient allocation of resources is more likely. However, unless subsidies are paid to the elderly to encourage them to purchase the socially optimal amount of care they have no reason to include these external effects in their decision-making. Recently, doubts have been expressed about the existence and importance of this caring externality. Sugden (1980), for example, prefers to interpret the prevalence of medical and welfare charities not as evidence of altruistic or philanthropic preferences (caring externalities) but as *moral duties* derived from basic contractarian principles. If his argument is accepted the case for collective action is reduced.

(3)   Public goods. Some social care services may be seen as public goods whose provision or consumption is both non-rival (my consumption or enjoyment does not preclude your enjoyment) and non-excludable (my consumption or enjoyment actually *forces* your consumption). A good example from outside the compass of social care would be street-lighting: once provided, anyone walking down the street can enjoy its benefits and nobody can avoid benefiting. The problem with public goods of this kind is that there is no incentive for any one individual to provide them, for whilst he or she bears the cost everyone else can benefit by taking a 'free ride'. Collective action will be needed. Some social care activities have the attributes of public goods, albeit often localised. For example, the direct and indirect material benefits to society from the nurture, education and training of the mentally or physically handicapped are shared by all and, if they include macroeconomic effects, cannot really be avoided, although, of course, they may be small. The containment and perhaps correction of delinquent or criminal behaviour will also be a public good because everyone can feel safer, say, about walking the streets at night. The number of social care activities that qualify for the description of public good is small, but some collective action will be necessary if each is to be provided.

(4)   Option demand externalities. The final source of externality comes from the benefit we derive from the availability of services which we do not currently use, but which we may need at some future date. Does our concern about the quality of social care provision for the elderly increase as we approach old age ourselves? These 'option demand' benefits may imply collective action such as state provision, or they may imply a need for personal insurance against the risk of needing care.

The range of potential external costs and benefits is wide, and it is clear that 'state versus market' debates are too simplistic and polarised to provide useful prescriptions for policy. Some external benefits could be encouraged within a market system by paying subsidies to consumers or by regulating behaviour; some external costs could be reduced by appropriately imposing other regulations, fines or taxes, or by recourse to litigation. Other externalities may encourage localised collective action, such as the establishment of neighbourhood groups, charities or voluntary organisations, although once the number of recipients and/or donors becomes large, organisation may become difficult.

Lack of information

One of the necessary prerequisites for a market to produce an efficient allocation of resources is the assumption that the consumer is the best judge of his own welfare. There are good reasons for believing that many clients are not in a position to make optimal decisions about their need for care. Mentally handicapped persons, young children and the elderly with dementia, for example, are unlikely to be able to reach such decisions themselves, and in many instances their parents or other carers will not possess the necessary information or knowledge to make decisions for them. Indeed, in many instances, it is the ignorance, neglect or malice of these carers which has generated or contributed to the need in the first place. Other clients, whilst in a position to contemplate making decisions for themselves simply will not possess the necessary expertise to make the *best* decisions. Nor are they likely to be able to acquire either that expertise or sufficient knowledge of its suppliers (the social care professions and agencies) from market experience, for they do not enter the social care market with the frequency that they enter, say, the foodstuffs or clothing markets. It *is* possible to envisage purchasing the relevant knowledge in the way that one purchases knowledge of the law from a solicitor or knowledge of the housing market from an estate agent. However, the very nature of the problems dealt with by social care agencies – their long and complicated gestations and their long-term implications – and the complicated interactions with other social services (such as education, housing and health), would make it unlikely that a market for 'social care information' could function with the flexibility, sensitivity and responsibility required for an efficient allocation of resources.

Most of these arguments would be likely to command widespread acceptance, but their implications for the delivery of care can be interpreted differently. Some would favour the public provision of social care, seeing these services (or at least some of them) as 'merit goods'. Others would favour market provision (for some services) supported by a system of voluntary or compulsory insurance. *Merit goods* were first discussed by Musgrave (1959, p. 13), who defined them as goods 'considered so meritorious that their satisfaction is provided for through the public budget over and above what is provided for through the market and paid for by private buyers'. The decision to treat some goods as meritorious would presumably be taken through the normal democratic process. It may be justified by consumer ignorance, as it has been introduced here, or by the presence of externalities or inequities. Merit goods leave providers open to the charge of paternalism. An alternative is for the state to coerce individuals into taking out private *insurance* policies against the need for social care.

Market imperfections

For a market system to guarantee efficiency neither suppliers nor consumers should possess market power; markets must be 'perfectly competitive'. For example, a producer with monopoly power would be able to set his selling price in order to maximise his profits to the detriment of consumers. Monopoly power might arise 'naturally' because the market is simply too small to support more than one producer. If consumers are unable or unwilling to move or travel great distances to enjoy residential or day care, or if service providers are unable or unwilling to travel great distances to deliver domiciliary care or fieldwork support, then natural spatial monopolies are inevitable. The greater the desired or required degree of specialisation within a necessarily integrated social care system, the more sparse the population, and the more pervasive the technical and social economies of scale in production, the more likely are these spatial monopolies. Thus, whilst it might be reasonable to envisage competition between private old people's homes in the more popular retirement areas, the same is unlikely to be the case for training services for the mentally handicapped or therapeutic communities for certain types of children. With highly specialised services enjoying economies of scale there will be a case for either public regulation or public ownership. Public monopolies may be able to exploit these economies to keep costs down or their bureaucratic and inflexible structures may create waste and inefficiency. Another source of market power may follow from the consumer's lack of information and expertise, so that the care provider's relative expertise will put him in a position of power over the client. In particular, the provider may not only supply the services but also gauge the client's needs and advise the client on how much to demand. This could mean the exploitation and manipulation of clients, either by prolonging the care period, or by tying the client to a particular and lengthy form of care with inflated fees. If, furthermore, care providers can organise themselves into a strong professional association, as doctors and solicitors in Britain have done, they can – if they so wish – exercise considerable control over the marketing strategies of their members.

Equity

To many people the most important objection to the market provision of social care is the market's inability to allocate services according to need, where 'need' has been previously defined in accordance with society's chosen criterion of equity. The concern that this inability generates is different from the caring externality discussed earlier, for the former comes from recourse to our basic principle of justice and the latter from our altruistic preferences. A perfectly functioning market will allocate services according to consumers' ability or willingness to pay, and there is no necessary correlation between the distribution of income and the distribution of need. We can possibly overcome this equity problem by paying the 'more needy' suitable subsidies on the price of social care services or on their insurance premiums, by providing cash grants or redistributing income, by issuing 'care vouchers', or simply by moving responsibility for provision into the public sector. Whilst it may be administratively more straightforward to provide services directly rather than attempt to alter the workings of the market, it must be recognised that the available evidence on the 'target efficiency' of publicly provided care is not encouraging in either the social care sector or elsewhere (Bebbington and Davies, 1983b; Le Grand, 1982). Equally, none of the quasi-market strategies is without its faults. Subsidies, grants and vouchers, for example, may not satisfactorily correct the inequitable balance of provision and may introduce the problem of stigma. An interesting recent development in this area is the examination of the conditions under which a majority of individuals will prefer state provision to the redistribution of incomes. It would seem that the more variable the distribution of needs and the less variable the distribution of income, the greater the preference for cash over kind (Usher, 1977; Weitzman, 1977; Rivera-Batiz, 1981; Weale, 1983).

Insurance

The uncertainty of individual demands and the ignorance of most individuals of the range of services available to meet their needs do not, in themselves, imply the wholesale abandonment of a market-based allocation mechanism. The market has its own solution to the problems of uncertainty and ignorance, which is the market for insurance. The general aim is to allow the individual citizen to turn a high and unpredictable cost (the loss of income and the cost of care or treatment) into a small and certain cost (the regular premium paid to the insurance company). Some elderly recipients of local authority home help services are already using their health insurance policies to cover charges, and a variety of new schemes, including reverse-mortgages, is being introduced (Judge, 1983a).

The basic principle of the insurance mechanism is that risk-averse individuals will choose to take out insurance against the cost of social care services. A risk-averse individual will reject a fair bet, preferring the certainty of, say, £100 to the fifty-fifty chance of getting either nothing or £200.[3] The insurance in this case must be actuarially fair in the sense that the premiums accurately reflect the actuarial risks of incurring specified social care expenditures. However, universal assumptions of risk-aversion and actuarial fairness are not easy to justify.[4] First, some individuals are clearly risk-preferrers, accepting fair bets because of their enjoyment of the uncertainty. Secondly, insurance premiums may not be actuarially fair or may not be *perceived* to be fair by the insured. Actuarially fair premiums may not be charged by insurance companies either because of their administrative or transaction costs which they have to pass on to the consumer, or because they enjoy a degree of monopoly power in the insurance market. This is the *loading* problem: if premiums are not fair, individuals may under-insure. They may also under-insure if their own perceptions of the risk of future social care costs is below the actuarial risk. They may not believe that the average (population) probability of a shortfall occurring can possibly apply to them, or fully appreciate the full cost of the care that will be needed. Many social care needs are highly predictable, such as those associated with old age or handicap, and are likely to encourage individuals to take out insurance. Others are very *unpredictable* and are quite likely to lead to under-consumption of insurance.

Another set of problems that could arise with social care insurance follows from the non-random incidence of welfare shortfalls. Some individuals, such as the congenitally handicapped, will be uninsurable. For others, the risk of shortfall may be so high that the premiums charged by insurance companies will be impossibly expensive. The former problem suggests the need for collectively-provided care. The latter could be overcome by the suitable redistribution of income and is not really an argument against the market or the principle of insurance. Related to this is the problem of *adverse selection*. In order to keep their administrative costs down, insurance companies will calculate the actuarial costs of groups and not individuals, but this risk-pooling will mean that low-risk clients within a particular 'premium band' pay a higher premium than is actuarially fair for them. This will drive these low-risk individuals out, and raise the average premium for those that remain. Compulsory insurance may be the answer to this problem.

A third difficulty is the problem of *'moral hazard'*. The insured individual will have less incentive to take preventive action to avoid the future need for social care and will have every incentive to consume as much of that care as benefits him once the need arises. Of course, the costs of receiving care are to be reckoned not only in money terms but with regard to the costs of inconvenience, compliance, stigma and so on, and these will limit an individual's demands. Nevertheless the problem of over-consumption is a real one and will push up expenditure and hence premiums. This problem of moral hazard can be tackled by introducing deductibles (the client pays the first £100 or whatever), co-insurance (the client pays a proportion of all costs) or other cost-sharing requirements. With the present publicly-provided system of care, of course, 'moral hazard is complete since all care is virtually free' (Culyer, 1982, p. 135) and we rely on eligibility criteria (social definitions of need) and care professionals to control the demands of clients.

The problems of under-insurance, loading, adverse selection and moral hazard may together imply the need, not only for a system of *compulsory* insurance but a system of compulsory *government* insurance. Furthermore the externality and equity problems, which no insurance system can overcome, require some collective action which might sensibly and conveniently be combined with such a compulsory system. We cannot rely on the 'invisible hand' of the market to generate either an efficient or an equitable allocation of all social care resources. Nevertheless, there may be scope for employing the price mechanism, backed by a system of insurance and supported by suitable subsidies, vouchers or cash grants, in some areas of social care provision. Within the mixed economy of welfare there will presumably always be room for this kind of initiative. How then is the price mechanism *currently* used either to ration demand or to stimulate supply?

Consumer charges

In the last ten years

> there have been repeated calls from the government, local authority leaders, and political pressure groups for an extension of the use of charges in the delivery of social welfare. Even the Labour party, which is ideologically opposed to the use of charges to achieve social welfare objectives, has seen successive Labour administrations retain and extend the use of charges (Judge, 1979, p. 371).

The proportion of gross expenditure met out of fees and charges, which averaged 11 per cent for English and Welsh local authorities during 1975–6, varies widely between areas and between services (Judge and Matthews, 1980a). For some services, fees and charges account for a very high proportion of costs (for example, 30 per cent for old people's homes), whilst for others the revenue from this source is tiny (less than one per cent for children boarded out or in residential care). For any particular service, different local authorities may charge markedly different amounts. For example, figures compiled for 1978–9 show that the average annual income per home help case ranged from zero in fourteen authorities to almost £42 in Northamptonshire, representing 19 per cent of cost. The mean figures were £9 per client per year, or 4.7 per cent of total cost, a proportion which has certainly risen since then (Judge, Ferlie and Smith, 1981, Tables 1 and 2). These authors also found that over half of the observed variation in the proportion of charges to costs could be explained by differences between authorities with respect to: the proportion of the population aged over 65 and the number of maternity cases (both positively related to the charging proportion), and the number of home help cases per capita and Labour party representation on the council (both negatively related).

Some economics principles of pricing

In a perfectly competitive market, the price of a good or service would be set by the interplay of the forces of supply and demand. However, in the presence of externalities, public goods and merit goods this simple market mechanism will function imperfectly and in many instances will not function at all. The problem for suppliers of social care services, therefore, is to use a suitable combination of regulated prices and subsidies to achieve an efficient and equitable allocation of resources. The simple expression

$$price = cost - subsidy$$

highlights the two-stage procedure in price determination. At the first stage the price to be charged must be related to the cost of producing the service. As we saw in the previous chapter, it is the marginal and not the average cost of production which is relevant in the definition and pursuit of efficiency. Setting price equal to marginal cost will maximise social welfare. However, this result is not unambiguous. For example, if prices are not equal to marginal costs elsewhere in the economy, the use of the marginal cost rule in the social care sector may be inappropriate. Secondly, if marginal costs are below average costs, prices will not generate enough revenue for the producer to cover his costs, and losses will be incurred. Alternatively, if marginal costs are much higher than average costs, large profits will be made. In some circumstances, therefore, the producer may be justified in setting price above or below marginal cost. At the second stage the central or local authority (which may not actually produce the service under consideration) must decide whether or not to subsidise consumption of the service.[5] If there are sizeable external benefits from the provision of care, subsidies can be used to reduce charges or premiums in an attempt to persuade clients to consume the socially optimal amount. A second kind of subsidy will be used to correct or compensate for differences in income or need, and might also take the form of a reduced or zero price for certain clients, lower insurance premiums, earmarked provision of certain services (perhaps using vouchers), or payment of cash grants. In each case a means test and/or a needs assessment will be required.

The objectives of charging

The two general justifications for using prices to ration resources are the pursuit of efficiency and the promotion of consumer choice. The second of these is often irrelevant when discussing consumer charges for public sector services, since clients are rarely afforded a choice of facilities. It is, however, of relevance in the increasing number of circumstances in which clients (or their relatives) choose between two or more facilities provided by private or voluntary organisations. The efficiency justification has manifested itself in practice in a number of ways. Parker (1976) distinguished four efficiency-related objectives of pricing for social services and a fifth which concerned the symbolic role of charging.[6]

(1) *To raise revenue* By adopting a policy of consumer charges, social services departments can hope to recoup some of the costs of provision. The emphasis on this objective is directly related to the degree of fiscal pressure. In the last five years many local authorities

have significantly raised their home help charges or introduced them for the first time. This revenue raising objective has also been the most important justification for charging clients for meals services, either in their own homes or in day centres and luncheon clubs, and about 20 per cent of local authority expenditure on these services is covered in this way. However, a very much smaller proportion of the cost of the home help service is met from consumer charges. The need to avoid aggravating the distribution of income has left the home help service with so many charge-exempted clients as to reduce charges to only 5 per cent of costs. There are other reasons why consumer charges may not raise as much revenue as policy-makers wish or expect. Firstly, they will obviously deter some clients who consider the service received to be of less value than the price. The higher the price elasticity of demand the greater this reduction.[7] The second reason is that administrative costs may rise; the costs of assessing and collecting charges will often exceed the revenue that is generated. If charges have other purposes then this may not matter, but as a pure revenue-raising device there may be difficulties. A third drawback is that many of the charges will actually be paid by other government departments. A prime example of this transfer payment property is provided by residential care charges for the elderly. An increase in the weekly charge for residential care will be fully met by changes in retirement pensions or supplementary benefit payments for the great majority of residents. Charges may also simply delay demand, so that clients only receive care when their needs are much greater and the costs much higher.

(2)   To Reduce Demand The simple rationing function of the price mechanism is the second justification for introducing consumer charges. This was the primary justification for increasing charges for day nurseries at various times during the post-war period, particularly when it was felt necessary to reduce the female labour supply (Judge and Matthews, 1980a, pp. 46–52). What little evidence there is suggests that the demand for day nursery places is highly price elastic. More precise evidence from a number of local studies in the USA bears out this experience, with price elasticity estimates often being greatly in excess of unity (see, for example, Kushman, 1979; Robins and Spiegelman, 1978). However, for some other services this price elasticity will be much smaller, particularly for existing and dependent clients, such as the elderly recipients of home help or the

elderly in residential care. There will also be deflected demands. The increasing charges for local authority day nursery places over the post-war period certainly pushed up the demand for private nurseries and for unregistered child-minders, and it is not at all clear that these effects were predicted or designed by policy-makers. Of course, the deterrent effect of charging may exacerbate existing inequities. If subsidies are not paid, charges may deter precisely those clients most in need of care.

(3)   *To Shift Priorities*   In a few instances charges have been used to convert policy priorities into practice by reducing the demands made by non-priority cases, population groups or areas. For example, local authorities might attempt to reduce their use of private day nurseries or to raise the female labour supply by lowering the price charged to parents for local authority nursery places. Other examples of using charges to shift priorities are hard to discover in the social care sector, although Parker (1976) cites the cases of dental charges (exemptions used to encourage 'preventive demand' by children) and contraceptive charges (abolition used to influence demographic trends) from other areas of social policy.

(4)   *To Check Abuse and Improve Regulation*   During the committee stage of the 1969 Children and Young Persons' Bill, a government spokesman argued that 'parents should be required – if their means so permit – to pay for the child's board and lodging, so that they are in no way better off as a result of the child's being in care, but that they should not be required to pay for any additional treatment which the child requires.'[8] In this case, charges are used to prevent abuse. With an apparently free service it may be feared that demand will be 'too high' and resources wasted. This view has been put forward on a number of occasions in relation to parental contributions for child care (see Judge and Matthews, 1980a, p. 53), but is of less relevance for other social care services. The argument that a zero-priced service will be abused or wasted neglects two important considerations. According to Blau's view of exchange theory, the receipt of care may not cost the consumer any money, but it is quite likely to impose a cost in terms of approval, esteem or compliance (Blau, 1964). The second point missed in arguments about abuse is that few services are issued on demand, but must first receive the approval of the 'gatekeeper' professional. There will still remain some

opportunity for fraudulent demand from consumers, but any other perceived abuse is probably simply a result of the informal rationing procedures employed by social work professionals (Hall, 1974; Smith, 1980).

(5)   *To Act as Symbols* Many of the charges introduced for social services during the post-war period have symbolic value, either to clients, to the electorate, to the Cabinet or even to foreign opinion. The Conservative party, for example, is committed to a policy of charging as a political belief, and the Labour government's re-introduction of prescription charges in 1968 was seen as the Minister of Health's ploy to appease Cabinet colleagues searching for economies (Parker, 1976). The singularly most important symbolic charges in social care are for services for the elderly, and especially residential services. It was the express intention of the Labour government in 1948 to establish local authority residential care for the elderly with as few similarities as possible with the Poor Law workhouses they were replacing. Severe constraints on capital expenditure meant that few new homes could be built or converted, and charges were used as a symbol of the new relationship between the helper and the helped – more like 'the relationship between hotel resident and manager than inmate and master' (Ministry of Health, 1949, p. 311). This symbolic purpose of charges for residents was reiterated at various times in the next thirty years, so that 'there should be no element of charity in all this', and was extended to other services, such as meals on wheels, although of course the majority of the charging revenue is a transfer payment from the social security branch of government.

Objections to charging

Despite some ambiguities and drawbacks, charging has served important economic, political and symbolic purposes during the post-war period. There have, however, been objections, ranging from the view that they represent a fundamental attack on the principle of the welfare state, to the argument that, whilst desirable on a number of grounds, they are too anomalous and piecemeal to be effective. Some of the difficulties of charging – in the presence of externalities, inelastic demand, consumer ignorance and market imperfections and so on – have been described earlier. These nearly all imply the modification, but not the abandonment, of the pricing mechanism. There are other more fundamental objections: charges deter those in greatest need, they introduce the problem of stigma, they are not cost effective, and they are hedged by anomalies.

The deterrent effect of charging is an important objective for some services, but it is commonly feared that it may be the most needy, and particularly the 'poor needy' who are deterred. Judge and Matthews (1980a, Chapter 6) distinguish three possible deterrent effects:

(1) Potential clients do not apply for or purchase the service.
(2) Existing clients stop purchasing the service.
(3) Potential or existing clients purchase only a proportion of their full allocation or requirement.

These are all problems of horizontal target efficiency, since some individuals deemed to be in need of care by some socially agreed criteria (which take into account the caring externalities of receipt) are not receiving it. If the demands of potential and current clients are elastic with respect to price, and the limited amount of evidence on day nursery, home help and nursing home demand would suggest that they are,[9] then this will always be a potential problem. Whether it is an actual problem is not at all clear. Judge and Matthews (1980b, pp. 119–20) report the case of the 130 per cent increase in the price of meals (both in clubs and in clients' own homes) which had the effect of reducing demand by those already receiving the service by over 20 per cent and replacing them with people previously on the waiting list, thus redistributing 'the benefit of a meal from a "needy" to a "less needy" client.' Hyman's study of the home help service in Redbridge revealed that the imposition of a flat rate charge of £1.50 per week reduced demand by about 10 per cent. Those who cancelled the service were less dependent (less isolated, less handicapped, and so on), but had previously received assistance with tasks for which there was no effective alternative support (Hyman, 1980). Whether or not this suggests that the 'less needy' were deterred depends on the way that these apparently countervailing effects are weighted by the equity criterion underlying the need judgement, and also on the effects of charges on the general living standards of clients. These and other results suggest that pricing *may* deter those in need of care, but the evidence to date is partial and ambiguous.

If some people with legitimate needs do not purchase social care because the charge is too high, then it will be necessary to subsidise them to encourage take-up. Thus arises the spectre of the means test. Universal services, supplied to all eligible individuals without charge or means test, have been argued to be preferable to selective services because they do not act as a disincentive to work, they are administratively simpler, they encourage a higher take-up rate, and they are not socially divisive. The work-disincentive problem is of little relevance in relation to the social care services, and the question of administrative burden is considered below. On the third point we have already seen that take-up rates may be depressed by pricing, but the universalist argument here is mainly centred on the lack of advertising and the complicated claims procedures. These are real but not insurmountable problems, and in some cases the introduction of charges actually *increases* take-up through a legitimising effect (Maynard, 1980). The main strand of the universalist argument is the problem of the *stigma* associated with the receipt of means-tested services. There is little satisfactory evidence to draw upon and the only thorough empirical study of the relationship between means testing and stigma, for the school meals service, has found little support for the universalist position (Davies, 1978). However, it would be inappropriate to generalise from this result that the problem of stigma has been exaggerated, for it is the *context* within which means testing is undertaken which is crucial, and there are probably other characteristics of the receipt of services which are stigmatising (Foster, 1983, Chapter 9).

A third objection to the use of consumer charges is that they are simply *not cost effective*. It has often been pointed out that the cost of assessing home help clients for charges and the cost of collection outweigh the revenue that is generated,[10] and that the cost of collecting parental contributions for child care is similarly expensive. However, in relatively few cases is revenue generation the sole objective of charging. Thus, before we can dismiss charging as administratively burdensome and cost ineffective we need to assess its benefits in terms of the reduction of demand, the prevention of abuse, and so on. A more fruitful line of enquiry would be to examine what *form* of charging would best achieve these objectives (Judge and Matthews, 1980a, pp. 27–9). At the same time there is a pressing need to remove some of the *anomalies* that characterise current pricing policies. When similar services are provided by two or more agencies or departments it would seem sensible for charging arrangements also to be similar. Judge (1978, pp. 126–7) illustrates the point by reference to the free services of nursing auxiliaries (provided by the NHS) which are often identical to chargeable local authority home help services. Similar problems arise with charging for other personal social services, such as aids and adaptations (supplied free by the NHS), day care services for children and some residential facilities for the mentally ill (both supplied by education departments).

In concluding their review of charging practices, Judge and Matthews (1980a) remarked that 'one of the attitudes we encountered most frequently . . . was the widespread view among officials that charges for personal social services have little more than nuisance value. In our view such attitudes represent the primary reason why pricing policy has been inadequately formulated' (p. 137).

The supply response

As well as using the market or price mechanism to reduce and deflect the demands made upon scarce social care resources, it can be employed to regulate and stimulate the supplies of those resources. In both uses the pursuit of efficiency has to be qualified in a number of ways, especially by consideration of the distributions of welfare and income. Rather more attention has been directed towards the rationale for and effect of consumer charges on *demand* than has been focused on the association between pricing and *supply*. The possibility of variations in supply often passes without comment, and the response of supply to variations in price only very rarely generates more than a passing remark.

> Suppliers of public services are not subject to competitive pressures . . . and often take decisions about the level of service to be provided either on arbitrary grounds or according to administrative criteria of need. The result is that supply is not flexible in relation to price since suppliers do not perceive a supply curve (Stewart, 1980, p. 16).

Thus, the price-elasticity of the supply of publicly-produced social care services is low, and the research response likewise.

The same cannot be said for the supplies of private and voluntary services or the supplies of the basic resource inputs essential for the production of final and intermediate outputs. If we use the term supply in its most general sense then there are many issues that deserve examination. Consider again the basic *production of welfare* perspective introduced in Chapter 2, relating the resource and non-resource inputs to the final and intermediate outputs. The question of a supply response arises in relation to each of these four basic components and the causal relationships between them, as the following illustrative questions make plain.

(1) *Supplies of resource inputs* How responsive are the supplies of (paid) staff resources to prices offered for their services? What factors encourage or discourage the voluntary activities of unpaid carers? To what extent does the boarding-out allowance attract potential foster parents? Will an approved adoption allowance merely encourage 'baby-farming' as envisaged by the 1981 Adoption Act?

(2) *Supplies of non-resource inputs* To what extent are the non-resource inputs into the production process exogenously determined and to what extent can they be influenced by care agencies?

(3) *Supplies of intermediate outputs* What are the price-elasticities of supply of the intermediate outputs of private and voluntary organisations? To what extent, for example, is there price competition between the proprietors of private old people's homes? What factors stimulate innovations in the provision of new care services?

(4) *Supplies of final outputs* Is there a relationship between the weekly fee charged by private and voluntary children's homes and the (perceived) final outputs of the services they provide?

(5) *Supplies of effective or efficient care* How can the price mechanism be employed to encourage the 'supply' of effective and efficient care practices? What types of incentive to social care staff and organisations appear to be effective? How do care agencies respond to changes in the relative prices of the resources they employ? What are the incentives to innovate?

We actually have very little information with which to answer these important supply side questions. For example, despite a considerable 'tightening' of the labour market in recent years, most social services departments are still bedevilled by high rates of staff turnover and shortages of suitably qualified social work staff. Yet, with the exception of a few studies of job preferences (Bebbington and Coles, 1978; Collison and Kennedy, 1977), of job satisfaction (Kakabadse and Worrall, 1978), and of staff turnover and wastage (Knapp, Harissis and Missiakoulis, 1981, 1982), virtually nothing is known about the supply of qualified social workers. Nor do we yet have more than a preliminary idea of the substitutability of these and other staff resources, or of the productive efficiency of their employment (Bebbington, Davies and Coles, 1979; Judge, 1978, Chapter 8). Interest is growing, but slowly, in the incentives offered to staff and to private and voluntary care agencies to encourage them to provide effective and efficient care. 'Incentive reimbursement' policies for residential services have yet to be examined in a British context, and experimental evidence on the effectiveness of organisational incentives for field social work staff is only now becoming available. One study, conducted in the Thanet area of Kent, looked at the effects of giving field social work staff considerable autonomy in the use of both conventional statutory services, such as home help and meals on wheels, and other community resources, including paid and unpaid volunteers. Social workers were supplied with detailed costings (or 'shadow prices') for these services and had to work within a budget constraint for each client. The study found that social workers made imaginative and flexible use of service packages to provide highly cost effective care (Challis and Davies, in press). Within the same research project it was possible to examine the motivations of the volunteers or 'helpers'. Financial reward was mentioned by over a third of all volunteers as a motivating factor and the researchers concluded that their findings gave 'little support to the view that care in the community for the frail elderly can be successfully generated without the substantial input of both human and financial resources' (Qureshi, Challis and Davies, 1983, p. 166).

The question of payment to encourage the supply of voluntary activities and altruistic actions has been a controversial one for some time, and particularly since Titmuss's arguments regarding the nature of the welfare exchange (Titmuss, 1968, 1970).[11] Originally discussed in the context of blood donation, the issues raised by the debate are of obvious relevance in many social policy contexts. For example, many local authorities are presently hampered in their attempts to board-out more children with families by their inability to recruit sufficient numbers of suitable foster parents. It would appear to be the case from research in the USA that in order to secure an adequate supply of foster families, child care organisations must not only ensure adequate levels of financial compensation through the boarding-out payment, but also provide the necessary social work support for parents and children (for example, see Simon, 1975).[12] It is likely – and evidence from a number of local authorities in Britain suggests that it is already happening – that the 'reservation wage' of new foster families (defined in terms of both boarding-out allowances and social worker support) is higher than that required or demanded by existing foster families (Knapp, 1983b). The most highly motivated potential foster parents (not synonymous, necessarily, with the *best* foster parents) will already be fostering.

One supply side issue to attract attention, partly in response to continuing fiscal pressure, is the *innovative potential* of social care agencies.[13] The transition from a period of incremental growth to one of fiscal and demographic pressure has encouraged greater emphasis on efficiency-improving innovations. For example, the shift from residential-centred to community-centred care for the elderly, justified on the grounds of efficiency, was made possible by (and itself generated) a plethora of innovative care arrangements by statutory, voluntary and private care agencies (Ferlie, 1982; Hedley and Norman, 1982). Local authorities have, for example, introduced greater flexibility in the home help service and introduced a wide variety of short stay residential and day care facilities.

The pursuit of efficiency

How then can we ensure that social care agencies, often removed from the efficiency-encouraging pressures of market forces, pursue their care responsibilities efficiently? What techniques can they use in planning and policy-making to guide them to a more efficient use of resources?

We saw in the earlier chapters that the conceptualisation of the inputs and outputs of social care is relatively easy when compared with their measurement in practice. On both the input and output side it is possible to distinguish a number of levels of measurement, ranging from fairly crude indicators to more sophisticated (but not necessarily better) monetary valuations. The resource inputs into the production of welfare process can be measured in three different ways: in their *natural units* (the number of staff, the minibus mileage, and so on); as *accounting costs* (the actual amounts expended to secure the services of the staff or to erect or rent a home, and so on); and as *opportunity costs* (the benefits that have to be forgone in the employment of inputs). Money is generally used as an index of opportunity cost 'simply because price is a common denominator in terms of which relative values can be assessed and understood' (Doherty and Hicks, 1977, p. 192). Opportunity costs are preferred to accounting costs because the latter do not generally reflect the true values that society places on the resources used in the production process. There is also the option in undertaking social care research or making policy recommendations of ignoring the inputs altogether. Non-resource inputs are costless, in so far as they have neither a market price nor an imputed social valuation, but should be appended to the costings wherever possible.

In order to compare and aggregate the wide variety of inputs used in a care service, we might attempt to express all of them in terms of opportunity cost using the common numeraire of money. Likewise, in order to compare and perhaps aggregate the multitude of *outputs* that the services produce, and additionally to enable us to compare them with the resources that have produced them, it has often been suggested that *monetary valuations* be placed on the outputs. The difficulties of output valuation are, however, tremendous and, many would argue, insurmountable. There are, then, four options in output measurement: not to attempt it at all, to seek intermediate output measures (the number of residents, the quality of care, and so on), to seek final output measures (the effects on the well-being of clients), and to seek monetary values for the outputs.

These four input and output measurement options may now be cross-classified, as in Table 6.1, to form a simple two-dimensional matrix of 16 cells. Outputs are arranged along the horizontal axis and inputs on the vertical. This matrix serves a number of purposes. Firstly, all previous research studies and policy commentaries can be slotted into one or more of the cells. Secondly, the matrix has the virtue of summarising the various 'efficiency analyses' (broadly defined) that have been suggested by different disciplines. It is not my aim to provide an exhaustive review either of previously conducted research on social care or of the modes of analysis available to the researcher or policy-maker. However, some of the comments about social care research made earlier can now be summarised with the aid of the matrix, and the analyses encountered in some of the chapters

TABLE 6.1 Input and ouput measurement and the tools of efficiency analysis

Inputs	Outputs			
	Not measured at all	Measured as intermediate outputs	Measured as final outputs	Measured in monetary units
Not measured at all		Routine activity statistics produced by local authorities and DHSS.	Social work evaluations. Reports by social work inspectorates'.	
Measured in 'natural' units	Routine statistics produced by local authorities and DHSS.	Intermediate output production functions. Majority of British operations research studies.	Final output production functions, logical extensions of some social work evaluations.	
Measured as accounting costs or expenditures	Routine local authority and national accounts. 'League tables'. Some PPBS.	'League tables'. PPBS. Some operations research (but with restrictive assumptions). Most cost functions work.	Some cost function studies.	
Measured as opportunity costs			Cost effectiveness analysis.	Cost benefit analysis

that follow may also be compared in this way.[14] For example, the local authority '*league tables*' much beloved of some commentators often use information on accounting costs (or expenditures) and either ignore output measurement altogether, or use a very narrowly defined range of intermediate indicators. The resultant figures may well be useful in some respects, but as indicators of efficiency they are of little value. Also of limited value are those policy recommendations based on examinations of outputs only. A lot of social work research is of this kind. In fairness, the compilers of the expenditure or rate of provision figures and the social work researchers do not generally make the (inadequate) policy statements themselves, but the danger is always there that somebody else will.

More interesting from the efficiency standpoint are some of the analyses which follow directly from the production of welfare perspective. *Cost function analyses* are discussed in Chapters 9 and 10. Sometimes the data needs of the cost function analyst are only slightly greater than those of the 'league table' compiler, but the methods of anlaysis and interpretation make the results much more interesting. Logically equivalent to the cost function is the *production function*. The production function, introduced briefly in Chapter 2, indicates the maximum feasible output from given input levels.

The great majority of the *operations research* studies of social care and related services, in Britain at least, have restricted themselves to intermediate indicators of output and inputs measured in 'natural' units. Unfortunately most of these studies have also been restricted by assumptions of linearity, a single output measure (usually 'independence'),[15] a tendency to focus on 'macro-system' allocations of care to the neglect of care processes themselves, and a heavily empiricist approach. With few exceptions, operations research in Britain to date has not proved particularly helpful in making efficiency prescriptions in the social care sector. Another 'macro-system' tool sometimes used is the *Planning, Programming and Budgeting System (PPBS)* or Programme Budgeting method. The technique is more an aid to a priorities exercise than an efficiency study (see Banks, 1979; Mooney *et al.*, 1980), although some authors have confused the two (Booth, 1981).

Cost effectiveness analyses, when properly conducted, are based on opportunity costings of the inputs, and measures, but not monetary valuations, of final output. *Cost benefit analyses* differ in that they attempt to place (monetary) valuations on the outputs. There have been no fully valid cost benefit studies for social care services, the major difficulty being this monetary valuation stage. The research studies by Wager (1972) of services for the elderly, and Schofield (1976) of preventive social work with families, both appeared with a cost benefit title, but did not overcome this valuation problem. Cost benefit and cost effectiveness analyses are described and reviewed in the next two chapters. I will argue there that the general approach, even in the absence of final outputs with attached monetary values, has a great deal to contribute to the formulation of social care policies. Our preferences for final over intermediate outputs and for opportunity over accounting costs imply that we should prefer to move from left to right in Table 6.1 and from top to bottom. Combining these desired directions of movement takes us 'south-east' towards the bottom right-hand corner, and particularly to the cost benefit analysis cell. Given the full social opportunity costs of the inputs, and final outputs valued in similar monetary units, we are then able to comment fully upon the *social efficiency* of the services under consideration.

7

Cost Benefit Analysis: The Principles

Introduction

Value for money is most definitely in vogue – if not yet fully in practice then in exhortation. The search for 'value for money' (or 'cost effectiveness' or 'efficiency') is being conducted at all levels of government and from a number of different perspectives. All such searches are special cases of cost benefit analysis. In the last chapter we saw how the pursuit of final output and opportunity cost measures would logically take us to a position where either cost benefit analysis or cost effectiveness analysis was not only feasible but desirable. This desirability stemmed not from the supposed intention to reduce everything to monetary terms (which is most certainly not the aim) but from the careful and comprehensive use of the principles of the *production of welfare model*. In this and the next chapter I want to focus attention on cost benefit analysis, looking first at the principles. I shall use the term cost benefit analysis and its common abbreviation (CBA) as a shorthand term for the cumbersome expression 'cost benefit analysis or cost effectiveness analysis', since the majority of the principles are shared by both.

By repute, CBA is neither a simple nor an uncontroversial mode of analysis. I shall be examining the main sources of controversy in a later section of this chapter, but it is important to anticipate part of that discussion in order to justify this incursion into what some readers may see as the unacceptable face of welfare economics. CBA is simply 'an effort to bridge the gap between a conceptual model – theoretic welfare economics – and actual social policy' (Weisbrod and Helming, 1980). Welfare economics is that branch of the subject concerned with the relationship between an economic system and the well-being of individuals. It has developed the technique of CBA as a means of appraising efficiency in contexts where markets either do not exist or cannot be relied upon to automatically generate efficiency.

CBA is just one of several evaluative techniques that are employed in social care research. Where it differs from other techniques is in its logical extension of the principles underlying those techniques to the examination of the full range of causes and effects (Levine, 1968; Weiss, 1972). The common theme of all evaluative research is to enquire if a particular project or course of action is worthwhile and economic evaluation is no different in this purpose. The difference is the meaning attached to the term 'worthwhile'. Economic evaluation, and particularly CBA, also shares a common basic assumption that political and administrative forces alone cannot be relied upon to generate efficiency or 'value for money'. It does not seek to replace the sound or educated judgement of the decision-maker, based as it is, and as it must inevitably be, on political priorities. Final decisions will be made by politicians, advised by administrators, in the light of the information made available to them. It is the principal aim of all evaluative research, and CBA is certainly no exception, to provide a more considered and sound information base for policy decisions. Weisbrod, one of the leading and most respected exponents of the art of CBA, has made the point that this technique will never 'make decisions', but if it is vigorously pursued it will 'make decisions better informed' (Weisbrod, 1979). Like the production of welfare perspective upon which it must inevitably be based, CBA is a way of thinking.

In principle, CBA is simplicity itself. The costs of a project are compared with the benefits; if the latter exceed the former the project is worth undertaking. If two or more projects are vying for selection, the project with the greatest excess of benefits over costs is to be preferred. Benefits and costs which fall to or upon any member of society are to be included and are to be measured in some common units to allow comparisons to be made. Unfortunately it is this simplicity which has been the cause of so much difficulty. A mode of 'project appraisal' or 'economic decision-making' with so much inherent appeal will inevitably capture the imagination of the hard-pressed policy-maker starved of information. In reality, CBA is a complex tool, based, some would argue, on somewhat shaky theoretical grounds and harbouring a whole host of practical problems and potential pitfalls. Some of the research studies erroneously labelled as cost-benefit analyses have been roundly and justifiably criticised. Economists, though sometimes given to verbosity, emphasise the complexity of this particular technique of appraisal by the sheer volume of introductory, intermediate and advanced textbooks dedicated to the subject.

Whilst the principles of CBA generally assume that the costs and benefits of policies, programmes or projects can be measured in similar units to allow their direct comparison, the *practice* of CBA has not been restricted to cases where outputs can be measured in monetary terms. Some critics of the CBA approach point to an increasing tendency 'toward using CBA in areas where costs and benefits are more easily expressed in pecuniary terms' (Buxbaum, 1981, pp. 467–8). This might lead, it is argued, to the diversion of resources to areas where effectiveness or efficiency has been demonstrated and away from areas where it has not. Leaving aside the lack of evidence to support this view, and the naïvety that is attributed to decision-makers, the sentiment expressed by such critics is an important one. In fact, it has really only been the application of the CBA technique in areas where output or benefit measurement is most problematic which has won converts in the social care field:

> The hard-nosed approach of those who talk in terms of cost benefit and management by objectives has been disconcerting, as it has seemed to reflect a preoccupation with money rather than people, an attitude that people's needs must be tailored to financial considerations instead of financial resources being stretched to meet people's needs. However, as this approach developed into the idea of a goal-oriented social services system, I cannot argue the concept. In fact, I only wish that it had been generated and developed within the field, instead of from outside (Shyne, 1976, p. 6).

Nor is CBA restricted to answering questions about the criterion of efficiency. Increasingly, applied economic evaluations have sought to examine and comment upon the *distributional* implications of the proposed policies whose efficiency characteristics are apparently the primary focus of interest.

CBA cannot provide answers to all the questions posed by decision-makers, nor has it ever been claimed that it can do so. It can, however, provide answers to a wide variety of questions. Williams (1974) suggests that CBA might usefully be employed to answer questions of the following kind:

(1)   *What* care service is more or most appropriate in given circumstances?
(2)   *When* should care be provided?
(3)   *Where* should care be provided?
(4)   *To whom* should care be provided?
(5)   *How* should care be provided?

The answer to one or more of these questions will surely aid the politician, administrator, practitioner and even the radical commentator.

Theoretical underpinnings and practical precursors

The theoretical basis of cost benefit analysis can be traced back at least to the nineteenth century. Possibly the first practical CBA – although not described by that name – was undertaken by the French economist Jules Dupuit in 1844. The technique really only became well-known after its employment in studies of flood control in the USA in the 1920s and 1930s. During the next thirty years the number of practical CBAs mushroomed, but almost entirely in relation to projects whose costs and benefits were amenable to monetary measurement. The first CBA in Britain was conducted by the Road Research Laboratory and confirmed the need for the M1 motorway after work had already started on its construction. Only in the relatively recent history of the technique has it been applied to areas, such as the human services, where cost and especially benefit measurement is much less straightforward.

The conventional theoretical basis for CBA is Paretian welfare economics. A policy change (say) which makes at least one person better off without making anyone else worse off is defined as a *Pareto improvement*. The terms 'better off' and 'worse off' refer to levels of welfare (and not income or wealth) and are measured in terms of consumer surpluses.[1] In practice, of course, very few policy changes have no adverse effects at all and so it becomes necessary to compare the welfare improvements of one group with the welfare losses of another. This gives rise to the *potential Pareto improvement criterion*.

If it is possible for those adversely affected by a policy change to be compensated by those who benefit, and for the latter still to be better off than before, then the policy change is deemed to be worthwhile. The potential for compensation must be there, but there is no necessary imperative that it actually be paid. Thus earlier justifications of the CBA approach were purely concerned with efficiency and only more recently have distributional issues (the identities of gainers and losers and the actual payment of compensation) been incorporated.

The potential Pareto improvement criterion is justified as an objective of society in one of two ways. One school of thought[2] pursues consensus value judgements for society as the basis for formulating social objectives. This school maintains that the value judgements of Paretian welfare economics are widely agreed and in particular that increases in efficiency, other things being equal, are desirable. Thus if a policy change will increase efficiency without having a harmful effect on, say, distributive justice, then that policy change should be made. Increases in efficiency, in this line of argument, are indicated by potential Pareto improvements.[3] This so-called *Paretian approach* to CBA thus recognises the existence and importance of social objectives other than the pursuit of efficiency, but maintains that it is not the role of the cost benefit analyst to pursue them. Thus an increase in efficiency (that is, the existence of a potential Pareto improvement) may or may not mean an improvement in social welfare. In the other school of thought, the so-called *decision-making approach* to CBA, the potential Pareto improvement criterion is justified by reference to the objective chosen by a social decision-maker who, it is argued, 'occupies his position by virtue of a socially approved political process. He is entrusted with the task of making choices on behalf of the general public, and this trust implies that he will formulate objectives for society. He is accountable to the public' (Sugden and Williams, 1978, p. 91). In this latter approach it is assumed that the decision-maker (the central government, say) has sufficient control over the distribution of resources to be able to convert potential Pareto improvements into actual improvements. In this way the tax system can be used, at a broad level, to allow society to pursue not only the efficiency objective but also distributive justice. Because the value judgements underlying the Paretian approach are not totally appropriate, and because equity or distributive justice is such an important objective in social care contexts, it would seem more sensible to adopt this decision-making approach to CBA. However, it is important not to fall into the trap of assuming a single decision-maker. Organisations and agencies are made up of a number of individuals with different views and objectives, and it will not be straightforward to reconcile conflicting views. This will be important not only in establishing a view about the optimal (or better) distribution of resources, but also in calculating opportunity costs. *Whose* views of the alternative uses of social care resources are to be taken as valid in what circumstances?

The stages of cost benefit analysis

I shall distinguish six stages for a CBA:

(1) Separate or define the alternatives to be analysed.
(2) List the costs and benefits.
(3) Quantify and value the costs and benefits.
(4) Compare the costs and benefits.
(5) Qualify or revise that decision in the light of risk, uncertainty, and sensitivity.
(6) Examine the distributional implications of the alternatives.

Stage 1: separate the alternatives

The exact nature of the range of policy choices facing care providers needs to be made explicit at the very beginning, and the question that the CBA will address should be made clear. It is crucial to get this question right, for once it is selected, the nature of the whole study is determined.

> The designer of a poorly thought-out cost benefit study may believe that it will answer questions that it logically cannot. Worse, he may believe, after the study is complete, that it *has* answered them – in which case public decision-making may actually be made less rational by the use (or misuse) of his analysis (Sugden and Williams, 1978, p. 231).

In some social care contexts, CBA can be used to evaluate both investment programmes and forms of care. The underlying methodologies are identical but clearly the information needs are rather different. In separating the alternatives for either type of evaluation one should first define the nature of the policy decision. Are we concerned with whether or not to provide service A, or are we choosing between service A and service B, and so on? In some instances constraints on either policy or practice narrow the range of options right down, perhaps to a single procedure. We might then use the CBA framework to provide information on 'How *much* of this procedure is optimal?' If two or more projects or procedures are being compared they must be rendered comparable. It has often been remarked that false comparisons are made between residential and other forms of care because for some clients there is really (*currently*) no option to residential provision. We shall see the importance of this point in the next chapter. It is also worth noting at this point that when final output measures are not available, or are deliberately not sought, as in some forms of cost-effectiveness analysis, then it is crucial that comparisons made within the general CBA framework are valid. Do the alternatives have *exactly* the same objectives?

It will be recalled that CBA is a tool of efficiency analysis and that a policy, procedure or practice cannot be efficient if it is not effective, that is if it does not raise or produce output. Thus CBA can be used to examine whether *any* care is actually worthwhile. Finally, we have to define the *extent* of the policy decision. Most projects and procedures, however small, localised or individualised, will have ramifications well beyond the immediate beneficiaries and sufferers. Many of these ramifications are too small to warrant the research effort needed to measure them, and others can be assumed to have been taken on board through the reasonably well-oiled workings of a market economy. Of course, the latter should never be taken as an act of faith but checked at the outset.

Stage 2: list the costs and benefits

At the second stage, all the likely costs and benefits need to be listed or enumerated, although no attempt is made to measure or value them just yet. Even if a cost or benefit is considered to be immeasurable, it should still be listed so as not to be forgotten in the final consideration of the results. This listing is not straightforward. Costs and benefits are not as distinct as it is often suggested, either in theory or in the practical analysis. Our discussion of opportunity costs in Chapter 4 emphasised that they are measured by forgone benefits. The distinction between costs and benefits is also difficult to maintain in some practical circumstances. Take, for example, the discussion of residential versus community care for the elderly. One important cost of community care is the burden and strain borne by relatives and neighbours. But the removal of this burden is also a benefit of residential care, and so the analyst must be careful not to double-count it. There is thus a preliminary classification problem to overcome.

Costs fall on the agency directly responsible for care (the local authority social services department, or private or voluntary organisation), on other agencies such as the local authority housing department, the National Health Service or the probation service, and on the client, relatives and neighbours. These costs are incurred either directly or indirectly. Among the direct costs are those immediately and readily attributable to clients or groups of clients through local authority accounts. Thus it is possible to obtain without undue difficulty the average weekly cost of residential care for elderly people. It is much less easy to obtain estimates of the indirect costs such as those associated with social work teams, and with peripatetic or occasional NHS resources, and those incurred by clients' relatives. This classificatory schema is detailed in Table 7.1 where examples of the different types of cost are drawn from the range of services for the elderly. It can be seen that the costs included in the table are of three kinds:

(1) *Living costs* – expenditure on provisions, clothing, personal needs and so on
(2) *Labour costs* – staff costs in residential homes and costs incurred by relatives providing care in the community
(3) *Capital costs* – durable resource inputs such as the residential home, the client's own home and so on.

Referring to Table 7.1 we can see that most evaluations and commentaries concern themselves only with direct costs incurred by the providing agency. That is, they ignore all costs except those in the top left-hand cell. Some social care managers might argue that they are not concerned with costs incurred by other organisations or by clients. This is really rather short-sighted because many of these other costs fall directly to the local authority (for example, via the housing

TABLE 7.1   *Classification of the costs of services for the elderly*

	Examples of costs incurred by:		
	Direct care agency	Other agencies	Clients and others
Directly	Expenditure on residential homes, home help services, meals-on-wheels, etc.	Expenditure by Housing Dept. on sheltered housing.	Expenditure by clients on food and housing.
Indirectly	Expenditure on field social workers, occupational therapists, etc.	Expenditure by NHS on district nurse visits, hospital out-patient services, etc.	Lost work and leisure opportunities of relatives, strain on neighbours, etc.

department) or to the taxpayer (via the NHS). Actually, I doubt if very many managers or practitioners would argue against the *principle* of including these other costs, but budgetary constraints and procedures often mean that they have to take decisions which minimise their own costs even though there may be a more than equivalent increase in costs incurred by other agencies or clients. There is thus a need for changes in *incentives* in order to avoid such moves which are clearly not in the social interest. It is important to notice that a decrease in the expenditure or costs included in the left-hand column will almost always mean an *increase* in the costs included in the other two columns.

If we now turn to the benefits we can distinguish those enjoyed by clients, those enjoyed by people directly associated with clients such as relatives and neighbours, and those enjoyed by other members of society with a general concern for the well-being of clients and their carers. This third set of benefits is a form of 'externality' (see Chapter 6). The benefits should range over all likely effects and our discussion of outputs in Chapter 3 provides the necessary basis for this. We can also make the distinction between 'observed' and 'concealed' benefits. The observed benefits are those which the researcher can identify by observation of clients and other affected parties. In the case of services for the elderly the researcher will be able to obtain information on mobility, incontinence and self-care capacity by questioning care staff or relatives of the client or perhaps by direct observation. In contrast, changes in morale or loneliness can only really be measured by asking clients themselves. The distinction between observed and concealed benefits is obviously not clear-cut. This two-way classification of benefits is detailed in Table 7.2 and illustrated again with examples taken from services for the elderly. Most evaluations of social care services focus only on the easily observed benefits to clients, that is only those in the top left-hand cell of Table 7.2.

TABLE 7.2   *Classification of the benefits of services for the elderly*

| | Examples of benefits enjoyed by: | | |
	Clients	*Clients' relatives*	*Society*
Observed	Changes in mobility, incontinence, self-care capacity.	Changes in employment opportunities.	Increased supply of housing if elderly clients move into residential homes.
Concealed	Changes in morale, loneliness, etc.	Changes in the burden of responsibility.	Psychological benefits of seeing elderly living in better circumstances.

The classification of costs and benefits in this way has the signal advantage of ensuring that the full range of effects is considered even if it later proves impossible to obtain measures for all of them. However, there is still one more task to undertake at this second stage in a cost benefit analysis. This is to ensure that the listing of the costs and benefits is consistent and sensible. There are four difficulties to overcome.

Transfer payments should be excluded. A transfer payment is a passing of money from one person to another which is not payment for goods or services received. Prime examples are taxation (a transfer payment for society as a whole) and unemployment benefits (whether paid out of an insurance scheme or as 'pure relief' and no matter how financed). Most cost benefit or related studies of social care services can immediately be criticised for their erroneous inclusion of social security and related payments. We should be wary of *double counting*, particularly if we want to measure the costs and benefits of alternative services over as wide a range as possible. Thirdly, and related to the two previous difficulties, we should take care when including *secondary effects*. Benefits and costs accruing to other than the immediate beneficiaries or sufferers should be included only if these have not already been taken into account by the market-determined valuations of the immediate or primary effects. Even when they are not reflected in market valuations care should be taken with these externalities. The basic rule of thumb is to include all costs and benefits that change the productivity of an asset (the 'technological externalities'), but exclude those which change the price or value of an asset (the 'pecuniary externalities'). Of course, transfer payments, some forms of double counting and secondary effects are of crucial importance in examinations of the distributional consequences of policies. In studies of efficiency, however, they should be ignored. The fourth difficulty we face is deciding on the *project life*, that is the length of time over which we are going to measure costs and benefits. The outputs of many social care services could be argued to accrue over the whole lifespan of clients, but clearly we cannot wait that long before completing an analysis. The cut-off point is thus arbitrary and liable to be determined by balancing the wish to measure effects over as long a period as possible with the need for a result. The arbitrariness of the decision in some cases can be mitigated by conducting a suitable sensitivity analysis in Stage 5.

Stage 3: quantify and value the costs and benefits

There are actually two steps here: the quantification or measurement of the costs and benefits listed at the second stage, and their subsequent valuation in monetary terms. I have collapsed them into one stage because it is often difficult and unnecessary to distinguish them. The technique of cost effectiveness analysis does not attempt to place monetary values on the outputs. For the moment I shall aim for the ideal: the valuation of inputs in terms of their opportunity costs and the valuation of final outputs.

There is no need to say too much about the measurement of either costs or benefits because of our earlier detailed discussions in Chapters 3 and 4. If each of the resource inputs and final outputs has an identifiable price over the lifetime of the project, if the project does not affect the price of any relevant good, if the prices of all relevant goods are set in a competitive market, and if none of the relevant goods (inputs or outputs) is a collective good

then valuation is a simple task (Hellinger, 1980, p. 206). One does not need much prior familiarity with the social care services to realise that none of these conditions is likely to hold in practice.[4] Let us therefore examine each of Hellinger's conditions in turn and seek ways around violations of them. In the terminology of welfare economics we are seeking *shadow prices*. There are thus four reasons why shadow prices will not be the same as market prices.

(1)   Market prices do not exist because the input or output is not marketed.
(2)   Market prices are not constant.
(3)   Market prices are distorted by market imperfections.
(4)   Market prices do not exist because the outputs are 'public (or collective) goods' or are difficult to apportion because the inputs are shared.

(1)   Non-marketed items Perhaps the most contentious aspect of cost benefit analysis is its attempt to place monetary values on the non-marketed items entering the production relationship. It should be noted that whether or not a CBA methodology is employed, and whether or not the valuation of intangibles is attempted by the analyst, the valuation of them is actually inescapable. Each resource allocation decision regarding care policy or practice makes an implicit valuation or trade-off of the costs and outputs of the alternatives. The aim of a CBA is to make those valuations *explicit*, and to clarify *whose* values are being employed. By making the valuations explicit one might hope to obtain some consistency, and by demonstrating who is doing the valuing one might stimulate some much needed debate about the relative claims of clients, professionals, politicians and so on. Ultimately, of course, the choice of whose values to accept is itself a value judgement and there will rarely be a uniquely superior solution.

There are essentially three approaches to the valuation of intangibles: the human capital method, the implicit valuation method, and the willingness-to-pay method. The first of these uses earnings as a basis for valuing benefits. Thus in health care the alleviation of some medical problem allows the patient to return to work, thus raising national productivity by an amount roughly approximated by the future stream of earnings. Given that most social care clients do not and will not join the workforce there seems little scope for employing what is anyway a much criticised approach.[5] Implicit valuation methods are based on the current or previous behaviour of either clients or decision-makers (including social work professionals). In their day to day activities and decisions they make implicit valuations of both resources and outputs which this second approach seeks to make explicit. This has proved a popular and valuable approach in health care studies. The third approach is based on the explicit judgements of clients, based on their observed trade-offs between resources or states of welfare, or elicited through a carefully designed series of questions. Once again the very characteristics of social care clients might militate against the employment of this willingness-to-pay method.[6]

(2)   Price changes Even if market prices exist and are good approximations to social opportunity costs, a complication may arise if the project or service that we are evaluating is sufficiently large to alter those prices. Do we take the initial or final price as the measure of opportunity cost? For example, if all local authority social services departments decided to double the proportion of children in their care boarded out with families, they are likely to find that the supply price of potential foster families will rise. Which boarding out allowance is to be used as a measure of the cost of foster care – is it the pre-expansion rate or the higher post-expansion rate? The solution, not surprisingly, is a combination of the two, with the exact formula being determined by considering the consumer and producer surpluses associated with the policy change (Pearce and Nash, 1981, Chapter 6; Sugden and Williams, 1978, Chapter 9). Of course, small-scale projects or procedures are unlikely to alter prices in this way. Incidentally, the price changes discussed here are direct; indirect price changes are what we have previously called pecuniary externalities, which are secondary effects to be excluded.

(3)   Price distortions If markets are perfectly competitive then market prices and social opportunity costs (or shadow prices) will be the same. The two will deviate for a number of reasons: market imperfections (including monopoly power), indirect taxation, un-employment and externalities. The last of these has already been considered. Our six examples of opportunity cost measurement in Chapter 4 included cases where one or more of these distortionary

factors was at work. The adjustments made to observed market prices thus aim to move them closer to the social opportunity costs.

If resources are supplied by a *monopolist*, or some group with market power, then price and marginal social cost will generally differ. The adjustments to the observed prices are made in accordance with the nature of the production – if the resources would not otherwise have been produced or used then their shadow price is set equal to the marginal cost of production; if, on the other hand, the resources are diverted from some other use, then the shadow price is set equal to the value in the next best use, equal to the demand price in the market. If *some* of the resources have been diverted from other uses, then a suitable weighted sum of the marginal cost and the demand price is employed. If resources are imported from abroad the exchange rate may distort their true value, and similar adjustments will be needed. *Indirect taxation*, whose only aim is the raising of revenue for the Exchequer or the local authority will similarly distort prices. If the resources would not otherwise have been produced or used, then the shadow price is the supply price (the marginal cost of production), whilst diverted resources are set at the demand price (including the taxes). Combinations of the two are used accordingly. If, on the other hand, the taxation is imposed to control externalities (such as pollution), or to discourage 'merit-bads' (like smoking) or to redistribute income, then adjustments of market prices might not be needed. A third source of market distortion is *unemployment*. Staff employed on the project or service being assessed by the CBA who would otherwise have been unemployed may have a zero shadow price. In fact, it might be more accurate to set the price equal to the value of forgone leisure and the costs of travelling to and from work, which implies a shadow price somewhere above zero. A further complication is that one must consider the government's macroeconomic policies, for if the present unemployment level is that which is necessary for 'policy optimisation' then employing an otherwise unemployed person may create unemployment elsewhere, so that the shadow price is equal to the wage which is paid. If unemployment is structural this 'complication' does not arise.

Whether it is necessary to make these adjustments, which are not all straightforward, is open to debate. Drummond (1980) argues that it is probably unnecessary to adjust prices when the item concerned is not important in the over-all appraisal, when the deviation from the social opportunity cost value is small, or when the time and trouble of making the adjustment is excessive. This is not a counsel of indolence but simply recognises that the costs of undertaking a proper CBA might very easily exceed the benefits of the project being analysed.

(4) Public goods and joint costs Collective or public goods cannot be consumed by one individual independently of other individuals. It will therefore be difficult to discover how much individuals value the public good by observing their choices in purchasing it. As we saw in the previous chapter there are likely to be relatively few public goods in social care contexts. A variety of approximations to the values of public goods has been suggested including the use of property values and the implicit costs of access (see Sugden and Williams, 1978, pp. 159–64).

A second and more common difficulty is that many resources are shared between a number of uses and users. Family centres may provide services for the under fives and for children on supervision orders, they may act as the base for one or more social work teams, they may provide day care services for the elderly or mentally handicapped, and they may have residential facilities. How then are the costs of running a family centre allocated between the different uses, as they would need to be in any CBA which attempts to compare this relatively recent innovation with more conventional services? The same problem arises elsewhere. How do we apportion the costs of, say, a residential children's homes to the individual children living within it? The problem is simplified slightly (though not a great deal) when we remember that the examination of efficiency usually requires only *marginal* cost data. There is, however, still the problem of obtaining values for these marginal costs. Both types of apportionment – between uses and users – can only satisfactorily be accomplished within a cost function framework (see Chapter 9).

The quantification and valuation of costs and benefits thus harbours a number of pitfalls, some of which are avoided without undue difficulty whilst others are more problematic. These pitfalls are summarised in Figure 7.1.

Stage 4: compare the costs and benefits

Having faithfully followed the recommendations of the first three stages we would have obtained a series of costs and benefits for each

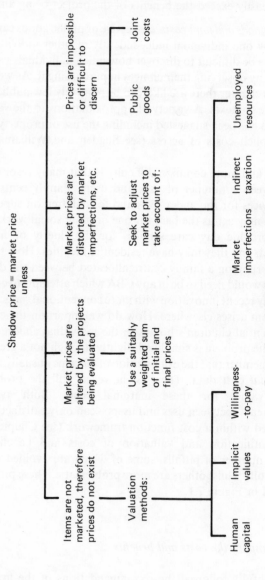

FIGURE 7.1 *Shadow price calculations*

project. Typically a new project requiring substantial capital investment will have high costs in the first one or two years followed by a period of low costs, whilst there may be no benefits at all until the service is in operation. Similar time profiles for the costs and benefits might be observed for preventive services. We therefore need to be able to compare costs incurred today with benefits enjoyed tomorrow, and the comparison is not immediately straightforward. We generally prefer one pound today rather than tomorrow because we have a whole day between now and then in which to use the money, a set of options not available tomorrow. This is the concept of time preference and allows us to weight future costs and benefits so as to render them comparable with present costs and benefits. Time preference is well illustrated by the behaviour of individuals who are prepared to pay a rate of interest in order to bring forward the receipt of money. The behaviour of borrowing and lending in fact provides the basis for the weighting of costs and benefits occurring at different times. In lending money to others we demand an amount in return which is greater than the sum originally lent. This is to compensate for the risk of not getting the money back, to take account of inflation, and in recognition of the fact that we are postponing our own enjoyment of the money.

Let us assume that the annual interest rate that we charge on the sum lent is 10 per cent. This implies that we are indifferent between £100 today and £110 next year, or between £100 today and £121 in two years time. These future values are obtained from the conventional formulae:

$$110 = 100 + (0.1)100 = 100(1 + 0.1)$$

$$121 = 100 + (0.1)100 + (0.1)[100 + (0.1)100] = 100(1 + 0.1)^2$$

After n years the amount will be $100(1 + 0.1)^n$. The discounting of future values back to the present time is simply the reverse of compounding the interest and we use the term *discount rate* rather than interest rate. We must thus decide how much we need now instead of the £110 in one year's time. Under these circumstances the amount is £100. This is obtained from the formula

$$100 = 100/(1 + 0.1)$$

We then say that £100 is the *present value* of £110 in one year's time if the discount rate is 10 per cent. In general the present value of a cost (or benefit) of x pounds recorded in year n is given by

$$Present\ Value = x(1+r)^{-n}$$

where r is the discount rate. In an actual CBA, the values and timings of the costs and benefits can be predicted with more or less accuracy. The researcher must select a suitable value (or set of values) for the discount rate, which is intended to measure society's *rate of time preference* and to reflect the alternative uses of the resources allocated to the proposed project or service. In fact, the Treasury recommends a particular numerical value for use in public sector CBAs, but a number of different values have been suggested by economists (Pearce and Nash, 1981, Chapter 9; Sugden and Williams, 1978, Chapter 15). The choice of discount rate is crucial, and most cost benefit analysts will examine the implications of more than one numerical value (see Stage 5). The larger the discount rate the smaller the present value of a given cost or benefit. Therefore, if the major costs are incurred early in the life of a project and the benefits are enjoyed mainly towards the end of the period a discount rate which is 'too high' will tend to undervalue the present value of the benefits relative to the costs and one which is 'too low' will undervalue the costs relative to the benefits. For simplicity I will assume a constant value for r throughout the period.

Now consider the streams of costs and benefits:

$$C_0, C_1, C_2, \ldots, C_n$$
$$B_0, B_1, B_2, \ldots, B_n$$

where the subscript $0, 1, 2, \ldots n$ denotes the time period (year). The present value of C_0 is simply C_0. The present value of C_1 is $C_1(1+r)^{-1}$ if we assume a social discount rate of r. The present value of C_2 is $C_2(1+r)^{-2}$, and continuing in this way we have the *present value of costs* (PVC) given by

$$PVC = \sum_{t=0}^{n} C_t(1+r)^{-t}$$

and similarly the *present value of benefits* (PVB):

$$PVB = \sum_{t=0}^{n} B_t(1+r)^{-t}$$

The difference between PVB and PVC is the *net present value* (NPV) of the project or procedure under consideration

$$NPV = PVB - PVC = \sum_{t=0}^{n} (B_t - C_t)(1+r)^{-t}$$

The decision rule is then simple. If NPV is greater than zero then the project should be undertaken; otherwise it should not. This is the *net present value criterion* for CBA. It is easily extended to more than one project by choosing that alternative with the greatest NPV. Thus for two alternatives *A* and *B*, both with positive NPVs:

if $NPV(A) > NPV(B)$ choose *A*,

if $NPV(A) < NPV(B)$ choose *B*,

if $NPV(A) = NPV(B)$ choose either of them.

When we are considering how *much* of *A* to do, and how much of *B*, within a given budget constraint, the decision rule is not quite so straightforward. Intrinsically there are no major conceptual difficulties, but it will be necessary to use a mathematical programming technique to select the optimal combination. The solution cannot be found by relying on one of the other decision rules often suggested.

Three other decision rules have attracted attention in the CBA literature. Occasionally, *benefit-cost ratios* are computed (equal to PVB/PVC) and the project with the largest ratio recommended for selection. Unfortunately, unless the distinction between benefits and costs is entirely free of ambiguity, which is unlikely to be the case in many social policy contexts, these ratios may not be reliable indicators of the social worth of the projects.[7] The *internal rate of return* rule first finds that internal rate of return, *i*, which makes the present net value of a project exactly equal to zero. That is, we find the value of *i* which solves the equation:

$$\sum_{t=0}^{n} (B_t - C_t)(1+i)^{-t} = 0$$

The project should then be undertaken if the internal rate of return (*i*) is greater than the social discount rate (*r*), but not if it is smaller. It is not intrinsically the correct rule (it merely gives the right answer on most occasions) and it is vulnerable to the problem of multiple solutions (the above equation can often be solved for more than one value of *i*). In some circumstances the internal rate of return criterion is preferable to NPV, but this is not generally the case. The other criterion is the *terminal value rule*. Mishan (1967) suggested a normalisation procedure to overcome the problems associated with the internal rate of return rule and to ensure that it yields identical results to the NPV criterion. With this criterion costs and benefits are no longer discounted back to the present but are compounded to a terminal value using suitable compound rates, and all projects are scaled up so as to be normalised for length of life. The terminal values of the costs of different projects are also equalised. The decision rule is then to choose the project with the greater 'normalised' terminal value of benefits.[8]

Stage 5: *take account of risk, uncertainty and sensitivity*

The costs and benefits calculated for the various projects are usually expected or predicted values, and their prediction is always likely to be subject to some error, however carefully undertaken. It is therefore important to qualify the decision rules and their recommendations by taking account of these errors. We can distinguish between *risk*, when the value of a variable is unknown but its probability distribution *is* known, and *uncertainty*, when neither the variable nor its probability distribution is known. Uncertainty is more common than risk. Other errors are possible, for example we may set the social discount rate too high, compute a mistaken shadow price, or allow too long an expected life span. The researcher can allow for these by conducting a number of sensitivity analyses, computing the NPV (for example) on different assumptions regarding the costs, benefits, rate of discount, and life span. These will indicate just how sensitive are the conclusions of the CBA to these different assumptions.

Stage 6: *examine the distributional implications*

In describing the theoretical underpinnings of CBA two approaches were distinguished in justifying the adoption of the potential Pareto improvement criterion. One consequence of the *Paretian approach* is the view that the role of CBA is to examine efficiency but not to concern itself with the distributional implications of alternative projects. The *decision-making approach*, on the other hand, recognises the need to take account of both social objectives in the analysis. In fact, as it turns out, *both* approaches need to examine the distributional issue. In aggregating and comparing costs and benefits at stages 3 and 4 we have already made a value judgement about the distribution of (say) income. That judgement or assumption is that the prevailing distribution is satisfactory so that weights of unity can be attached to all costs and benefits.[9]

There are two alternative courses of action. The first is to include a different set of weights at the third stage so as to take account of the fact that the benefits may be falling mainly to the more affluent (or less needy or less deserving) members of the population and the costs to the less affluent (or more needy or more deserving). The analyst would probably want to examine the implications of a number of *different* sets of distributional weights via a sensitivity analysis. Weighting schemes have been based on different ethical principles, the most commonly used being utilitarianism. Weights are thus sought which approximate individuals' marginal utilities of income. Alternatively, a set of distributional weights can be based on Rawlsian or other ethical postulates. In practical circumstances, weights have been based on relative incomes, marginal rates of gross taxation, marginal rates of net taxation (i.e., benefit-burden ratios), and the weights implicit in other government decisions (Pearce and Nash, 1981, Chapter 4). The other course of action would be to assume equal weights but comment at the end of the analysis on the distributional or equity implications of the different projects or procedures. A danger of including other distributional weights before aggregation is that 'this becomes just another part of the "tool kit", another issue that CBA 'solves' for the decision maker' (Drummond, 1981, p. 141). There is also the danger that equity might get subsumed under efficiency and that CBA merely becomes a vehicle for the analyst's own prejudices. However, it would be wrong, I think, for the cost benefit analyst not to make clear the implications of alternative projects, procedures or services for individuals in different socio-economic or income groups, for individuals in different areas of the country, and for individuals with different needs. In some cases, of course, the distributional implications of a project may be too small to be of consequence, although this should be checked and not assumed.

It should be noted that there is no unique CBA methodology; the analysis must always be adapted to fit the particular policy or practice question that is being studied.

Cost effectiveness analysis

The stages of a cost effectiveness analysis (CEA) exactly mirror those of a CBA except that no attempt is made to place monetary values on the outputs. It is assumed that costs may be distinguished from benefits, and that the latter are not reducible to monetary measures 'as a matter of practice, or should not, as a matter of principle' (Sugden and Williams, 1978, p. 190). Thus the CEA technique aims to show how a given level of benefit can be achieved at minimum cost (or maximum benefit at given cost). Problems will arise with more than one output or benefit, especially when these benefits are not systematically or consistently related to each other. 'Rates of exchange' between benefits have been suggested, and these of course could be obtained from the aggregated output measures that were discussed in Chapter 3. In this way it would be possible to calculate the 'cost per unit of output' for each project (having suitably discounted both elements back to the current period[10]) and use this as the decision rule.

Many economists would agree with Sugden and Williams that CEA is of most value when 'choosing between mutually exclusive ways of achieving a particular, very clearly defined benefit' (p. 191). It cannot, however, be used to say whether or not the benefits of a project or procedure actually outweigh the costs. What it can do is ensure that a full range of costs is estimated and that measures (but not values) are sought for all relevant dimensions of output. The information thus gathered can then be presented in such a way as to make plain the efficiency and distributional implications of the alternatives under consideration and allow policy-makers to make the necessary trade-offs. For example, the analyst could supply comprehensive cost estimates for two alternatives, call them X and Y, with the cost of X exceeding the cost of Y. He could also supply detailed output measures (actual or predicted) for these alternatives. The decision-maker must then decide whether the greater cost of X is outweighed by the greater benefit of Y. In so doing, of course, he is supplying the missing valuations.

Is cost benefit analysis suitable for social care?

This discussion of the theoretical underpinnings and stages of cost benefit analysis has highlighted two things: the technique is less straightforward than some writers would have us believe, and it harbours a number of difficulties of both theory and application. Should we therefore abandon any attempt to apply this technique in the examination and evaluation of social care services? I want to conclude this discussion of principles by arguing that we should *not* abandon it, but that we do need to think carefully about its application and about the interpretation of its results. Most of these remarks apply with equal validity to cost effectiveness analysis and I shall retain the generic term 'cost benefit analysis' to refer to both techniques.

Thus far we have encountered two kinds of difficulty. There are some rather specific problems associated with the definition and measurement of costs and benefits, the choice of a suitable discount rate, the selection of the criterion for choosing between alternative projects, and so on. There are also some more general problems of research ideology. These include arguments about the inclusion or exclusion of the distributional consequences of alternative projects, the reducibility of benefits to monetary values, and the role of the cost benefit analyst in the decision-making process. I do not intend to say much more about the first set of difficulties. They are not unimportant, but they have all received some consideration in the foregoing, many appear to have been quite satisfactorily resolved by economists working in other service areas, and many – indeed most – are shared by all social care evaluations. The third point needs some explanation. Many of the criticisms raised against the cost benefit technique are criticisms directed either at evaluation *per se* or at the evaluation of social care. Most of them are out of date, criticising or expressing reservations about aspects of the evaluation which have been successfully resolved by the *production of welfare* approach. Most of them have been discussed already in earlier chapters and I will consider them again through another medium – their *practical* ramifications – in the next and subsequent chapters. Many of them are difficulties which are only avoided by alternative evaluative methodologies by making unacceptable assumptions about reality. If the principles of the production of welfare perspective are generally held to be reasonable, if the need for obtaining measures of the 'success' of care is accepted, and if the scarcity of resources is acknowledged so that benefits forgone are considered as well as benefits received, then the usefulness of CBA cannot be denied. 'The question is not *whether* such analyses are desirable, for in one form or another – formal or informal – they cannot be avoided, but *how* to do the analyses in a useful manner' (Weisbrod and Helming, 1980, p. 617).

Some of the criticisms voiced about CBA have been born out of a misunderstanding of the true nature and intent of the technique and of the scope of its applicability. Booth (1981), for example, seems to be of the opinion that efficiency analysis and PPBS are one and the same thing, and that difficulties in the application of the latter in the USA in the 1960s rule out applications of all efficiency analyses in Britain today. Booth confuses the *macro* tool of PPBS, whose aims are modest and intermediate (see Chapter 6) with the explicitly *micro* focus of CBA and other techniques of efficiency analysis. CBA will not help us choose between the expansion of care facilities for the elderly and the provision of more day nursery places for the under-fives, nor does it claim to do so. Some other misconceptions have been fed by the poorly designed and inadequately executed CBAs of the 1960s and 1970s. Some previous evaluations of British social care services that have boasted the title 'cost benefit analysis' were really nothing of the kind. Wager (1972) and PA International Management Consultants (1972) simply conducted cost-cost studies and their complete neglect of outputs does a disservice to the cost benefit tradition. Inadequacies of this kind can easily mislead and create a bad press. Unfortunately most of the management consultancy firms currently conducting 'value for money' studies in local authorities are perpetrating errors of this kind.

Two of the common misconceptions about cost benefit analysis are that it *only* considers monetary items and/or that it attempts to place monetary values on items that are 'priceless' or 'beyond money'. The first thing to notice is that some items are only without prices by historical accident. Blood, for example, was not marketed in Britain until 1983 when the NHS introduced charges for private hospitals (and then the 'market' was very limited), and is marketed in many other countries. Just because an item is not marketed in our society does not mean that it can *never* be marketed. We might feel that it *ought not* to be marketed, that there is something morally objectionable about attaching a market price. One is a normative statement which can never be 'right' or 'wrong', the other is a positive statement which is ultimately verifiable by experience and evidence. Secondly, even if one does reduce all costs and benefits to monetary values (and it is my belief that this is not essential and, given our lack of knowledge about some services, not totally feasible) this does not imply 'that an increase in the national income is the overriding goal of social policy' (Booth, 1981, p. 18). Such is the implication of the 'human capital' approach to the valuation of intangible items (see p. 126 above), but few economists would subscribe to this approach. If some items (particularly benefits) cannot sensibly be valued in monetary terms then cost effectiveness analysis can be employed, and to good effect. Of course, as we have already seen, decision-makers are attaching *implicit* valuations to these items. Whenever a social worker, home help organiser, residential homes' manager, social services director, or government minister allocates resources between services or clients a decision has been made as to relative costs and benefits of the competing claimants on those resources. Whether the values underlying these allocations are 'correct' is obviously a value judgement. The aim of the CBA, therefore, is to make these values explicit so that decisions might be more consistent and better informed.[11]

Another criticism of CBA basically reduces to the contention that no information is better than some information. Buxbaum, for example, asks; 'Why should their [decision-makers'] collective minds be able to evaluate each piece of information, weight it, balance it, and put together a better judgement? It is possible for information to overwhelm decision-makers and distort decisions' (Buxbaum, 1981, p. 467). What Buxbaum does not demonstrate is that decision-makers make worse use of 'some information' than they do of 'no information'. Of course, if the information fed to them is itself misleading or misguided then the resultant policies might be totally wrong, but this is not the point that Buxbaum is making. My own interpretation of the available evidence is that policies based on 'no information' are demonstrably worse (in the sense of being irrational, inefficient, and contrary to the stated aims of policy-makers) than those informed by evaluation studies. Some of the evidence presented in the next three chapters makes this quite plain.

Underlying Buxbaum's argument is the view that:

Political pressure to limit social welfare expenditure has converted economic analysis into the budget-cutter's rationalisation . . . At present, it is probably wise to reject economic analysis and pursue political action to alter the political context. When the nation is restored to the pursuit of both efficiency and improved social welfare, rational decision-making may be tried again (1981, pp. 468–9).

This association of cost benefit analysis (or perhaps even efficiency in general) with expenditure cuts is common. To some extent it is the confusion of economics the *topic* with economics the *discipline* (see Chapter 1) and to some extent it is a view born of frustration and disenchantment with the present trends in public sector activity. However, efficiency is a valid and justifiable objective whatever level of expenditure decision-makers are planning.

Cost benefit analysis has a dual function. It assists the decision-maker to pursue objectives that are, by virtue of the community's assent to the decision-making process, social objectives. And by making explicit what these objectives are, it makes the decision-maker more accountable to the community (Sugden and Williams, 1978, p. 241).

Cost benefit analysis is more an art than a science, more a way of organising thought than of mechanistically allocating resources. It should seek to uncover extant value judgements, and not unthinkingly impose those of the analyst or the politician. It cannot replace the judgements of decision-makers but it can supplement and inform them. It can help the decision-maker formulate his policy questions sensibly and logically and then (generally) provides a *range* of answers from which the decision-maker might choose. If the decision-maker misinterprets these answers it is the cost benefit analyst's responsibility to point this out. It is not, however, his responsibility to determine policies. The interplay of economic appraisal and political priorities is the most sensible way to proceed.

8

Residential and Community Care of the Elderly: An Application of Cost Benefit Analysis

Introduction

The principles of cost benefit analysis, set out in the last chapter, can now be used to structure a discussion of policy questions and previous evaluations in social care. I shall illustrate the art of cost benefit analysis in a single area, albeit one which has generated a great deal of discussion and a large volume of research: the choice of an optimal balance of care services for the elderly. This particular selection inevitably means that a number of interesting studies and areas have had to be overlooked. However, the issues and difficulties raised in this consideration of the balance of care services for the elderly are shared by many other social care questions.

One of the most oft-quoted objectives of care of the elderly during the post-war period has been a preference for domiciliary or community care over residential care:

it is the general objective of both health and welfare services, working in co-operation, to maintain the elderly in the community and to accept admission to hospital or residential care as the right course only when an old person himself accepts the necessity for this and when he has reached the point where the community services are no longer sufficient (Ministry of Health, 1960, p. 122).

This quote comes from an Annual Report of the Ministry of Health, but it would have been possible to have selected similar quotes from any number of other such reports, speeches, memoranda, circulars, White Papers and building notes. Over the years this preference for community care has developed from an *assumption* that it is the best policy to an accepted *doctrine* requiring, it would seem, little or no rationalisation, and, more frequently, to a rational policy based on the (generally untested) premises of client well-being and cost. The *Growing Older* White Paper, published in 1981, provides a good example of such 'untested rationality' (DHSS, 1981, opening paragraphs).

The two main rationalisations for a policy emphasis on community rather than residential provision have been that elderly people prefer to live in their own homes and that this alternative is cheaper. The Guillebaud Committee felt that the development of domiciliary services 'will be a genuine economy measure, and also a humanitarian measure in enabling old people to lead the sort of life they prefer' (Guillebaud Committee, para 647). That old people would themselves prefer to remain in their own homes was cited in both of the Nuffield-sponsored surveys of the 1940s and stressed again by Bevan in the National Assistance Bill debate. Rowntree (1947, para 259) found many 'old people maintaining a hopeless struggle against adversity in order to cling to their last vestiges of independence' and so avoid being admitted to the much-feared Poor Law Institution. Sheldon's (1948) general impression from his survey of the elderly in Wolverhampton was

one of admiration for the mental vigour and 'guts' of the old people: one cannot avoid the suggestion that the facts of living in an environment that they are used to, of having something to do and of being able to feel necessary in the world are important factors in producing this state of affairs.

This view is not shared by all. The House of Commons Expenditure Committee obviously had some doubts about domiciliary care: 'Maintenance of one's own home poses the question of whether the resulting quality of life is in fact satisfactory. . . . The goal, if achieved, depends on many factors besides the services provided' (Expenditure Committee, 1972, paragraph 15). A survey by Harris (1968) found that 11 per cent of old people's home residents said they were unhappy as compared with 7 per cent of those living at home, but she 'did not find any evidence to support the picture of old people's homes being inhabited by masses of unhappy and discontented residents' (p. 69). The second rationale for favouring community care – that it is very much cheaper – has attracted much less attention.

Unfortunately, prejudice against residential institutions has resulted in the almost aggressive assertion that costs are not relevant (anyway it is shown that residential care is more expensive!) and that the relative benefits are already known. This seems to me to be a most dubious proposition (Plank, 1977, paragraph 2.1).

A third rationalisation for the general preference for community care has re-emerged in recent years. It is often argued that domiciliary care has the virtue of reducing the burden on residential care. This emphasis on non-residential care stems from a realisation that the elasticity of supply of residential places in response to changes in need is much less than the elasticity of supply of domiciliary services. Residential services are argued to be of considerable value for some elderly people and, because they are scarce resources, should be used carefully in order to maximise their effectiveness. In other words, the relative cheapness or cost effectiveness of domiciliary care derives not from its substitutability but from its complementarity with residential care. This third perspective clearly suggests a need to carefully specify the research question. This is especially important in the light of recent developments in the use of residential resources for short-term care and the small but growing body of evidence of substantial burdens imposed on unpaid carers in the community.

Specifying the relevant research question

It has sometimes been argued that for many old people there is really no choice as to the mode of care required. Thus, the argument runs, for these persons there are no alternative forms of care to be compared. Such arguments are obviously based on an assumption that investment in new capital resources is possible, but innovatory care schemes (that is, new 'technologies of care') are ruled out. This assumption is neither realistic nor necessary. Ferlie's review of innovatory practices reveals that social services departments, health authorities and voluntary organisations have developed a broad range of efficiency-promoting services, often with little or no additional expenditure and (often) fairly low opportunity costs (Ferlie, 1982, Davies and Ferlie, 1982).

A careful reading of Ferlie's *Sourcebook* suggests that the basic ingredients of today's innovations in care of the elderly are actually pretty limited in number, so that the examination of costs and outcomes need not be especially problematic. Care services are not discrete but are arranged along a continuum, running from full self-support or the highly informal support provided by unpaid carers in the community, to the most self-contained of residential establishments. As we move along the continuum so we take in different varieties and degrees of domiciliary and residential provision. Recent changes in the use of local authority residential homes, developing their short stay, day care, and attached housing responsibilities, can all be interpreted as filling in gaps on the continuum of care. It is thus misleading to conduct research on 'residential *versus* community care', for this breaks the continuum and implies independence of costs between settings. It could also encourage the examination of a more narrow range of outcome indicators than would be justified by the policy question, and encourage a focus on quite short time-horizons within which the balance and mix of services for clients remains unchanged.

For the purposes of exposition it is helpful to select just two or three points from this continuum of care services. Given the similarity of the basic ingredients of service packages along this continuum, such a selection need not necessarily over-simplify either the research or the policy question. Of course, for the purposes of conducting a particular evaluation it will be necessary to examine a discrete number of options, but provided that these options are not treated as rigidly independent it should be possible to interpolate costs and outcomes between them to provide 'vicarious' evaluations of other points on the continuum. Consider the following three service alternatives:

(1) *Care provided informally* by unpaid persons in the community such as relatives and neighbours (but not by other volunteers attached to any organisation), which I shall call *informal care*.
(2) *Domiciliary care* provided by social services departments, health authorities, voluntary organisations and others, perhaps

additional to the informal support of relatives and neighbours, whilst the client lives 'in the community'.

(3) *Residential care* provided in a residential home (statutory, voluntary or private).

The labels attached to these three service packages are used merely for convenience and brevity; in practice a more rigorous set of labels would probably be needed. We can illustrate the policy choices between them with the aid of three simple diagrams.[1]

The relationships between cost and client 'dependency' for these three service packages are plotted in Figure 8.1. Each has been drawn as a simple straight line, with higher dependency levels implying higher costs of care. What is important is not whether costs are monotonically associated with a particular measure of physical or mental incapacity, but that there is at least one characteristic of elderly clients which, other things being equal, will raise the costs of care and will do so to different degrees in different settings. To deny such an association is to argue that costs are invariant with respect to individual characteristics and that the technologies of the production

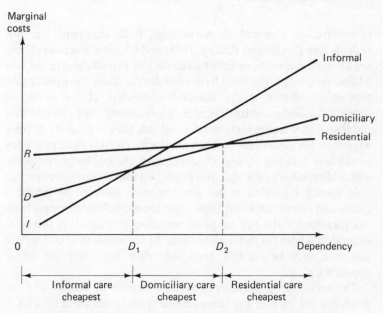

FIGURE 8.1 *Costs by dependency for three care modes*

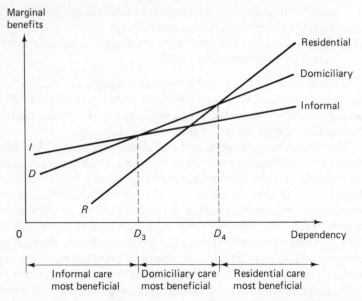

Figure 8.2 *Benefits by dependency for three care modes*

of welfare are identical across settings. Both arguments are unrealistic (see Davies and Knapp, 1978; and Chapter 9 below). These
are all *marginal costs*, indicating the cost of providing care for one
additional client.[2] The lines have been drawn under the assumption
that informal care is the cheapest alternative at low levels of
dependency (indicated by dependency levels lower than D_1) and that
residential care is cheapest once dependency goes beyond D_2. If costs
were the only consideration then an elderly client with dependency
somewhere between D_1 and D_2 could most cheaply be provided for
with a 'domiciliary package'. It is important that these costs cover not
only agency expenditures but also the costs incurred by informal
carers and clients, and that these costs should reflect the opportunities forgone for the full range of resources employed. If the cost-
dependency lines for different services do not cross, then one service
will obviously be cheaper than the other two over the whole
dependency range.

The relationship between (marginal) benefit or output and dependency for each of the three service types is drawn in figure 8.2.
Again these relationships are drawn as straight lines, and again they

are assumed to cross. In this instance, the benefits for elderly clients, their carers, and other members of society are greatest with informal care until dependency exceeds D_3, between D_3 and D_4 the domiciliary package care is the most beneficial, and beyond D_4 it is residential care which produces the greatest marginal benefit. These benefit curves are alone sufficient for policy-making on the assumption either that costs do not matter or that they are set at some constant or standard level. Neither assumption is satisfactory. The approach adopted in this book clearly requires that we look at both costs and benefits simultaneously. This is done in Figure 8.3, although in order not to clutter up the diagram I have restricted it to just two of the services.

The marginal benefit and cost relationships have been deliberately drawn in such a way that at extreme levels of dependency the optimal

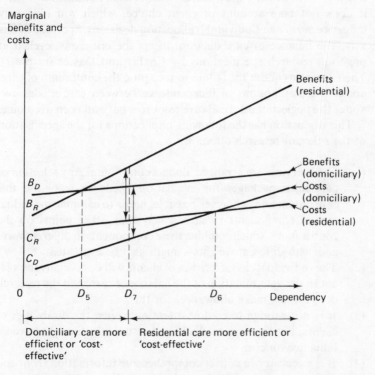

FIGURE 8.3 *Costs and benefits by dependency for residential and domiciliary care*

placement is clear. The most efficient provision for an elderly person with dependency less than D_5 will be the domiciliary package. Below D_5 the benefits of domiciliary care are higher and the costs lower than those for residential care. Similarly, beyond dependency level D_6 residential care is the more efficient since its benefits are greater and costs lower. But what about all those elderly people with dependency characteristics between D_5 and D_6? In this range the benefits of residential care are the greater but so too are the costs. We seek that level of dependency (the 'cut-off' point) at which the excess of benefits over costs is the same for the two service packages. This is D_7. Thus for dependency levels below D_7 the more efficient service is domiciliary provision, whilst above D_7 it is residential care. Figure 8.3 thus provides an indication of the optimal (most efficient) *balance of care* for the elderly. It does not take account of the *distribution* of benefits and burdens, which I shall examine below, and it does not take account of client choice, which will obviously influence *particular* (individual) allocation decisions. Specified in this way, the balance of care diagram meets the criticisms levelled at previous research specifications by Challis and Davies (in press). Their concerns about the failure to recognise the continuum of care, about the assumptions of independence between care modes and about the neglect of informal care resources have all been overcome.

This discussion has the following implications for the specification of the relevant research question:

(1) Care services are arranged along a continuum. Any selection of particular packages for evaluation needs to recognise this continuum and, wherever possible, needs to examine individual service components in such a way that other points on the continuum – which combine these components in different ways and with different weights – might also be evaluated.

(2) The individual characteristics of clients will be crucially important in the determination of the balance of care, and the research design must make allowances for this.

(3) It is not enough to confine attention to just the disabilities of clients, but to examine all characteristics which might have an influence on cost.

(4) It is necessary to collect comprehensive information from and about informal carers, for their services form an integral part of almost all packages along the continuum.

Measuring the costs

As we move from one point on the continuum to any other, different services and resources assume different degrees of importance. We might also find that the relative weights attached to the various objectives and outputs of care also vary. Because of the pervasive emphasis of the 'residential *versus* community' question in the postwar policy literature, the vast majority of research studies has focused on a 'typical residential package' and 'typical community package'. The latter is usually a combination of a few domiciliary services provided by social services departments and health authorities and the latter is usually twenty-four hours a day residential provision with no other inputs considered. I shall describe and discuss some of these evaluative studies later in this chapter (p. 155), but for the moment I want to concentrate attention on the specification and measurement of the *costs*. I do so because there are already many comprehensive reviews of the measurement of 'effectiveness' or 'outcomes' elsewhere in the literature. I have already considered the dimensions of output in Chapter 3, and in the British literature useful reviews are provided by Challis (1981), Davies and Knapp (1981, Chapters 2 and 3), Goldberg and Connelly (1982) and K. G. Wright (1974).[3]

It is possible to distinguish at least seven care agencies, groups and individuals who will incur costs at some or all points along the care continuum: social services departments, the National Health Service, housing departments, the social security branch of government and the Inland Revenue, voluntary and private organisations (including volunteers),the elderly clients or recipients themselves, and their principal (unpaid) carers (cf. Challis and Davies, in press, Chapter 4).[4] I shall discuss the listing and the measurement of these various costs as one stage, in order to avoid unnecessary repetition. Some cost items are likely to appear under more than one heading and should not be double-counted.

Social services departments

With few exceptions, all of the evaluative studies of residential and community care for the elderly have either ignored the cost side of the policy question or have focused exclusively on the direct costs incurred by public agencies. Also with few exceptions, none of these studies has gone beyond the uncritical acceptance of expenditure figures provided by these authorities or has attempted to cost *packages* of services.

The costs incurred by social services departments relate to:

residential care
day care (including luncheon clubs)
home help and home aides
meals on wheels
field social worker resources (including administrative time)
occupational therapy
transport
telephones
aids and adaptations
paid 'street wardens', 'good neighbours', and the like
joint finance expenditure
grants to other bodies (including housing departments, private and
    voluntary agencies)

The last two items, joint finance and grants to other bodies, may be double-counted elsewhere. There may be a need to adjust expenditures for taxes (such as VAT or the high level of taxation on petrol) if it is felt that their inclusion in the market prices means an overstatement of the true costs (see Sugden and Williams, 1978). This could be an important distortion in services with a large transport element, such as meals on wheels, but only Wager (1972) has attempted any such adjustment. There may also be a need to make adjustments for variations in costs due to extraneous factors such as wage levels, client characteristics and the inheritance of capital (see Chapter 9). It will be necessary to adjust the observed capital cost figures so as to get closer approximations to the opportunity costs.

The costing of residential services is relatively straightforward, although the increasing use of residential facilities as community resources (for day care, meals, occupational therapy and short stay residence) will complicate matters. The main elements of residential care costs were given a preliminary airing in Chapter 4 and will be the focus of more detailed analytical attention in the next chapter. The most comprehensive costing of *domiciliary* packages has been undertaken by Challis and Davies (in press) in their evaluation of the

Kent Community Care Scheme. These authors calculated unit costs for a broad range of services and weighted them by actual receipt for each of the clients covered by their study. The costing of service components should not present any new difficulties. The field social work input into both residential and community care poses probably the most complicated estimation problems. Individual caseloads provide little guide to the amount of time devoted to particular clients and many social work activities (such as discussions with colleagues, liaison with other departments or agencies, travelling and general administration) are generated by more than one client. Because of these difficulties very few studies have adequately costed social worker support, and yet their omission or inadequate inclusion could seriously bias the conclusions.[5] The same comment applies to the omission of the costs of supervisory staff (such as home help organisers) and of administration, occupational therapy and transport services.

The National Health Service

Similar costing problems are likely to arise for the variety of peripatetic and occasional services provided by the NHS. The main costs incurred by health authorities will arise from the following:

hospital in-patient care (general, geriatric, psychiatric)
day hospital provision (general, geriatric, psychiatric)
rehabilitation units
nursing homes
services provided by general practitioners, district nurses, health
    visitors, community psychiatric nurses, bath attendants, etc.
laundry services
chiropody
general aids
transport
joint finance expenditure

Once again the costing of these services in practice is likely to require the judicious use of cost function techniques to tease out the joint costs of, say, hospital in-patient and out-patient care, together with the careful collection of data on time-use by the many community-based health professionals dealing with the elderly.

Housing departments

Many of the care packages currently provided have implications for housing departments, either directly through the provision of sheltered or special housing and the cost of rent and rate subsidies, or indirectly through the housing market effects of client movements. (I shall discuss the indirect effects under client costs below.) Special housing schemes impose both capital and recurrent costs and the principles of estimation are no different from those discussed for residential services. Rent and rate rebates, whilst recorded in the accounts of housing departments, are merely transfer payments (that is, they do not correspond to flows of *real* resources) and should therefore be ignored in discussions of efficiency. They do, however, have important distributional implications.

DHSS and Inland Revenue

The 'costs' incurred by the social security branch of the Department of Health and Social Security and the Inland Revenue obviously have distributional implications, but again do not represent flows of real resources. The present jungle of allowances and benefits includes old age pensions, supplementary benefit payments, 'pocket money' allowances for residents in homes or hospitals, allowances paid for sons' and daughters' services or dependent relatives, and invalidity and attendance allowances (Equal Opportunities Commission, 1982a). These 'costs' to society as a whole are sources of income for clients and their carers and as such will be spent on the clothing, food, housing and other items which are recorded under other heads. This illustrates the transfer payment problem.

Private and voluntary organisations (including volunteers)

Many of the costs incurred by non-statutory care agencies will be reimbursed by the statutory sector and these costs must not be double-counted. Private and voluntary homes and WRVS meals services are often funded by grants from social services departments, but it should not prove unduly difficult to cost their services. Rather more problematic will be the costing of volunteer services. As I argued in Chapter 4, volunteers are not necessarily free resources just because they are unpaid. The opportunity costs of their employment are 'context- and volunteer-specific', although within a well-defined range of alternatives.

Elderly clients

The elderly clients themselves, who we should perhaps more accurately call the 'recipients of care' since their informal carers are often recognised as clients too, will obviously incur many costs. Any 'item of daily living' not provided by a local authority department or other agency will impose a cost on the recipient of care or the principal carers. Even in the comparatively closed environments of residential and hospital care, the elderly residents will bear some personal consumption costs, estimated to be around 6 per cent of capital and recurrent costs in residential homes and about 3 per cent in hospitals (K. G. Wright *et al.*, 1981). The elderly living outside these establishments will bear a substantially higher proportion of the total costs of normal daily living. For most items the actual expenditure will reasonably approximate the social opportunity cost values and so the researcher can either collect information on spending patterns by individual recipients or households, or else rely on national sample survey estimates of 'typical' expenditure patterns such as those collected in the Family Expenditure Survey (FES). For example, Challis and Davies (in press) collected details of actual income from all the individuals covered by their study so as to predict expenditure from the income-banded FES figures. Wager, Mooney and Wright also used FES figures, and there would now seem to be little to be gained by allocating scarce research resources to the collection of more refined data. There is also a fairly good consensus regarding housing costs. Most researchers now start by ignoring the actual weekly housing payments made by elderly individuals, which are often relatively small, and instead seek opportunity cost values. These may be high if it is felt that the elderly 'under-utilise' their housing resources and if there is an excess demand for housing.[6] The annuity values of replacement costs, regional house values, specifically assessed house valuations or hedonic prices have thus been employed as opportunity cost estimates not only for owner-occupied housing, but also for rented accommodation (see the studies reviewed below and see Gillingham, 1980 for a useful discussion of some of the conceptual issues). Rate payments, which are simply transfer payments from householders to local authorities, can be ignored.

Principal carers

The most neglected and probably the most under-valued costs are those borne by families and other unpaid carers. Wager (1972) discusses only the direct costs borne by principal carers – expenditure on accommodation and the normal items of daily living. Like a number of other researchers since then, he estimates these costs from FES data, although these will often underestimate principal carer costs because of the additional financial burden imposed upon them by a disabled or confused dependent. 'The most usual extra costs are for heating, special diets, the management of incontinence, . . . extra wear and tear on clothing and furnishings, . . . extra transport costs, . . . substitute care, . . . and aids and adaptations' (Equal Opportunities Commission, 1982b, p. 24). Wager estimates the marginal accommodation costs from rental values, either calculated as a proportion of the annuity costs of replacement as discussed earlier, or as the rent actually paid for shared accommodation. Later work began to recognise that there were other, less tangible, costs to carers but did not attempt to cost them (Moroney, 1976). Thus Mooney (1978b, p. 159) regretted their omission from his study as 'particularly unfortunate because all too often . . . decision-makers not only omit such considerations but at times appear even to deny their relevance.' This opinion was clearly endorsed by the experience of K. G. Wright *et al.* (1981, pp. 23–4) who recognised 'the importance of the informal caring network but . . . did not attempt to cost its contribution . . . because our research sponsors [the DHSS] requested us not to do so'. Only very recently have researchers been willing (and able) to attempt to cost these informal support services.

The costs borne by the principal carers may be arranged under four heads:

(1) The *material costs* of food, accommodation and transport, which most studies of care have managed to estimate reasonably well
(2) Costs associated with *lost employment oppportunities*. Available evidence suggests that these lost opportunities may be considerable, and certainly households with handicapped or elderly dependents are over-represented among those with low levels of income (Layard, Piachaud and Stewart, 1978).

(3)   The *social cost of caring*, including restrictions on leisure activities and marriage opportunities
(4)   The *emotional or psychic costs* of strain, stress, guilt and fatigue.

Principal carers are predominantly female, related to the elderly client and in neither full nor part-time employment. They undertake a full range of care tasks at all hours of the day and night and often with no formal care input at all.[7] The costing of these informal care services is still at a relatively primitive stage. Lost employment opportunities might be costed at the expected wage level adjusted for the unemployment rate or expected difficulty of finding a job. The care burden might alternatively be costed by calculating the number of hours involved and either attaching a value to that time (using the experiences of a large number of previous economic studies of the value of work and leisure time) or calculating the cost to a *formal* care agency of providing equivalent care. In doing so one should not cost those informal care services which are *willingly* provided by carers (in so far as they themselves derive some benefits from giving them). However, whilst the DHSS appears to have argued that most such services are willingly provided, the available evidence suggests otherwise. Challis and Davies (in press, Chapter 4, pp. 26–7), for example, conclude from their review of the British and American literatures that

> Many of the tasks are physically exhausting, particularly when sleep is interrupted by the need to perform them. The tasks can be obnoxious . . . . Most of the tasks can be unrewarding if the dependent has a personality which removes the satisfaction of help; and without relief they can all cause intolerable stress . . . . The care frequently continues over long periods . . . . The material costs of caring can be large . . . . Often carers can at most work part-time . . . . Those who allocate some of the principal services attached too little weight to the burdens borne by principal carers when allocating resources.

Conclusions from seven evaluative studies

Few empirical studies have been able to examine the full range of costs described above, and hardly any have obtained adequate measures of even a small number of the principal final outputs. The most comprehensive social care evaluation by these criteria is the Challis and Davies study. Other recent British studies which have enhanced our understanding of the costs and outputs associated with packages of care are the York University study of conventional domiciliary, residential, and hospital provision and the Aberdeen study of the balance of care (K. G. Wright *et al.*, 1981; Mooney, 1978b). Other work, conducted by local authorities has continued the fine 'in-house' tradition established by Wager (1972) in Essex. Two good examples are the Avon County Council (1980) study of admission to residential care and its alternatives, and the London Boroughs' study (Plank, 1977). More recently, some public agencies have purchased the expertise of management consultants to investigate aspects of 'value for money'. This has generated a great deal of controversy, mainly – to date – about the political ramifications (Black and Gray, 1983; Crine, 1983; Fry, 1983; Knapp, 1984a). It is, however, of more than passing political interest to examine the credentials of these management consultants, the most readily available example of their work being the study reported by the Audit Inspectorate (1983a).[8] To conclude this section, I shall briefly comment upon these seven studies, arranging them in chronological order. It would be unfair to compare them too closely, for they each attempt to answer a different question and they were each conducted within different constraints.

The Essex study (Wager, 1972)

Aim: To obtain detailed costings of domiciliary and local authority residential care and an indication of the circumstances and characteristics of clients receiving the two services.

Data base: Essex County Council, all 464 elderly people on waiting list for residential care on 8 January 1971, but no data collected about residents of homes. Questionnaires were completed by social welfare officers. Costs were collected from local authority and other published cost figures.

Measurement of costs: Capital and operating costs for residential homes were calculated as average opportunity costs and a personal ('pocket money') allowance added. Domiciliary services costed were home help, meals on wheels, home nursing, health visiting, day care and 'social visitors', calculated as averages and adjusting for some market distortions (taxation), but assuming volunteers to be free resources. Client and informal carer costs were measured as normal living expenses plus opportunity costs of accommodation, and sheltered housing costs were included. Marginal costs were not considered.

Measurement of benefits: Was not attempted, though an index of capacity for self-care for the elderly on the waiting list was developed and discussed.

Discounting: The differential timing of certain costs and benefits was taken into account by discounting some capital elements, using rates of 5 and 10 per cent. For all other costs only a single year (1969–70) was examined.

Main conclusions:

> For those living in sheltered housing or lower value 'normal' housing there was, on average, a margin of £3 or £4 per week to be taken up by domiciliary services before domiciliary care reached the cost of residential care . . . . In more expensive housing the margin was smaller or negative . . . . For elderly people living with others the costs of domiciliary care seemed likely to be substantially below those of residential care (pp. 65–6).

The relative benefits of these care packages were not considered but Wager felt that his findings suggested a move away from the expansion of residential care and towards a 'selective domiciliary care programme'.

Comments: Despite some limitations (biased sample, neglect of benefits, neglect of principal carer costs, etc.), Wager's work is superior to almost every other related research study conducted since 1972. It has been widely discussed and described (see Drummond, 1980, pp. 97–104; Drummond, 1981, pp. 196–7; Williams and Anderson, 1975, pp. 86–93).

The London Borough's study (Plank, 1977)

Aim: To produce information on the costs and consequences of local authority homes, local authority sheltered housing, and domiciliary care.

Data base: Eight London Boroughs, August 1972, 803 residents of local authority homes, 594 residents of a particular form of sheltered housing (considered to be an alternative to residential care), 415 people on waiting list for old people's homes, and 426 people considered suitable for sheltered housing, all randomly selected. Interviews were conducted with elderly people by a survey research company; costs were collected from local authorities.

Measurement of costs: Average operating costs of local authority services, net of charges, were added to the personal incomes (e.g. 'pocket-money' or pensions) of residents. Costs incurred by all other agencies and carers were not included. Marginal costs and opportunity costs were not considered.

Measurement of benefits: Data was collected on levels of mobility, self-care, 'ability to live elsewhere', levels of care (particularly in case of emergency), standard of accommodation, morale, continuity with previous life style, social contact and loneliness. Changes in these dimensions of welfare were not examined.

Discounting: Not attempted: only a single year (1971–2) was examined.

Main conclusions: Residents in homes receive a higher level of care than residents in sheltered housing, who, in turn, receive a higher level of care than persons in private households without warden supervision . . . . Though the data on satisfaction and loneliness collected in this study may be inadequate measures of a concept as complex as 'quality of life' they do at least raise some doubts about the assumption that this is cheaper for elderly people living in the community. Levels of care, standards of accommodation and satisfaction were all higher among residents and loneliness was lower. The very narrowly defined cost measures make cost comparisons meaningless.

Comments: Whilst Plank's tentative conclusions are based on a study which, by the dual criteria of the production of welfare perspective and the cost benefit methodology, has a number of inadequacies, his measures of levels of welfare based on very large samples of clients provide strong evidence to guard against the simple assumption that community care is better than residential care. It is perhaps because his conclusions are a little 'uncomfortable' and his remarks a little out-spoken that this important study has been surprisingly neglected.

The Aberdeen study (Mooney, 1978)

Aim: To determine the optimal 'balance of care services' for the elderly, focusing on community, residential and hospital care.

Data base: Aberdeen, June 1976. All 366 residents of local authority homes, questionnaires completed by matrons. 659 clients visited by a random selection of 35 district nurses and 50 health visitors, questionnaires completed by these staff. No data collected for elderly people in hospital. Costs data collected from health authority, local authority, published sources (such as FES) and staff.

Measurement of costs: Average costs were calculated for clients on the 'margins' of care, but marginal costings were not attempted. Geriatric long stay bed costs measured as average accounting cost. Residential home costs based on local authority accounts but adjusted for resident dependency and including 'support services' (though definition of these is unclear). For both forms of care, capital costs were estimated at their replacement value. Some 'support service' costs were also estimated for those living in the community and to these were added living costs (using FES data) and housing costs (based on rateable values). Not all agency costs are therefore measured, and the study also excludes volunteer and principal carer costs.

Measurement of benefits: Not attempted, but clients were assessed (by staff) as to whether or not they were on the boundaries or 'margins' of care.

Discounting: A 10 per cent discount rate and 60 year life were assumed in calculating annual capital costs. All other costs examined for only one year (1975–6).

Main conclusions: The care of residents of local authority homes assessed as being on the 'community margin' cost £2500 a year compared with about £1800 for those living in the community assessed to be on the 'residential home margin'. The cost for residents assessed as being on the 'hospital margin' was £3260 compared with £7200 for geriatric hospital care.

Comments: Mooney's study demonstrates a relatively inexpensive method for examining the optimal balance of care services by focussing exclusively on clients on the margins or boundaries of care. This approach is interesting and helpful but needs further development before it can claim to be a sufficiently valid, realistic and sensitive tool to warrant widescale employment. See Knapp (1980a) for further comments. Mooney *et al.* (1980, Chapter 6) provide a few more details of this study.

The Avon study (Avon County Council, 1980)

Aim: To determine the reasons for admission of clients to residential homes, and to determine the amount and cost of any services that would be required as an alternative to admission.

Data base: Avon County Council, January–May, 1979. All 231 long-stay admissions to local authority residential homes and 50 people on priority waiting lists. Samples included elderly mentally infirm. For 90 per cent of clients, information obtained from interview with relevant social worker; otherwise obtained from case files.

Measurement of costs: Both gross and net costs are calculated for a range of local authority and NHS services: residential care, mobile meals on wheels, day care and day hospitals, good neighbour and home aide schemes, wardened housing, and a variety of others. Average operating costs were taken straight from the annual accounts but capital costs were computed at replacement values. Transport costs were based on mileage records. Housing costs for the elderly living alone were calculated as opportunity costs but for those living with relatives these were set to zero. Volunteer, principal carer and some elderly recipient costs were not examined. All costs are averages, not marginal figures.

Measurement of benefits: Not attempted, but client characteristics (dependency, etc.), reasons for admission to residential care, household circumstances examined. Social workers were asked 'whether certain new community services or an expansion of existing ones would have enabled the elderly person to have remained in the community subject to the client's condition likely to be no worse than in a residential home' (p. 57).

Discounting: Not attempted.

Main conclusions: Inter alia, 'for nearly three quarters of persons for whom an alternative was named – equivalent to approximately one third of all admissions – the costs of care in the community would have been less than in residential care' (p. 57).

Comments: This study obviously has its methodological and empirical limitations, as a comparison with other studies described here will demonstrate, but is a good example of the high quality research now being undertaken by some local authority research sections.

The York-Based study (K. G. Wright, Cairns and Snell, 1981)

Aim: To examine the extent to which community care services can be a practicable alternative to institutional care and to calculate their relative costs. Community, residential and hospital care were studied.
Date base: Four unnamed local authority areas (two in Yorkshire, one in the Midlands, one Inner London Borough), period of data collection not given. Samples of 768 of the 'more dependent' people in the community and of the 'least dependent' elderly in hospital, and a random sample of 543 residents in homes (presumably local authority). Interviews undertaken by a survey research company with clients wherever possible (63 per cent though varying greatly across locations) or alternatively with someone well acquainted with client.
Measurement of costs: Capital costs for residential and hospital care estimated at replacement, up-grading or improvement costs. Staff and general service costs for hospitals were calculated as the average accounting costs given in the normal annual returns. Staff costs for old people's homes were calculated for different dependency groups, using matrons' estimates of relative care staff time allocations, and running costs were taken from local authority accounts. In both institutional settings personal consumption costs were added. In the community setting, housing was estimated at replacement value, living costs were based on FES data, and domiciliary and other care services were costed at their average operating cost values, sometimes also including administrative expenses, but not capital costs. A broad range of such services was considered, including GP, social worker and other peripatetic resources. Volunteer and principal carer costs were not examined. Marginal costs were not computed. The costs from only one area are reported.
Measurement of benefits: Not attempted, but a Guttman scale of client dependency was developed.
Discounting: A rate of 7 per cent and life span of 60 years are reported in the calculation of annual capital costs but other discount rates were also studied. All other costs examined for only one year (1976–7).

Main conclusions: Wright and his colleagues identified one point on their Guttman scale which represented a turning point. Below this point individuals were well supported in the community and this form of care was cheapest; above this point community care may sometimes be cheaper but risk and other factors (which they do not present evidence on) make it difficult for people with this degree of dependency to be maintained in their own homes alone. Thus 'a good system of familiar and friendly help must be available if people in these dependency categories are to be kept at home. At the higher levels of the scale it may even be difficult to keep people in residential care' (p. 43). Hospital care is generally much more expensive than residential care.

Comments: This study is most useful for its standardisation for dependency differences, although the method of standardisation is not really the most satisfactory of those currently available (see Chapter 9). Cost information for a very broad range of services and resources was collected and converted to opportunity cost values.

The Audit Inspectorate study *(Audit Inspectorate, 1983)*

Aim:

To identify factors underlying differences in the patterns of care provided to elderly people by social services departments in different local authorities, and to review the impact these factors have on the costs of care provided and the value for money obtained; (and) to investigate elements of the care provided by particular authorities and to identify those whose adoption by other authorities might improve the value for money obtained by those authorities (p. S1).

Data base: Four local authorities (two Inner London Boroughs and two Metropolitan Boroughs), 1980–1. Information obtained from central records of authorities and 'a limited amount of survey work' generally varying between authorities. Representativeness of this survey work unclear. Covered hospitals, residential homes, home help, day care, meals-on-wheels, lunch clubs, sheltered housing, though costings not attempted for all services. Packages of community care costed.

Measurement of costs: Average operating cost (including debt charges) obtained from local authority accounts. Client, informal care, other local authority department and fieldwork costs not considered. Marginal costs and opportunity costs not considered.

Measurement of benefits: The authors mention 'dimensions of achievement', but make no attempt to measure benefits. For some services and packages, costs are compared for elderly individuals with different dependency characteristics (basis for differential costing not clear).

Discounting: Not attempted.

Main conclusions: The summary conclusion is that:

> the total provision of hospital and residential care in the country and in the four authorities is approximately consistent with value for money, but the allocation of the resource to individuals may well not be consistent with value for money, i.e. some people are being provided with care which is more expensive than they need and which may indeed be giving them less value than they would receive from the cheaper form of care, while others may not be receiving the expensive form of care which they require (p. S10).

Comments: It is difficult not to be highly critical of a study which obviously cost so much to undertake and which makes a number of apparently unjustified and possibly dangerous recommendations. 'Value for money' is certainly not measured. Costs are narrowly defined, ignoring costs to clients and their principal carers, erroneously including debt charges, and (at times) erroneously calculating them net of consumer charges. Output or benefit measurement is not attempted. The authors refer to Maslow (1943) and his first two 'needs', but do not attempt to measure them. The higher order 'needs' of belongingness and love, esteem and self-actualisation are not mentioned. Implicitly, care units or local authorities providing services which aim to meet these higher order needs are criticised for making discretionary expenditures. There is no reference to, or apparent appreciation of any of the literature on the conceptualisation and measurement of the effects on clients published during the entire life of the 'welfare state'. In contrast to the claims of its authors, the study is neither 'ambitious' nor 'innovative' (p. S1). See also Knapp (1984a, 1984b) for further comments.

The Kent study (Challis and Davies, in press)

Aim: To compare the cost effectiveness of arrangements for channeling services and other resources to clients given social workers as case managers with enhanced autonomy and discretion, smaller caseloads, a budget on which they could draw to mobilise community resources or to pay for any agency services, and a list of (shadow) prices of units of social services, compared with the more usual arrangements for providing services and support, for a group of persons with a high probability of admission to institutions for long term care.

Data base: Two adjacent East Kent seaside towns, 1977–80. 74 matched clients in each of the experimental and comparison groups. A before/after quasi-experimental design. Interviews conducted with all clients at two points in time, immediately before admission to the scheme and a year later and also with all principal carers, supplemented with other interviews and other collections of data from helpers, community care workers and others.

Measurement of costs: Marginal social opportunity cost values estimated for services provided by the social services department, housing department, NHS, voluntary organisations, paid volunteers, elderly recipients of care and their principal carers. Transfer payments are excluded. Capital costs for all services calculated at replacement value. Personal living costs calculated from income-specific FES data and housing costs from assessed market valuations.

Measurement of benefits: A wide range of output dimensions was measured at the end of the first and fourth years with continuous monitoring of location and service receipt over this period. These have been discussed on pages 46–7 above. It is intended to monitor location of each case until death. Three discount rates were examined (5, 7 and 10 per cent) and a life span of sixty years assumed for new residential investment. All other costs discounted over three years (1977–80).

Main conclusions: For a group of whom one in three would have died within a year, one in three would have been admitted to a hospital or home for long-term care, and only one in three would have continued to live in their own homes, community care [in this innovative form]: (a) halved the probability of entering an institution, and doubled the probability of continuing to live in their own homes; (b) improved the perceptions of surviving client's subjective well-being

(c) improved their quality of care as perceived by both the elderly person and an external assessor; (d) reduced average costs to the social services department without imposing additional costs on health services; (e) relieved informal carers of some 'psychic' costs and reduced other costs to them over the period during which the elderly client survived, though prolonging the period during which they provided support; and (f) appeared to reduce the social opportunity costs of care over that period of survival. 'Moreover, the approach proved popular among the workers and managers' (Chapter 13).

Comments: This carefully designed and executed evaluation clearly includes a much broader range of both costs and output measures than has any previous work. The study is based on a small sample of clients and evaluates a particular set of arrangements for matching services and resources to client needs, but it is being fully replicated in four other areas and partially replicated in a number of others. Its conceptual base and empirical application should act as models for future work.

It is quite clear, therefore, that only recently have researchers begun to approach the full ranges of costs and outputs required by the production of welfare approach and by the demands of policy-making. This last study has quite clearly built on the experiences of earlier evaluative research in this and other areas of social care. The continuation of this clear developmental trend in this area of evaluative endeavour will provide policy-makers with a clear, comprehensive and hopefully consistent collection of evidence on which to base their future decisions. At the same time there is an increasing amount of evaluative work being undertaken under the 'value for money' banner by management consultants and firms of accountants. This work develops primarily out of the financial auditing activities of the former Audit Inspectorate (now the Audit Commission). The continuation of the trend observed thus far in this second stream of research is of much less value. Whilst the first stream of evaluative research is explicitly and reliably based on the premises of the production of welfare model of care, the second stream is grounded in the rather narrow confines of financial management and control. There is no reason why the two streams of work should not eventually merge to provide not only local authorities but other care agencies with reliable and responsible information.

Further applications of the cost benefit methodology

The technique of cost benefit analysis is firmly based on the production of welfare approach. Whilst there is probably more agreement among policy makers, service professionals and researchers about the components and interrelations of the production of welfare perspective on services for the elderly than on most other social care services, the cost benefit methodology is equally valuable in those other areas. There has, however, been much less research on other client groups and services which, even by the generously wide criteria used in this chapter, could be discussed under a 'cost benefit analysis' heading. This is in part because the *objectives* of care are often less clear, in part because studies of the *effectiveness* of care have been few and narrowly-defined, and in part because, with few exceptions, the *costs* of care have been ignored. Among the notable exceptions are: the Coventry *home help* study (Latto, 1982), the slowly accummulating evaluative work on the care of the *mentally handicapped* and *mentally ill* which includes the measurement of cost (Conley, 1973; Glass and Goldberg, 1977; McGuire, 1981; McGuire and Weisbrod, 1981; Stillwell, 1981; Weisbrod, 1981; Weisbrod and Helming, 1980) studies of families with *physically handicapped* dependents (Baldwin, 1977, 1981; Hyman, 1977), *preventive social work* (Schofield, 1976; Pinniger, 1981) and services for *children* in care (Knapp, Bryson and Matthews, 1982). The further extension of the cost benefit approach into these areas can only be of benefit for policy and practice.

9
Variations in the Costs of Care

Social care costs

Increasing concern has been voiced in recent years about the costs of social care. As we have already seen, this partly stems from the experiences of recession and fiscal pressure. It also stems from a realisation of a gradually increasing proportion of the total population that is totally or partially dependent upon social and health care agencies for continued personal and social well-being. A third source of concern comes from a realisation that these costs vary greatly between and within local authority areas.

This heightened concern about costs stands in marked contrast to two other notable features of recent policy. It is quite clear that policy-makers and care providers have very little experience of the constructive employment of the cost information routinely collected and published either by themselves or by such organisations as the Chartered Institute of Public Finance and Accountancy (CIPFA). Secondly, there is a similar lack of experience when it comes to the design of special collections of costs data upon which to base sensible policies for care. In consequence, too many policy documents and general commentaries have based their recommendations on naïve, and often quite unfounded, economic premises. Some of these suggestions are potentially dangerous, and there are plenty of examples of recommendations and policies which have led to the even more inefficient use of available resources than was previously the case.

One aim of this chapter is to demonstrate how routinely available cost information may be gainfully employed in the planning of care services. The starting point for most policy recommendations which have employed costs data is a statement or description of the *differences* in cost between ostensibly similar services, or between different areas of the country. In this chapter I want to look at some of these oft-noted and oft-quoted cost variations. I shall first suggest why it is that costs can and do vary markedly for what are apparently very similar services. It is not difficult to suggest a number of such reasons, but it is less easy to employ these sources of variation for the development of policy recommendations. It will therefore be useful to examine the *cost function* technique, which is a potentially powerful tool for the explanation and subsequent exploitation of observed cost variations for policy. Its many uses will be described and illustrated below and I shall provide an empirical example of a cost function recently estimated for local authority old people's homes.

The statistics published annually by the CIPFA provide a current indication of the extent of cost variations between English and Welsh local authorities. A selection of cost figures is presented in Table 9.1. This table has many interesting features. We should first note that the figures are inadequate as a basis for policy. The discussion of costs in Chapter 4 makes it plain that these figures are merely incomplete 'accounting costs'. Certainly they do not measure the full opportunity costs of services. Slight variations in accounting conventions and the inevitable errors of calculation undoubtedly explain some of the observed differences between local authorities, but they cannot be blamed for the full range of variation. The tabulated figures beg a number of questions, for example:

(1)   Why is it that all but four of the 'maximum cost authorities' are in London?
(2)   How can the cost of day nursery provision in West Glamorgan be nearly three times higher than in near neighbour South Glamorgan?
(3)   Why does Humberside have the highest cost meals on wheels service and yet the lowest cost community home(s) with education?
(4)   Can Salford and Brent really be undertaking similar activities within their observation and assessment centres?
(5)   What is it about residential provision for the mentally ill in Devon and Camden which accounts for such a dramatic difference in average cost?

These are just some of the questions that are likely to be posed by

TABLE 9.1 Variations in average accounting cost between English and Welsh local authorities, 1981–2

Service	Average Cost* per	Mean Average Cost	Minimum Average Cost†		Maximum average cost	
Old people's homes	resident week	115.53	77.97	Oldham	174.52	Merton
Residential care – mentally ill	resident week	120.90	19.90	Devon	286.22	West Sussex
Residential care – mentally handicapped adults	resident week	119.27	63.48	Redbridge	282.69	North Tyneside
Residential care – mentally handicapped children	child week	215.81	109.40	Northamptonshire	622.32	Islington
Hostels & community homes (children)	child week	134.53	77.89	Barking	369.03	Camden
Observation & assessment centres	child week	267.70	125.41	Salford	891.26	Brent
Residential nurseries	child week	240.69	152.20	Lancashire	344.93	Enfield
Community homes with education	child week	248.40	145.39	Humberside	889.24	Lambeth
Residential care – younger physically handicapped	resident week	188.59	108.58	Cambridgeshire	375.77	Tower Hamlets
Day nurseries	child day	13.39	7.78	South Glamorgan	22.64	West Glamorgan
Adult training centres	trainee day	7.59	2.95	Redbridge	19.34	Westminster
Day centres for mentally ill	attendance day	9.05	3.19	Coventry	25.86	Camden
Sheltered employment workshops	employee day	20.20	11.93	Gwent	41.40	Hackney
Home help	hour	2.80	1.95	Leeds	4.51	Camden
Meals on wheels	meal	0.78	0.37	Wiltshire	2.30	Humberside
Children boarded out	child week	30.54	18.42	Gateshead	69.98	Westminster

* All cost figures exclude capital expenditure but are gross (i.e. they are not calculated net of charges to clients)

† Excluding zero costs

SOURCE: Chartered Institute of Public Finance and Accountancy, Personal Social Services Statistics, Actuals, 1981–82, CIPFA, London, 1982.

elected members of social services committees, by the Audit Commission, by local authority treasurers, and by government ministers. In this chapter I want to demonstrate how answers to such questions can be obtained and, in some cases, have already been provided. The fact that Oldham apparently has the lowest cost old people's homes in the country does not necessarily mean that it is unduly stingy or laudably super-efficient. Without further information we cannot say whether the observed variation in costs is due to 'good housekeeping, the Oliver Twist mentality, or the three or four star hotel mentality' (Sumner and Smith, 1969, p. 63). Unless and until we obtain some measure of output (even if it is only an intermediate measure) we cannot use cost data for policy prescriptions.

Such marked differences in cost have serious implications for both efficiency and equity. What can we learn from the observed variations in cost which can help us to lower the costs of provision whilst maintaining the quality? As the Layfield Committee reported in 1976:

Taxpayers have the right to expect public services to be provided efficiently: that is, the standard of service desired should be provided at the minimum reasonable cost. People . . . cannot shop around for most of the services provided by public authorities. So public authorities are not under the same pressure as private suppliers to keep their costs down. Special care should therefore be taken to ensure that the financial arrangements promote efficiency (p. 51).

The desire to promote an equitable allocation of resources is likely to be frustrated unless we can be sure that local authorities with unavoidably high costs are compensated. The crucial question is the distinction between avoidable and unavoidable influences on cost.

The sources of cost variation

It is a source of dismay to note the frequency with which crude expenditure figures are used as the sole basis for policy prescription. Not only are the outputs of care neglected, but the expenditure figures are quoted and compared as if they are unique and unambiguous indicators of provision. In fact, differences in cost between care units or local authorities vary in response to a range of factors.

Input prices

As one might expect, the amount an agency must pay for the resources it employs will affect costs. The high cost authorities in Table 9.1 were mostly in London, where wage rates are noticeably higher than in other parts of the country. The price paid for an input will often not be independent of the rate of employment, simply because inputs are not in perfectly elastic supply. Of course, local authorities and other care agencies may well be partly responsible for pushing wage rates up. Labour markets for even the most skilled staff tend to be localised and an excess demand for such staff is likely to raise the real cost of their employment. Shortages of suitably qualified or motivated staff generate competition among employers through internal or external labour markets, resulting in offers of non-pecuniary advantages (such as accommodation and less disruptive hours), more paid overtime, the employment of inferior staff and/or the regrading of posts. These practices may not show up in the accounts of the authority, and may not induce cost variations, but they will have an impact on caring practices and 'welfare production processes', and hence upon the well-being of clients. Thus prices may or may not be related to input qualities and to such factors as staff experience and training. Input price variations induce cost variations in a fairly straightforward way, but their importance is hard to gauge because so many other factors are usually varying at the same time. Certainly studies of cost inflation over time have found prices to be important. The costs of labour-intensive services have tended to rise faster than other services and goods and will continue to do so, through this so-called 'relative price effect'.

The volume of output

The cost-output relationship has long exercised the mind, pen, and latterly computer, of the economist. It is not possible to reproduce or even summarise the many hypotheses, fallacies and controversies which surround this relationship, but it is important to note the prolonged and continuing debate as to the shape of the average cost curve. The conventional textbook average cost curve is U-shaped, implying that cost per unit of output initially falls as output or scale increases, but later rises again. This shape was illustrated in Chapter 4. In contrast, many estimated cost-output relationships for manufacturing industries, railways, electricity suppliers and other areas of conventional economic interest, have been found to be L-shaped. Research for these industries reveals declining average cost as scale increases without an eventual increase: average costs level off at some minimum level but do not rise much above it over the observed scale range.

The shape of the average cost curve is of more than merely academic interest. If, for example, the unit cost of running a meals on wheels service continues to fall as the scale of operation increases then there is cogent support for plans to establish a small number of large meals organisations or to use existing organisations or services more extensively (cf. Lee and Martin, 1979). If, on the other hand, average costs are found to rise again beyond some particular scale then there are cost grounds for preferring to establish services around some slightly smaller scale. Whilst there are clearly many other factors which determine the most desirable scale for meals on wheels services, it would be foolhardy to disregard the cost element. What, then, are the sources of variation in the cost-output relationship?

Economies of scale may arise from the use of fixed or indivisible resources, such as the building, because variable inputs increase less than proportionately with outputs (particularly the case with over-head administrative and supervisory staff), from the specialisation of inputs, from the bulk-buying of some inputs, and because larger scale allows a higher percentage occupancy of available places. On the other hand, *diseconomies* of scale may set in beyond a certain level. Among the reasons usually cited are: the burden of management becomes too much and inefficiencies arise in the use of non-managerial inputs; the supply price of scarce resources will rise with increases in demand (as with qualified social workers); the fixed or indivisible inputs are *over*-used; staff motivation may decline with scale, giving rise to what is known as X-inefficiency; and 'organis-ational or budgetary slack' may creep in.

The discussion thus far concerns only the *volume of output*. This volume measure is an indicator of the scale of production. Alchian (1959) has suggested that certain other dimensions or characteristics of output be distinguished, each having its own influence on average cost. These other dimensions include the total contemplated volume of output and the rate at which it is produced.

The rate of production

For a given volume of output, a faster rate of production will raise average cost. In a study of residential care, for example, the volume of output could be measured at an intermediate level as the number of available places or the number of residents, and the rate of output would be the utilisation of available capacity and could be measured by the occupancy, throughput (or admission or turnover rates), or the average length of stay. These three 'rate' variables are obviously not independent. In fact they are linked by the simple formula:

average occupancy rate = average length of stay × throughput

In any examination of the effects of the rate of production on cost, therefore, it would only be necessary to specify *two* of these three variables. There are costs associated with receiving someone into care, particularly because more staff resources are required to help them through the difficult adjustment phase and because of the administrative tasks to be accomplished. *Admission rates* (and *discharge* and *turnover rates*) are thus likely to exert a positive influence on costs. The argument for examining the *occupancy rate* is that there are many costly resources, principally staff, which are geared to a particular level of operation and which cannot easily be adjusted to short-term changes in occupancy. If a home is temporarily under-occupied, having more spare places than usual, then, other things being equal, we would expect average cost per resident to be higher than usual.[1] In the jargon of microeconomics, the producer experiences an unplanned deviation from this optimum point on the long-run average cost curve. In the everyday language of social care management it is often simply remarked that 'unoccupied beds cost money'. The *length of stay* of residents will exert an influence on average cost simply because of its tautological association with occupancy and throughput. Because the influence of the former variable on cost is likely to be negative and that of the latter variable positive, the effect of length of stay or treatment should also be negative, although this effect is rarely examined in practice.[2]

Specialisation, case-mix and client characteristics

One of the very important reasons why the costs of public social care services can vary as widely as the figures presented in Table 9.1 is because care units with a particular label (such as 'community home' or 'day centre for the mentally ill') undertake a wide variety of activities. Some pursue a single specialisation and others undertake a range of care activities for a number of client groups. For example, a nationwide survey of residential establishments for children conducted in March 1983 indicated that some provided day care for other children, for the elderly or for mentally handicapped adults, some acted as centres for the delivery of community and domiciliary services, some prepared meals for local meals on wheels services, some had responsibility for the supervision of independence units, some provided extensive after-care services, some acted as family placement support or preparation units, some had an especially large responsibility for training, and so on. These are simply differences in activities *outside* the establishments. Within them the nature of residential care activities showed just as much if not more variation.[3] Care units differ greatly in specialisation, case-mix and clientele. These will all have cost implications. Homes with a wider range of non-residential functions and responsibilities will, other things being equal, incur higher costs. Within the home or other care unit there are likely to be economies of specialisation for reasons akin to those explaining economies of scale. There will also be diseconomies associated with this factor in so far as a high degree of specialisation can mean a lower occupancy rate.[4]

Client characteristics (one indicator of case-mix) will almost certainly be related to differences in cost. The increasing aggregate dependency of old people's homes' residents has raised the real cost of care over the last ten or twenty years and there is a lot of evidence on the strong association between cost and dependency (see Knapp, 1981, and below p. 183). It has also been found that the age, sex, marital status, psychological status, physical and mental health, medical needs, behavioural characteristics and legal status of clients can exert an influence on cost.

Social and physical environments

Final outputs are of particular importance in the explanation of cost variations, but are difficult to measure. Intermediate outputs, including indicators of care arrangements with hypothesised or proven associations with final output, might be useful surrogates. Are high-cost care services providing better quality care? The reasons for examining the cost-raising implications of the *physical* environment are slightly different. It is certainly true that the built environment will be an input into the production of final output, but it is also important to quantify its impact on operating, current or running costs.

Staffing levels and characteristics

It is often remarked that some care units are more expensive than others 'because they have higher staff-client ratios'. This is undoubtedly true but we should treat such remarks with a degree of caution. At least two sources of caution spring to mind. First, *why* do staff-client ratios differ between care units or between care sectors or between local authorities? In residential care, staff levels tend to be higher when residents are more dependent or more 'difficult'. Thus the *true* source of cost variation in this case is not the staff-client ratio or staffing level, but the aggregate dependency or 'difficulty' of residents. The second reason for proceeding with caution is because staffing levels and costs measure the same thing – the resource inputs. To use one to explain differences in the other, therefore, is tautological. I will return to this point later. Where it *may* be legitimate to attribute cost variations to differences in staffing is in relation to the *characteristics* of staff, and particularly their attitudes, perceptions, experiences and qualifications, and in relation to trade union pressures or constraints, and historical precedents.

Location

The variation between local authorities illustrated in Table 9.1 is important not only because it needs explanation, but because it shapes the annual Rate Support Grant settlement and so on. The reasons for variation in costs between areas are numerous and many will already have been covered by other factors discussed here. For example, old people's homes in London tend on average to be larger than elsewhere so that some cost variations might be attributable to economies or diseconomies of scale. Of more importance are the higher salaries that London authorities must pay to attract and retain staff. At the local authority level there are probably four location effects:

(1) Organisational factors reflecting differences in the role of care units in the care system.
(2) Ecological factors reflecting differences in the characteristics of areas which partially determine needs and demands.
(3) Pecuniary factors reflecting input price differences.
(4) Miscellaneous historical and idiosyncratic factors.

Ownership and 'marketing'

It has often been claimed that voluntary care services are cheaper than public services (see Gladstone, 1979; Holman, 1981; Personal Social Services Council, 1977, paragraph 2.42) and the growing importance of private care services introduces a further cost consideration. Voluntary organisations might be able to provide cheaper services for a variety of reasons.

> Lacking voluntary help their [local authority homes'] staff and administrative costs may be higher and certain amenities like tobacco, newspapers, etc., are included in their charges. They are also more often involved in the provision of clothing for their residents who may have fewer personal resources than old people entering some of the voluntary homes (Shenfield, 1957, p. 159).

Other reasons for the supposed cost advantage enjoyed by the voluntary and private sectors include differences in managerial efficiency, smaller overheads, lower staff-client ratios, and a greater personal commitment from staff. These and other hypotheses about inter-sectoral differences will be considered in the next chapter. For the moment we should simply note that any comparison of voluntary, private and statutory provision should ideally standardise for all of the factors listed above before drawing conclusions about relative cost effectiveness.

At this point it is also as well to notice that the costs of public care services are sometimes expressed net of charges to clients rather than in the preferred gross form. As we saw in Chapter 6, the incidence of charges is obviously important in the examination of the distribution of the burden of care costs, but should not delay us here, for they do not form part of the central argument about cost variations. The net costs of care will clearly vary with the charging policies adopted by agencies and any conclusions based on net costs should be treated with caution. We should be looking at costs and charging policies as two different issues, and the cost-charge margin is a variable of interest in its own right.[5]

Efficiency

If the influences of all of the above factors have been fully accounted for and still there remains some variation in average cost, then that variation must be attributable to differences in the efficiency with which care services are delivered. (Included in this definition of efficiency are both X-inefficiency and organisational slack. See Chapter 5.) It is important to stress that differences in the average cost of care should not simply be interpreted as differences in the 'efficiency of care'. Before we can be sure that high cost means low efficiency we have to standardise for the influences of the other likely cost-raising factors distinguished above.

Cost equations and cost functions

There are clearly a great many possible explanations for the wide variations in average cost that we previously tabulated and which are often remarked upon in policy discussions. How then can we test these hypothesised influences on the cost of care and how are we to reconcile some of the apparently conflicting influences? There exist a number of different techniques to explain cost variations (see Koutsoyiannis, 1979). Easily the most powerful and manageable technique to use in studies of social care is *statistical cost analysis*, which directly and informatively provides an empirical representation of the *cost function*.

A *cost function* is the estimated relationship between, on the one hand, the cost of providing a service and, on the other, the outputs of that service and the prices of the resources employed. Other factors such as the size of the care unit, the characteristics of clients, the arrangements and organisation of care will also have cost-raising implications. The basic aim of a cost function analysis is to estimate the relationship between the cost of providing a service and the hypothesised influences in an attempt to 'explain' the observed variations in cost. 'Explanation' is achieved through the statistical technique of multiple regression analysis, applied to a sample of observations on care units, clients or local authorities. Under various assumptions the estimated cost function traces out the (stochastic) locus of points which indicate the minimum cost of production at each level of output. Given the level of output, the input prices, the state of technology and so on, the function gives the 'expected' cost of production, that is, the average level of either average or total cost given these particular levels of the cost-determining factors. The form of the function is determined by the interaction of *a priori* theoretical considerations and empirical experiences.

The cost function must be carefully distinguished from the cost equation, the former being a causal relationship and the latter simply a tautological accounting identity. It has been said that cost functions are prescriptive, cost equations merely descriptive. If we denote the inputs into care by $L_1, L_2, \ldots, L_n$, and their respective prices by $p_1, p_2, \ldots, p_n$, then the *cost equation* is simply

$$TC = p_1 L_1 + p_2 L_2 + \ldots + p_n L_n$$

where TC denotes total cost. The *cost function*, on the other hand, is written as

$$TC = f(Q, p, Z) = f(Q, p_1, p_2, \ldots, p_n, Z)$$

Where Q denotes the set of outputs, Z is the generic term for all other influences (potential or actual) on cost, and f indicates some functional form linking them all. The cost function is a theoretical construct obtained from a system of two relationships (the production function and the cost equation) and an optimisation assumption (cost minimisation, profit or welfare maximisation or similar).[6] The arguments surrounding the applicability or otherwise of an optimisation assumption will be examined later (see p. 187). Production and cost functions are actually 'mathematical duals'– for each cost function there is a unique corresponding production function (Shepherd, 1953). If the cost minimisation assumption does not hold and needs to be replaced by some other behavioural postulate then this duality property no longer holds. It does not make the cost function irrelevant or useless; it merely alters the nature of its interpretation.

As specified here, the cost function expresses cost as a function of output, input prices and certain other factors, but *not* a function of the input levels themselves. Thus staffing levels and staff-client ratios are excluded from this list of causal factors. The reasons for excluding them (and particularly the fact that costs and staffing levels are tautological related) were described above (see p. 175).[7] Thus when commentators on costs variations cite the differences in staffing levels between care units or local authorities they are merely redefining the difference.

The stages of estimating a cost function

The following stages are employed in each and every empirical cost function study, although they are not always made explicit. It is instructive to distinguish them clearly (Dean, 1976).

(1) *Select a production unit suitable for analysis.* Production, as we saw in Chapter 2, takes place at three levels – that of the individual client, the facility (such as the residential home) and the local authority or other care organisation. The distinction between facility and authority is similar to the distinction between plants and firms made in any conventional analysis of production, and is easy to maintain in practice because most social care facilities are separately monitored in terms of both expenditure and activity. 'Individual level production' is less familiar but crucially important in a service context. It is, however, particularly difficult to monitor or model at the individual level because virtually all resource inputs to production at this level are 'joint' or shared with other clients. Therefore, the examination of cost functions is most easily accomplished at the facility or authority level. The choice between facility and authority analyses should be determined partly by the extent to which facilities within a care organisation display marked differences, partly by the degree of independence in decision-making afforded those facilities, and partly by the availability of data. The greater the difference between facilities, the greater their independence, and the more disaggregated the data collections, the stronger is the case for facility rather than organisation analyses. Facility level cost relations are relatively easily aggregated up to the authority level if, for example, the empirical work is to feed into grant calculations. For some

services, of course, and particularly those with a substantial fieldwork input or an important informal contribution, it is difficult to arrive at a sensible definition of 'a facility' which is not the authority itself.

(2)   *Decide on a measure of output.* Final outputs are almost always preferred, but if unavailable a selection must be made from available intermediate indicators. Multiple outputs will be the rule rather than the exception and are included in the analysis either by estimating a separate cost function for each, or by computing an output index, or, preferably, including them as separate influential factors.

(3)   *Determine the time unit of observation.* Ideally, cost, output and other factors should be measured over a period corresponding to a complete production cycle, or at least over a period within which the rate of production is uniform. It would certainly be possible to define 'production cycles' for social care services, but most cost studies are likely to be restricted to annual or, at best, quarterly data because of the difficulty of commitment accounting in any shorter time period. The costs of collecting more regular cost and other data could well outweigh the benefits of their analysis.

(4)   *Choose the period of analysis.* The choice here is between a time-series or cross-section design (or, in a perfect world, a combination of the two). In practice the researcher will have little choice because of data limitations. Some authorities and organisations are now building up useful time-series of data, but these are probably not yet long enough to permit suitable analysis. All social care cost functions that have been estimated to date have thus been based on cross-section data sets for a large number of residential homes, home help areas, social work teams or local authorities. The choice between designs is not irrelevant since it has been argued that a time-series design leads to the estimation of a *short-run* cost function, and a cross-section design to a *long-run* cost function (see Chapter 4 above). In the cross-section, production units are of different sizes, each assumed to be operating close to its minimum cost level. The distinction however, is not clear cut (Johnston, 1960, p. 30; Koutsoyiannis, 1979).

(5)   *Decide on the measure of cost.* Once again the ideal is somewhat at variance from the actual. Opportunity costs would be preferred but are more difficult and expensive to measure than the often readily

available accounting costs. The cost function technique has almost always been used with accounting or expenditure figures, though occasionally supplemented by some opportunity costs (or 'shadow prices'). There is also the issue of which expenditures to include and which to exclude. The theory of long-run costs suggests that capital costs should be included, but the capital cost data currently collected and published for social care services is of limited use. Accounting data give depreciation figures (debt charges) which are distorted by such things as original construction costs (not reflated), method of depreciation costing adopted (which is usually linear whereas real world depreciation and running costs of fixed capital are non-linear, increasing with age), age of facility, method of financing and so on. Operating costs are thus usually estimated alone, although if it is possible to supplement them with estimates of opportunity or user cost then this would be a tremendous advantage. Actually in the labour-intensive social care sector where there is often only limited scope for the substitution of capital for labour (and vice versa), it would be reasonable to examine separately variations in operating and capital cost (Hirsch, 1968). Where possible we should also be including overhead costs, the costs or expenditures associated with peripatetic staff, and the costs falling to clients and their families.

(6) *Select the cost concept of interest.* The researcher must select either average or total cost as the concept to be explained in the cost function. Obviously one can easily be converted into the other, but estimated functions will not be exactly equivalent because of the influence of certain 'nuisance factors' in multiple regression. The arguments for estimating a total cost function in preference to an average function concern the bias and spurious correlation intro-duced by errors of measurement in the deflating variable (the basic output variable), whilst the arguments in favour of average functions stress the susceptibility of total cost expressions to the undesirable influences of multicollinearity and heteroscedasticity (Casson, 1973; Feldstein, 1967; Griliches, 1972). Average cost functions are more commonly estimated, probably because of their immediate intuitive appeal.

(7) *Deflate the cost data.* Input prices can either be used to deflate the observed costs before estimating the cost function, or else used as separate regressors. If the former method is chosen then deflation is undertaken at this stage. Dean (1976) and Johnston (1960) both

recommend deflation in this manner although the theoretical form of the cost function suggests the alternative. Certainly in practical circumstances it may be better to retain flexibility in the estimation by *not* deflating, especially if the input price index is not as accurate or sensitive as one may desire.

(8)   *Match costs with output and other determinants.* If there is a lag in either the payment for resources employed or in the recording of output the matching of cost and output may not be straightforward. Other potential influences upon cost should also be matched accordingly. Data for all hypothesised influences should be collected if possible. The estimation may then commence.

(9)   *Select the form of the cost function.* The final stage is to choose the exact form of the estimated cost function. Estimation will be achieved through multiple regression analysis, the particular variant of the technique depending on certain characteristics of the data (see econometrics textbooks on this). The general functional form (additive, multiplicative, log-linear, transcendental logarithmic, etc.) should be selected on *a priori* grounds if at all possible, but generally the researcher will have to rely on post-estimation comparisons of alternative forms (cf. Meiners, 1982). In my own experience a straightforward linear-in-parameters functional form (*not* the same as a linear-in-variables form) is certainly adequate as a first approximation, and I have not yet found any alternative which has proved superior in the final analysis. Within the set of all such specifications (which differ from one another in terms of the inclusion and exclusion of specific variables) the final form will be selected on the empirical grounds of goodness-of-fit (statistical significance), accordance with prior restrictions or notions, and parsimony. In most social care contexts the 'production technology' is not sufficiently precise or understood to allow the rigid specification of functional forms.

Examples of cost functions for social care services

Previous cost function research

In the study of manufacturing industries, agriculture, transport and distributive services, statistical cost analyses have been undertaken on literally thousands of occasions. There have been a great many applications of the technique in health and education research (though relatively rarely in Britain), but very few for social care services.

Old people's homes have received most attention from cost function modellers. Wager's (1972) examination of the relative costliness of residential and domiciliary services in Essex included the fitting of a simple linear relationship to data on average costs and scale.[8] Later studies have added more explanatory variables. Thus Knapp (1978) included non-linear scale effects, occupancy and home designation (physically infirm and mentally infirm), Davies and Knapp (1978) included scale and resident dependency, and Darton and McCoy (1981) added indicators of day care provision, resident admission rates, geographical location and certain physical structure indicators. The cost function study described below also concentrates on old people's homes and will be seen to be both a logical development of this series of studies and a considerable advance upon them.

Other cost studies of services for the elderly include work on day centres (Knapp and Missiakoulis, 1982, described in Chapter 10), the meals on wheels service (Hatch and Mocroft, 1979; Lee and Martin, 1979) and home help services (Davies and Coles, 1981). The Kent Community Care Study reported by Challis and Davies (in press) includes the fitting of cost functions for the packages of services received by clients. Studies of services for children are less common, the only published studies in Britain to date focusing upon local authority observation and assessment centres (Knapp *et al.*, 1979) and community homes run by local authorities and voluntary organisations (Hatch and Mocroft, 1979). Other studies have concentrated on training centres for the adult mentally handicapped (Knapp *et al.*, 1983) and a range of services for the mentally handicapped and mentally ill (Casmas, 1976).

An estimated cost function for old people's homes[9]

Previous examinations of the costs of old people's homes have been constrained either by limited data sets or by limited analyses. The survey of old people's homes conducted by the PSSRU in the autumn of 1981 was an omnibus study, designed to provide information about a number of aspects of residential care for the elderly (Darton, 1984). In particular the survey collected a comprehensive set of cost and home data in order to undertake more sophisticated cost function studies than had previously been possible.

Average cost was defined as gross expenditure on employees and running expenses during 1981–2 averaged over the number of beds normally in use. We were unable to obtain measures for all of the hypothesised influences on cost discussed above (pp. 170–7). In fact, five broad groupings of factors (and interactions between them) were examined for their effects on average cost:

(1)　*Characteristics of homes* (size, occupancy level, arrangements of beds on floors, whether beds above the ground floor were reached by lift, whether the home was purpose-built, whether the home was organised around a group living design, and whether staff accommodation was provided)

(2)　*Characteristics of staff* (proportions of staff with nursing and social work qualifications, whether or not additional volunteer staff were used, and whether there were any students working in the home)

(3)　*Non-residential services provided* (whether day care was provided from within the home or in an associated day centre used by residents, whether there was sheltered housing sharing staff or facilities of the home, and whether meals were prepared for meals on wheels services)

(4)　*Characteristics of residents* (dependency characteristics including behavioural problems and depression, resident turnover rates, the proportion of short-stay residents, and whether the home was used for clients of one or both sexes)

(5)　*Characteristics of local areas* (a general labour cost index, unemployment rate, female economic activity rate, population sparsity and indicators of the ease or difficulty of recruiting staff)

The final or 'best' form of cost function is detailed in Table 9.2. This was selected from a large number of alternative functional forms on the usual criteria of overall and individual explanatory power (statistical significance), conformity to prior restrictions (of which there were very few in this case), and parsimony. This final equation demonstrates that 76 per cent of the variation in observed average cost per resident week can be attributed to variations in those factors

TABLE 9.2 *An estimated average operating cost function for old people's homes, 1981–2*

The estimated cost function indicates that average expenditure on manpower and running expenses per bed normally in use per resident week is equal to:

−552.826*	
+1.743**	× labour cost index
−3.264**	× number of beds normally in use in group-living homes
−1.604**	× number of beds normally in use in non-group homes
+0.024*	× number of beds normally in use in group-living homes, squared
+0.014**	× number of beds normally in use in non-group homes, squared
+10.725*	× percentage occupancy level (at 31/10/81)
−0.058*	× percentage occupancy level (at 31/10/81) squared
+5.995*	if staff of home have duties in sheltered housing
+4.358*	if all laundry done within the home
+7.736*	× number of permanent admissions in 12 months to 31/10/81 per number of beds normally in use
+3.188*	× number of short-stay discharges in 12 months to 31/10/81 per number of beds normally in use
+4.927*	if mixed-sex non-group-living home
+34.823**	if single-sex group-living home
+63.294**	if mixed-sex group-living home
−12.488**	× proportion of residents in limited dependency category
+51.714**	× proportion of residents in appreciable or heavy dependency categories
−0.814**	× number of beds normally in use weighted by proportion of residents in appreciable or heavy dependency categories

Significance levels: * $0.01 \leqslant p < 0.05$, ** $p < 0.01$
F − value for equation: $F = 37.58$, $p < 0.0001$
$R^2 = 0.76$, *Adjusted* $R^2 = 0.74$
$n = 218$

listed in the table. The meaning and implications of this estimated cost function for old people's homes will be considered in the next section.

Usage and abusage: cost functions and policy formulation

Estimated cost functions have a number of policy uses: they ensure that costs are discussed in their proper context, they provide a measure of scale economies and diseconomies, they allow us to examine the cost-raising implications of changes in the characteristics of clients and physical and social environments, they provide measures of marginal cost and efficiency, they help to explain cost inflation and to apportion joint costs, and they provide some of the basic information needed for planning an optimal 'balance of care' and for pricing or charging policies. I shall discuss and illustrate these below, but first I shall consider some of the difficulties and criticisms of this mode of analysis.

Difficulties and criticisms

In the light of our discussion of the meaning of cost in Chapter 4, cost functions can be criticised for their inadequate *measurement*. Four criticisms have been made: opportunity costs are not used, the time reference of costs is rarely made explicit, capital costs are often excluded or inappropriately measured, and overhead costs are omitted. These criticisms have been levelled at empirical work, although there is nothing inherent in the principle of cost function estimation which precludes proper cost measurement. If accounting and opportunity costs differ it might prove difficult to estimate the true cost-output relationship and certainly it will be important to allow fairly broad confidence intervals around the plotted relationship. The second criticism is that costs collected annually by the accountant do not accord with either the short run or the long run of economic theory. This is correct, but unlikely to be a serious problem. Excluding capital costs, or modelling them separately from operating costs, will distort the estimated function if capital and other inputs are substitutable. On the other hand, using the capital cost figures supplied by the accountant will represent little improvement because of the biases towards a linear relationship that will follow if 'straight-line' depreciation procedures have been used. Finally, overhead costs are rarely included, and are difficult to include. The importance of omitting overhead costs will depend on the policy context; if overheads are roughly equivalent for two units or services which are being compared, it may make little difference if they are omitted, but this should not be assumed *a priori*.

Many empirical studies have omitted potentially important determinants of cost, either because the data has been unavailable or because the researcher had exercised insufficient ingenuity and imagination. If the omitted factors are correlated with the included factors then the estimated regression coefficients will be biased. A special case of this omitted variable problem concerns the lack of data on final outputs. Economies of scale as indicated by the regression of average cost on intermediate output variables should be qualified with comments on the social and psychological ramifications of scale. As with the point about measurement, this is a criticism of research methodology and not of cost function analysis itself.

Theoretically, the cost function is derived and examined under an assumption of *cost minimisation*. The plausibility of this assumption has frequently been questioned. If cost-minimisation is not an objective of the producer then the estimated cost function cannot be interpreted as the cost-output (or cost-minimising) *frontier*, subject only to random differences in efficiency and 'pure' random variations, nor can it be strictly interpreted as the dual of the production function. Instead, the fitted function represents the 'average' (mean) relationship between cost and output, and residuals indicate deviations from the average degree of efficiency. If producers do not attempt to minimise costs the cost function loses a little of its appeal, but certainly remains very useful. Hanushek (1979, p. 370) argues in a related context that non-minimisation allows economic inefficiency but does not invalidate the cost or production function 'unless resources are also wantonly squandered'. The fitted function can simply be interpreted as a behavioural rather than a technical relationship.[10] Of course, there are those who believe that cost-minimisation might not be such an unrealistic assumption after all. The exhortations of central and local government and the realities of recession in recent years may be held to have encouraged a more diligent search for cost-minimisation by social care agencies. A more ingenious argument could be based on the theories of organisations which do not assume, directly at least, the maximisation of profits (Young, 1976). These theories, such as those of Newhouse (1970), Niskanen (1971) or Williamson (1964), all posit the pursuit of utility maximisation by producers, which could be consistent with an assumption of cost-minimisation (Verry and Davies, 1975). Alternatively, rejecting the assumption of optimising behaviour by producers, we can posit a degree of 'organisational slack' and 'entropy'. However, organisational slack will only be maintained if the 'exit' and 'voice' forces are negligible (Hirschman, 1970). In the case of the management and accountability of social care units, 'exit' forces (the option or power to withdraw custom) can be negligible, except, of course, in the increasingly important case of services purchased by public authorities from private and voluntary agencies.

On the other hand, 'voice' forces – the option or power to complain and 'press . . . demands to management through internal hierarchical or external political demands' (Young, 1976, p. 34) – are likely to be very important. Hirschman's theory says that an organisation sensitive to exit or voice forces will tend to reduce organisational slack and adopt the objectives of the pressure groups. In our area of interest, the pervading forces are currently demanding cost-efficiency in a more or less explicit form. The *pursuit* of cost-minimisation is probably not an unreasonable assumption, although its *attainment* will be constrained in a number of ways, for example by trade union restrictive practices.

These are the principal criticisms of cost function analysis. The technique of cost function estimation is based on generally reasonable assumptions, despite differences between the production of welfare and more conventional production processes. Methodological inadequacies pointed out by previous authors are not peculiar to the cost function approach itself, but would have to be faced in most such studies. In the comparison of cost differences the cost function remains the most appropriate, valid and useful technique to adopt.

Uses and policy implications

(1)   *Proper context.* The primary purpose of a cost function, it could be argued, is to ensure that costs are viewed in a proper context; that is, costs are compared only after the influences of extraneous factors have been taken into account. That is, it is wrong to talk of *the* cost of care without regard to the factors associated with it or predictive of it. This is crucial, for example, if we are to counter the wholly inadequate remarks often made about inter-authority differences. In the PSSRU survey of local authority old people's homes in eleven areas, *actual* average cost per resident week ranged from approximately £72 in County K to £106 in London borough B, but we can see from the estimated cost function (Table 9.2) that many factors beyond the immediate or even long-term control of authorities have significant cost-raising effects. If we then calculate the *predicted* costs for these two authorities we find them to be £76 and £105 respectively, that is the differences between them are almost entirely accounted for by the factors in our cost function. The

remaining differences (the residuals) may then be attributed to different accounting conventions (although these should be minimal given the standardisation of local authority accounting procedures), to differences in omitted variables such as final output, and to variations in efficiency. The actual and predicted (or standardised) costs are presented in Table 9.3.

The figures in Table 9.3 indicate that there is still a fair amount of variation in average operating cost even after standardising for the factors in our cost function. Does this residual variation in cost reflect a variation between homes in the quality of care? Definitions of quality of care are replete with difficulties. The approach adopted in this study was to define seven indicators corresponding to the social environment dimensions most frequently distinguished in the gerontology and social work literatures as important influences on resident quality of life (Davies and Knapp, 1981, pp. 132–46). High values on each dimension indicate a 'better' social environment in the sense that the features of residential care that they represent have been found or argued to be associated with good resident quality of life. The relationships between these social environment measures and average operating cost were then examined through multiple regres-

TABLE 9.3 *Inter-authority differences in actual, predicted and residual operating costs*

Local Authority	Average Operating Cost per Resident Week*		
	Actual	*Predicted†*	*Residual‡*
London Borough A	96.48	94.43	+ 2.05
London Borough B	105.70	105.23	+ 0.47
London Borough D	93.38	94.23	− 0.85
Metropolitan District E	89.07	81.03	+ 8.04
Metropolitan District F	78.26	83.50	− 5.24
Metropolitan District G	78.51	76.47	+ 2.04
Metropolitan District H	91.55	89.90	+ 1.65
Non-Metropolitan County I	82.42	82.65	− 0.23
Non-Metropolitan County J	84.70	85.68	− 0.98
Non-Metropolitan County K	71.83	75.51	− 3.68
Non-Metropolitan County L	81.02	81.15	− 0.13
All Authorities	83.46	83.46	0

* Average cost per resident week in local authority homes in the area, averaged to give an authority figure.
† As predicted by the cost function reported in Table 9.2.
‡ Actual average cost *minus* predicted average cost.

sion analysis. The results, summarised in Table 9.4 suggest that higher-than-expected average costs are *not* related to higher-than-average scores on the social environment or 'quality of care' indicators. (The seven indicators together 'explain' only 8 per cent of the residual variation in average operating cost.) That is, subject to all the caveats mentioned here, it appears that high costs are *not* associated with high quality care. This important conclusion should be a springboard for the continuing examination of the costs of residential care (Darton and Knapp, 1984). This does not necessarily imply that additional expenditure on residential care will not generate better quality of care. It *does* emphasise that intermediate output indicators (such as quality of care) which have not been validated against final output measures provide a poor and possibly dangerous basis for policy argument.

Standardised cost figures are useful for a number of other purposes. They are currently employed in the calculation of ter-

TABLE 9.4   *The effects of social environment indicators on average cost*

Social environment dimensions	mean values	Effect on average cost per resident week†	
		Actual	Residual§
(Constant term)		103.65**	0.40
Regime	0.31	9.79	2.25
Motor control	0.98	−30.66**	−5.86
Privacy	0.32	4.35	4.93
Participation	0.56	3.31	−1.77
Interaction	0.78	−6.80	−0.96
Homogeneity	0.16	23.26	−8.10
Continuity	0.94	4.00	5.57*
F-value for equation		3.88**	2.57*
R^2		0.12	0.08

Significance levels: * $0.01 \leqslant p < 0.05$ ** $p < 0.01$

$n = 213$ for all three regressions

Regression of each of three average cost indicators on the seven dimensions of social environment.
 † Dependent variable is actual (observed) average operating cost.
 § Dependent variable is actual average operating cost minus predicted average operating cost.

ritorial need indicators. The cost estimates used by Bebbington and Davies (1980) in this way could, for example, now be up-dated and improved using the cost function described earlier. Another important application of standardised costs is in the examination of inter-sectoral differences, as described in the next chapter.

(2) *Economies of scale.* The relationship between average cost and the level of output or scale of activity indicates the presence or otherwise of economies and diseconomies of scale and so, other things being equal, the cost-minimising size of a facility. Our estimated cost function makes the important distinction between homes designed on the group living principle and others.[11] For both types of home average cost displays a distinct U-shape when plotted against scale. Costs are minimised (other things being equal) at a scale of 68 beds for homes designed on the group-living principles and at the smaller scale of 58 beds for other homes, although average costs do not vary a great deal over a fairly wide medium-size range (see Figure 9.1). In the sample of homes used for our analysis, average scale was 45 beds in group design homes and 46 in the remainder. The conclusion that average costs display a U-shape when plotted against

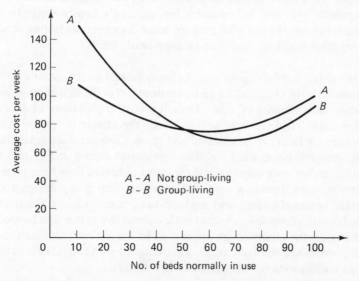

FIGURE 9.1 *Plot of predicted average cost per resident week by home size by group-living category*

scale has been a common feature of nearly all cost function studies of old people's homes (Knapp, 1981, pp. 211–13). Interestingly, previous claims that small homes were *not* more expensive to run than medium-size homes (Rowntree, 1947) and that medium-size homes were no cheaper than large homes (Wager, 1972; Thomas *et al.*, 1979) are actually inconsistent with the evidence presented by these claimants themselves.[12]

The weight of empirical evidence in this particular area, therefore, makes it clear that medium-size homes are the cheapest to run (in the public sector at least) and our discussion of fixed and variable costs in Chapter 4 would suggest that the larger a home the lower the average *capital* cost per place. Of course, there are other factors to take into consideration before the 'optimal' size of a residential home can be decided, although to date the evidence on the advantages and disadvantages of large scale is equivocal (Davies and Knapp, 1981, pp. 90–2; Weihl, 1981).

Cost function studies for other services have not been able to examine the effects of scale with as comprehensive an information set as has been possible for old people's homes. Lee and Martin (1979) found L-shaped average operating and capital cost schedules for the meals on wheels service in Leeds, whilst the limited amount of currently available information for children's homes suggests a similar shape, though with perhaps some diseconomies setting in at very large scales of operation (Knapp *et al.*, 1979).

(3) *Other cost-raising factors.* A closely related policy use of a cost function is the examination and quantification of the influences of all other determinants of cost. Thus the cost implications of more dependent residents can be identified, the effects of prices and occupancy rates can be assessed and so on. Consider once again the old people's home example. The cost curves drawn in Figure 9.1 indicate that once other variable features of homes have been taken into account there is a small difference between group design and other homes. In small and medium-sized homes (below about 50 beds), non-group design homes are less expensive to run, and beyond that scale the group design appears to be the cheaper, although the differences are relatively small. This, coupled with capital cost data, has implications for the design of new homes.

We also examined the association between cost and dependency. For our purposes we first examined the fourfold dependency classification developed by the DHSS in their analysis of the 1970 Census. This has been used and defined before (Davies and Knapp, 1978). We also examined the proportions of residents exhibiting behavioural difficulties and showing symptoms of depression. Neither had any effect on cost. The impact of dependency on cost is illustrated in Figure 9.2. Two features of the cost-dependency relationship which emphasise the need for further investigation are the relative costs of the minimal and limited dependency groups, and the shape of the heavy and appreciable dependency curve. It should be noted that only 5 per cent of the homes in the sample had more than 70 beds, so that the apparently lower cost associated with heavy dependency in very large homes is of limited relevance.

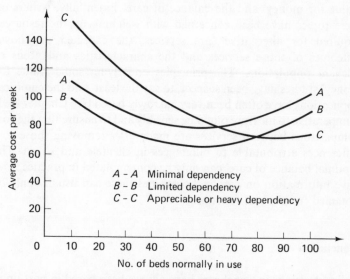

FIGURE 9.2 *Plot of predicted average cost per resident week by home size by dependency category*

(4) *Joint costs.* The estimated cost function is the *only* feasible and reliable technique available for allocating joint costs between two or more outputs, activities or services. Multiple and joint outputs are the norm rather than the exception in social care, and multi-purpose facilities are becoming increasingly common. The identification of the costs associated with the different dependency groups is a joint

cost analysis of this type. There is also the range of within-home and external services provided by children's homes which need to be individually costed for comprehensive policy-making.

(5)   *Cost inflation.* If costs vary consistently and predictably with variations in, say, the dependency characteristics of clients or the scale of facilities, then an estimated cost function will help both to explain past cost inflation and to predict likely future costs. The trend towards a more dependent population of old people's homes has often been observed in local surveys, and in a comparison of the 1981 PSSRU survey with the DHSS 1970 census of residential establishments (Bebbington and Tong, 1983; Darton, 1984).

(6)   *The balance of care.* Much has been written recently about 'value for money' and the balance of care. Essentially, writers on these topics have been concerned with weighing up the resources required for alternative care services, the expected or known outcomes of those services and the characteristics and needs of relevant populations. The principles underlying some 'value for money' studies have been suspect, to say the least, and the empirical applications have often been very narrowly based (see Chapter 8). It is imperative to measure outcome sensibly and to ensure that the cost comparisons between services are made *after* removing those cost differences attributable to differences in clientele and so on. The 'optimal balance of care' can only be contemplated in practice if we have information on *marginal* costs and these can usually only be obtained from a cost function.

Conclusion

Policy decisions in social care have always been based in part upon perceived costs and available cost information. Recently, the importance of costs in these decision-making processes has grown. Shortages of care resources have inevitably heightened concern about cost variations between services, agencies and care units. It is these variations which provide the basis for cost function examinations. As we have seen, these in turn provide a number of policy guidelines, suggestions and prescriptions. In the next chapter, the cost function technique is employed to guide the examination of inter-sectoral differences.

10

Inter-Sectoral Cost Comparisons: An Application of the Cost Function Technique

The mixed economy of welfare

One important characteristic of the search for 'value for money' or efficiency in social care has been a more purposive consideration of the contribution to be made by the private and voluntary sectors. Despite the tremendous recent impetus given to 'privatisation' in social care and in many other areas, there is actually very little evidence on the relative merits of the different sectors. In this chapter the technique of cost function analysis will be used to examine the cost differential between public, voluntary and private care services.

Judge (1982a) has provided a crude but useful 'classificatory framework of the mixed economy of welfare'. This framework distinguishes the mode of finance (public, private-collective, private-personal or 'no exchange') from the mode of production (public, private, voluntary or informal). Cross-classifying these two dimensions produces a framework for describing the broad variety of arrangements for the production and finance of social care. Local authority personal social services are both produced and financed by the public sector, whereas one of the clear aims of the Conservative governments of 1979 and 1983 was to increase the amount of 'informal care involving no financial exchange' (Judge, 1982a, p. 15). Whether they have been successful in this respect is open to debate, but certainly there have been very noticeable changes in the relative scale of other non-public activities. There have, for example, been considerable changes in charging policies. Local authorities have introduced or raised consumer charges for a number of services, and there have been changes in attitude towards the 'contracting-out' of care to private and voluntary agencies. Judge (1982b) argues that

> there is a case to be made for using POSC [purchase of service contracting or contracting-out] as a more imaginative instrument of social policy, but to be effective it requires public agencies to take positive steps to create a framework of financial and organisational incentives so as to establish the most efficient pattern of provision within their territories (p. 397).

What justification is there for the non-public provision of services? What advantages does a mixed economy confer? A review of the North American and British policy and academic literatures identified a number of possible advantages (Judge, 1982b; Judge and Smith, 1983):

(1) *Traditional supply*. Local authorities plan and organise their own provision around the services already provided by private and voluntary organisations.

(2) *Specialised services*. Most local authorities are unable to provide the full range of services required to meet the variety of needs displayed by the population. They therefore purchase specialist care from other authorities or from non-public agencies. This is common, for example, in child care.

(3) *Flexibility and innovation*. It is widely believed that non-statutory organisations have greater flexibility and innovative capacity, although it would be wrong to view local authorities as particularly deficient in this regard (Ferlie, 1982). It is often argued that profit-oriented ('private') organisations are less responsive to the needs of the community than non-profit (voluntary or public) organisations (Gilbert, 1983, 1984).

(4) *Consumer choice and access*. The existence of alternatives to public services allows the consumer or client to exercise some choice. Certainly it could be argued that the provision of suitable care services for minority ethnic or religious groups is more likely within a mixed system.

(5) *Lower costs and better value*. It is often argued that non-public organisations or providers can produce care at lower cost or can

ensure better value for money. It is this fifth argument for a mixed economy which I want to consider here.

It would be misleading to see the recent emphasis on 'privatisation' as originating with the Conservative administrations of 1979 and 1983, for earlier Labour administrations had extolled the virtues of non-statutory services. David Ennals, Secretary of State in the previous Labour government, is quoted as arguing in 1976 that: 'Pound for pound we can buy more services through a voluntary than a statutory channel. I am ready to prove it if there are some doubts' (quoted in Leat, 1978). In the same year the DHSS (1976) wrote that 'support for voluntary effort and encouragement of self-help schemes may represent better value for money than directly provided services.' However, these *earlier* arguments for an expansion of the voluntary sector were not extended to the *private* (profit-oriented) sector; the emphasis on market-based private care has been comparatively recent. Of course, the value of voluntary provision is not recognised by all.

> The romantic fiction of efficiency and cost effectiveness . . . is as pervasive here [as in the USA]. Urban Aid and other tokens of government concern not only combine the award of miniscule amounts of money to the voluntary sector with the maximum amount of ministerial rhetoric, but also continue to promote the myth of the super-effectiveness of voluntary effort (Westland, 1981, p. 15).

Is it the case, therefore, that the efficiency argument is mere rhetoric? Certainly there appears to be little evidence to suggest that local authorities purchase services from voluntary and private agencies because they are cheaper or perceived to give better value for money (Judge, 1982b). This, of course, is not the same as arguing that voluntary and private services are *more expensive* and/or *less efficient*. What, then, are the arguments concerning inter-sectoral differences in cost and 'value for money'?

The sources of inter-sectoral differences

It has been argued that *managerial efficiency* is lower in the public sector. This relative inefficiency, the argument runs, stems from the monopoly position of the public enterprise, from a lack of both skill and motivation among management, from 'political interference, patronage, rigid civil service systems, public employee unionism' (Savas, 1977, p. 2), and from the simple fact that public enterprises are not required to maximise profits or minimise costs.[1] The result is an allocation of resources which is neither efficient nor equitable, a self-maintaining and self-satisfying organisational structure, which alienates the workforce and disregards the feelings of clients (Reid, 1972). The competitive pressures faced by private sector producers, on the other hand, force them to be efficient in their use of resources. *Inter alia*, this will mean that their costs are lower than in the public sector, but it may also mean they cut corners and provide less satisfactory care services. These caricatures do not accurately portray public and private producers in social care, although there are undoubtedly elements of truth which carefully designed research might tease out. Particular care should be taken to 'hold other things equal' before making pronouncements about the relative managerial efficiency, or more generally the relative cost-effectiveness, of different sectors. In many circumstances, for example, it is clear that public, private and voluntary care agencies are *providing different services*, either because of different sets of objectives, or because of different clienteles, or because they adopt different degrees of specialisation.

One of the most frequently cited sources of inter-sectoral differences in cost is a difference in *wage levels*. Differences in wages, pension rights and fringe benefits between the three sectors arise for a number of reasons:

(1) Private agencies are tougher in bargaining with employees because there is more pressure on them to do so. Failure could drive them out of business.

(2) Staff employed in the voluntary and private sectors are less likely to be unionised or organised into a tough, countervailing bargaining force. It has also been the case that voluntary organisations have often suffered shortages of money and thus been unable to match public sector wage settlements (NCCOP and Age Concern, 1977; Townsend, 1962, p. 175).

(3) Staff employed by voluntary organisations may be more highly motivated. Hatch and Mocroft (1979), for example, felt that the most important reason for inter-sectoral cost differences was

'the greater commitment that a voluntary organisation can in some circumstances elicit from its staff, and their consequent willingness to work harder and/or for less money than the equivalent staff in a statutory organisation' (p. 404). This obviously raises some important questions regarding the long run supply response of such highly motivated individuals, as we saw in Chapter 6 above. A similar cost-advantage is likely to result from the intensive proprietorial involvement in small *private* care organisations.[2] Once again, however, this cost advantage may not continue for long, as proprietors may later reduce their personal and family inputs into care. It is the *long-run* marginal cost of care which is of most relevance for policy.

(4) The aggregate wage bill will be lower because voluntary organisations are able to make more use of (unpaid) volunteers. This could mean that (paid) professional staff can concentrate their efforts elsewhere, 'thus either providing a qualitatively or quantitatively better professional service (at the same cost) or providing the same service with fewer professionals (at less cost)' (Leat, 1978, p. 10).

A corollary of the differences in wage levels is the argument that public care services have much *higher staff-client ratios*. In part this will undoubtedly reflect differences in clientele or the nature of care. For example, voluntary old people's homes have lower staff-client ratios than their local authority counterparts, but the dependency of residents is also significantly lower. In fact these observed ratios exaggerate the real differences between sectors, for staff in the voluntary sector often work much longer hours, thus pushing up the *effective* ratio. It must also be said that higher staff numbers in the public sector may well mean a higher quality of care and therefore a higher level of final output. This argument has often been used in discussions of the growth of private residential care services for the elderly. It is argued that staffing levels in the private sector are lower and (particularly) that night cover is unsatisfactory (Clough, 1983), although the evidence to date is ambiguous (Judge, 1983b).

Private and voluntary organisations have a smaller bureaucracy to carry and thus have *fewer overheads*. This may reflect a degree of managerial inefficiency on the part of the public sector, but it may also reflect the fact that local authorities are obliged, by convention or law, to provide supporting services for these organisations, to supervise their activities, and to develop effective channels of communication and co-ordination. Private and voluntary organisations *are* organised differently and this *can* mean different costs and outcomes. However, this could mean that non-public services are actually more and not less expensive: 'the price of organised flexibility . . . is inevitably higher than the price of routinised programmes' (Morris, 1982, p. 340). Furthermore, the limited amount of research evidence currently available suggests that as non-public agencies expand, they lose some of the cost advantage that accompanies flexibility and informality (see below pp. 204–8).

A further important reason for the *apparent* cost advantage enjoyed by care agencies in the non-statutory sector is the simple fact that they are not always fully compensated for the expenses they incur. Local authority decision-makers will compare the costs of their own services with the fees charged for equivalent services provided by other organisations, including other authorities. The fees charged by private (profit-oriented) care agencies will normally cover costs, although the treatment of capital expenditure by, for example, proprietors of residential homes often appears to underestimate the real value of property. Voluntary organisations, on the other hand, will often charge fees to local authorities which are below expenditure (and probably well below opportunity cost). This is partly because of the agreement between them and the local authority associations as to the form of reimbursement,[3] partly because they are able to subsidise care from charitable donations, and partly because they can often stimulate supplementary care almost as a form of 'multiplier effect' (Judge, 1982b; Terrell, 1976). Once again, whether such an advantage is sustainable in the long run is an important policy question.

The final argument for believing that voluntary care services are cheaper than their local authority equivalents is because government statistics say so! Gladstone (1979) quotes figures prepared by the DHSS in 1977 of £81 per week in statutory community homes and £47 per week in registered voluntary homes, concluding that 'it costs less to provide a high standard voluntary service than a comparable service in the statutory sector' (p. 19). These figures and others like them, prepared annually by the DHSS for Parliament, are inadequate in a number of respects (see Knapp, 1983b), yet Gladstone's conclusion is quoted with approval by Holman (1981). In this way social policy mythologies are established. Even if voluntary and private sector care services are cheaper or more cost-effective, and in certain circumstances this seems to be the case, one should be careful not to devalue them by assuming that cost is held to be directly associated with value.

Testing inter-sectoral hypotheses

How then can we test whether these various factors do in fact influence the relative costs and relative effects of services produced in the public, voluntary and private sectors? Certainly the cost-benefit framework, emphasising as it does the full range of costs and outputs, provides an excellent basis for such an examination and should be a priority for future research. Given the difficulties of final output measurement and the need to be sure that 'like is compared with like', the *cost function* technique could be seen as a very useful partial and temporary alternative. In fact, in this as in many other contexts, the cost function methodology is a form of intermediate cost effectiveness analysis, examining the relationship between the cost of providing a service, the outputs of that service and other relevant characteristics which vary between sectors. To date there have been no inter-sectoral comparisons of the final outputs of care in the British context, but there have been some interesting and indicative cost function studies. There have been a few comparative studies of *intermediate* outputs between sectors. For example, Carter (1981) looked at day care services for a variety of client groups in the public and voluntary sectors. Townsend's (1962) monumental study of old people's homes provided some comparative material on private, voluntary and local authority services. Only the censuses of 1969–71 (all three sectors in Scotland in 1969, public and voluntary in England and Wales in 1970, and private in 1971)[4] and the PSSRU survey of 1981 (all three sectors, twelve areas of England and Wales) have been able to shed further light on these inter-sectoral differences, and only the last of these included a cost collection.

The cost function methodology combines the causal production function with the tautological cost equation. All of the hypothesised sources of inter-sectoral cost differences distinguished in the literature and discussed in the previous section relate to one or other or these two relationships. They can therefore be examined with a suitably specified empirical cost function, as illustrated in Figure

10.1. The figure, and thus the cost function methodology, have three implications for studies of inter-sectoral differences in cost, cost effectiveness or efficiency. We must first be sure that costs are defined sensibly and consistently. Some of the overhead or bureaucracy costs of the public sector may be incurred in order to support and supervise the non-statutory sectors. Some of the internalised costs of one sector may be external to another. For example, child psychiatry may be provided and costed within a local authority home, but also provided as a publicly-funded resource in a voluntary home. In some circumstances it will be sensible to compare public sector costs with private and voluntary sector *charges*. In other circumstances it will be more sensible to compare them with private and voluntary sector *costs* in order to avoid difficulties concerning charitable contributions and cost-price mark-ups. The second implication of Figure 10.1 is the need to standardise observed cost differences for differences in input prices, outputs and other factors. In most circumstances we would want only to standardise for those factors beyond the control of producers, but the exogeneity of cost-raising factors is crucially dependent upon the time-reference of the study. The third point is to use suitable estimation techniques, particularly when trying to isolate differences in managerial efficiency.[5]

Generally, cost comparisons between the voluntary, private and statutory sectors have either taken inadequate account of factors known to be associated with differences in cost or have erroneously included staffing levels or ratios as explanations of these differences. Gladstone (1979), as we have seen, merely compared crude average cost figures, without any attempted standardisation or adjustment for differences in provision and care. Hatch and Mocroft (1979) did attempt some standardisation of costs for the various services examined in furthering the work they originally started for the Wolfenden Committee. These services included children's homes, hostels for single people, meals on wheels, and women's refuges. The inter-sectoral comparisons for the last two services were merely hypothetical and therefore of doubtful utility. They attributed the 'cost advantages' of voluntary organisations to a number of factors, principally lower overheads, meeting needs 'in a way that is intrinsically less expensive' and through the greater commitment elicited from staff. However, their standardisation of costs is inadequate and 'explains' cost variations in circular fashion by including staffing levels among the regressors. Despite the many

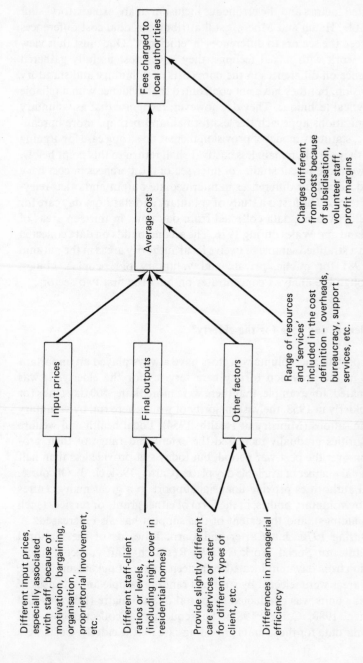

Figure 10.1 *The sources of inter-sectoral cost differences*

Fees charged to
local authorities

Charges different
from costs because
of subsidisation,
volunteer staff,
profit margins

Average cost

Range of resources
and 'services'
included in the cost
definition – overheads,
bureaucracy, support
services, etc.

Input prices

Final outputs

Other factors

Different input prices,
especially associated
with staff, because of
motivation, bargaining,
organisation,
proprietorial involvement,
etc.

Different staff-client
ratios or levels,
(including night cover in
residential homes)

Provide slightly different
care services or cater
for different types of
client, etc.

Differences in managerial
efficiency

omitted factors and the erroneous inclusion of an 'explanatory' staff variable, Hatch and Mocroft still attribute residual cost differences between the sectors to differences in 'efficiency'. One must thus view their work with mixed feelings: they have most usefully gathered evidence on differences in the bare costs of voluntary and statutory provision, but they have not confronted that evidence with a reliable analytical technique. They do, however, recognise that as voluntary organisations approach the less formal, and perhaps more bureaucratic, statutory model of provision there is no strong case for arguing that they should remain less costly. I shall return to this point below.

Two more recent studies of inter-sectoral differences in cost have standardised for differences in intermediate output and other relevant factors. The first is a study of voluntary and statutory day care for the elderly using data collected from day units in thirteen areas of England and Wales during 1976. The second builds on data collected from a stratified sample of twelve local authority areas in the autumn of 1981 for public, private and voluntary old people's homes, although the analysis concentrates on only the first two sectors.

Evidence: day care for the elderly[6]

The private and voluntary sectors have always played an important part in the provision of day care services for the elderly. It was estimated, for example, that there were more than 3500 day clubs for the elderly in 1953, the vast majority of which were run by voluntary organisations (Ministry of Health, 1954). Local health and welfare authorities gradually increased the extent and range of their provision over the post-war period, but today still provide less than half the total number of available day places (Carter, 1981, ch. 3). Of course, local authorities provide financial support to a great many centres run by voluntary bodies, in the form of either grants or services (such as buildings), and the extent of this support has also increased.

During 1976, Jan Carter and Carol Edwards of the National Institute for Social Work (NISW) Research Unit collected information from day units located in thirteen areas of England and Wales. The areas were selected by stratified random sample and a census of all day units was conducted by postal questionnaire (Edwards and Carter, 1980; Carter, 1981). Subsequently, I collected cost and income data for those units providing care for the elderly. Costs were measured as (gross) operating costs during 1976–7, deflated by the number of daily attendances per year.[7] A number of cost functions was estimated for this sample of day units, the final selection 'explaining' 76 per cent of the observed variation in average cost. This estimated cost function is detailed in Table 10.1.

TABLE 10.1   *Estimated cost function for day centres*

The estimated cost function indicates that average cost (staff and running expenses) per daily attendance is equal to:

2.39*	
+ 6.90*	if unit run by an Area Health Authority
− 2.75	if unit run by voluntary organisation
− 0.1026	× no. of daily attendances per year (÷ 1000) for local authority units
− 0.3471*	× no. of daily attendances per year (÷ 1000) for Area Health Authority Units
+ 0.0577	× no. of daily attendances per year (÷ 1000) for voluntary units
− 0.6724	× no. of times local library visited in previous month
− 1.4709*	× o. of times parks visited in previous month
+ 0.4822*	× no. of times shops visited in previous month
+ 1.5206	× no. of times local exhibitions visited in previous month
− 6.5500*	× proportion of users completely unable to walk or only with staff assistance
+ 3.3027*	× proportion of users able to walk alone with aids or appliances
+ 2.9540	× proportion of users unable to use toilet (and incontinent) or only with staff assistance
+ 1.2123	× if day unit gives physical treatment to users

Significance levels: *p < 0.05
(All other coefficients significant at level < 0.20
$R^2 = 0.76$ Adjusted $R^2 = 0.68$
$n = 55$

SOURCE: Knapp and Missiakoulis, 'Inter-sectoral cost comparisons: day care for the elderly', *Journal of Social Policy*, 11, (1982) pp. 335–54.

The fifty-five day units for which we had sufficient information to estimate the cost function were owned or run by local authority social services departments (twenty units), area health authorities (twenty-four units) or voluntary organisations (eleven units). The average operating cost per daily attendance in these units in 1976/7 ranged from £1.16 for voluntary units to £2.29 for local authority centres and £7.53 for those units run by the health service. At first glance, therefore, day services for elderly people provided by the non-public sector are much cheaper than publicly provided services. However, lower costs do not necessarily translate into greater cost-effectiveness and I have already argued that the bare comparison of costs in this way is unsatisfactory.

Differences in the costs of services may be explained by a combination of factors. Final output information was not available, but it was possible to use other pieces of information which, as the estimated cost function testifies, go some way to accounting for differences in cost. The data suggested significant differences between sectors in the activities provided for users, including the provision or otherwise of physical treatment which in part may be attributed to differences in the aims of day care as perceived by staff, and differences in physical design. Some of the indicators of differences in activities entered our cost function. Another group of explanatory factors in the cost function concerns the dependency of users, and again there are inter-sectoral differences evident from the national data collection (Carter, 1981). Finally, interview data from the subsample of twenty-two units suggested the interesting, though tentative, conclusion that voluntary units were not so well appreciated by users as were local authority units (Edwards *et al.*, 1980). These differences emphasise the importance of standardising the bare cost figures before making pronouncements about the relative cheapness or cost-effectiveness of voluntary as against statutory services.

The estimated cost function reveals how the costs of day care vary systematically and significantly with the dependency characteristics of users, the activities of units and the attendance levels.[8] These significant factors go some way to explaining why the costs of care vary between sectors. If we now partially standardise the bare average cost figures for the observed differences in dependency and activities, effectively removing their influences on inter-sectoral cost differences, we can plot average cost against the attendance level. This produces an interesting result. Whilst day care in voluntary units is often cheaper than care in local authority units this is by no means the case for all sizes of day unit. Once the influences of user dependency and unit activities and treatment have been removed, it would appear that units with an annual attendance in excess of 18 800 (or 360 per week) were more cheaply run by local authorities than by voluntary organisations. However, before this result is viewed or quoted out of context, it should be noted that the cost differential between local authority and voluntary units partly or wholly disappears if account is taken of the prediction errors inherent in the approach.

The 95 per cent confidence regions around the adjusted cost functions for voluntary and local authority units are plotted in Figure 10.1. It can be seen that these confidence regions overlap for much of the observed range of attendances.[9] In other words, whilst voluntary

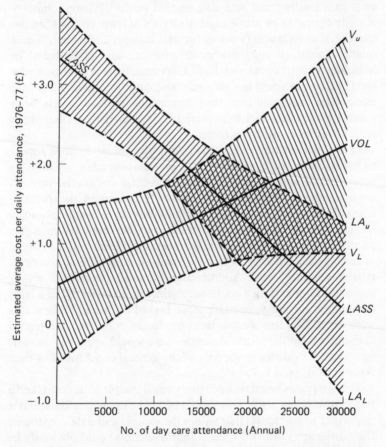

FIGURE 10.2 *Confidence or prediction limits for estimated cost-attendance relationships for voluntary and local authority day units (95% limits)*

SOURCE: M. R. J. Knapp, and S. Missiakoulis (1982) 'Inter-sectoral cost comparisons; day care for the elderly', *Journal of Social Policy*, 11, pp. 335–54. Reproduced with the kind permission of Cambridge University Press.

care is '*on average*' more expensive than local authority care when provided in larger day units, this difference could possibly be due to errors of prediction. However, it is also as well to emphasise that it is unlikely that voluntary day care in these larger units is actually cheaper than local authority care. It is probably the case that large voluntary units are no more successful than large local authority units in attracting and retaining unpaid staff.[10] Where voluntary units do appear to be providing day services at lower cost is when the number of attendances (a proxy for unit scale) is fairly small. These smaller voluntary units are more informal, and often based in community centres or church halls. Of course, there is no reason why local authorities could not themselves attempt to organise day care alone these informal lines, but historically at least it has been voluntary agencies which have preferred this model of care and which have attracted unpaid volunteers.

These same arguments help to explain why voluntary units appear to be characterised by diseconomies of scale and statutory units by economies of scale. Economies (falling average costs) arise through the more extensive use of fixed or indivisible resources, the specialisation of caring and other tasks, the bulk-buying of resources and so on. The diseconomies of scale experienced by the voluntary units may be attributable to the more-than-proportional increase in the burden of care as scale increases, which may make it more difficult to attract reliable voluntary staff. Additionally, the available pool of willing and able volunteers may not be sufficiently great to fully staff a large day unit or one that is open for most days of the week. These points were raised in a less specific form by, for example, the Wolfenden Committee and the results described here would appear to provide quantitative evidence in support of the general conclusions of their report (1978, pp. 83, 154–6).

This study was based on a relatively small sample of day units and a less-than-ideal data set. This should be borne in mind, although it is important to emphasise that within the sample and data constraints the results are valid and robust. Improvements could obviously be achieved by collecting final output and opportunity cost data and for a larger sample of units, by attempting a more comprehensive series of standardisations, and by examining the precise ways in which voluntary agencies recruit, employ and retain volunteer staff. For the moment the results provide clear evidence to seriously question the oft-made assumption that voluntary services are universally cheaper than statutory services.

Evidence: old people's homes

The most recent figures released by the DHSS, for the year ending 31 March 1982, indicate that 11 per cent of the 117 000 residents aged 65 and over supported in residential homes by English local authorities were living in voluntary or private establishments.[11] This proportion has declined slightly from a peak of 14 per cent in 1975–6. However, over the same period there has been a high rate of growth in the proportion of residents in voluntary and private homes whose fees are met, partly or fully, by supplementary benefit payments. This helps to explain the remarkable expansion of the private residential care sector in the last decade. The number of registered private old people's home places has almost doubled in this period, with most of the growth having taken place since 1976 (see Table 10.2). Over roughly the same period there have also been marked changes in the characteristics of the residents of these homes. Comparing the 20 per cent national census of homes conducted by the DHSS in 1971 with

TABLE 10.2   *Registered private old people's homes, 1968–82*

	Homes		Places		Local authority supported residents†	
Year	*Number*	*Growth*[1]	*Number*	*Growth**	*Number*	*%‡*
1968	1628		19 600			
1969	1672	2.7	21 000	7.1	—	—
1970	1706	2.0	21 700	3.3	—	—
1971	1748	2.5	22 500	3.7	—	—
1972	1808	3.4	23 600	4.4	—	—
1973	1779	−1.6	24 200	2.5	—	—
1974	1804	1.4	24 300	0.4	—	—
1975	1770	−1.9	24 600	1.2	—	—
1976	1769	−0.0	26 412	7.4	2096	1.8
1977	1869	5.7	28 126	6.5	1437	1.2
1978	1946	4.1	30 073	6.9	1877	1.6
1979	2052	5.5	31 998	6.4	2164	1.8
1980	2278	11.0	35 764	11.8	3267	2.7
1981	2519	10.6	39 253	9.8	2609	2.2
1982	2830	12.3	44 346	13.0	2178	1.9

*   Annual growth rate (percentage) from previous year.
†   Separate figures for voluntary and private homes not given prior to 1976. Figures refer to residents aged 65 and over.
‡   Residents supported in private homes as a percentage of all local authority supported residents.

SOURCE: Department of Health and Social Security statistics.

the PSSRU survey of homes in a representative sample of twelve areas in 1981 reveals some interesting changes. The average age of residents is now substantially higher, and on virtually every indicator of dependency, today's residents pose more problems for staff (see Table 10.3).

TABLE 10.3   *Private old people's homes, 1971 and 1981*

Characteristic	1971	1981
Number of homes covered by survey	362	157
Average number of places per home	12.7	16.6
Age distribution of residents		
% aged 65–74	15.6	10.1
% aged 75–84	43.7	37.1
% aged 85+	40.7	52.8
Percentage of male residents	14.0	13.8
Distribution of places in rooms		
single	35.0	40.5
double	35.0	28.5
multiple	30.0	31.0
Continence		
% residents generally continent	80.5	59.6
% residents doubly incontinent	3.9	9.9
Mobility		
% residents generally ambulant	70.2	43.5
% residents bedfast	2.2	3.0
Mental State		
% residents mentally alert	74.0	50.8
% residents severely confused	4.3	13.7
Self care		
% residents able to bath without help	36.2	20.4
% residents able to dress without help	74.0	47.7
% residents able to use WC without help	79.8	66.5
% residents able to feed without help	93.9	83.3

SOURCES: 1971 *data* collected in DHSS census (one in five sample of all private homes in England and Wales). Data coded from questionnaires and analysed at the PSSRU (see also Judge, 1984).
1981 *data* collected in PSSRU survey of old people's homes in 12 local authority areas (see text for details). See Darton (1984) and Judge (1984).

Despite the historical significance of the private and voluntary residential sectors, relatively little is known about their performance when contrasted with the statutory sector. Townsend's national study of old people's homes, conducted in 1958–9, provided a few indications of the comparative performance of the three sectors. *Inter alia*, he found higher staff-resident ratios in the private sector (but also older and more dependent residents), but few inter-sectoral differences in care practices and arrangements. One significant difference that emerged was that voluntary and private homes offered more freedom (in 'daily life') than did local authority homes (Townsend, 1962). Only with the fairly recent growth in private provision has interest in inter-sectoral comparisons re-emerged. However, it is not always recognised that the questions posed by such comparisons are not easy to answer properly.

Most of the discussion of the privatisation of residential services has combined ideology with evidence. Opposition to current trends towards a greater role for the private sector stems either from an ideological position that profits should not be made from the meeting of social care needs, or from the belief that market systems cannot operate in the interests of consumers or clients – a profit-oriented care provider 'cannot realistically place the welfare of the patient above the prospect of making a profit' (O'Brien *et al.*, 1983, p. 341; see also Gilbert, 1983, and Chapter 6 above). Arguments in support of privatisation are based either on the assumption that markets foster consumer choice or the belief that markets operate efficiently to allocate resources. On both sides there are value assumptions which cannot be 'wrong', but there is also a dearth of evidence on relative efficiency. The North American evidence is rather long on rhetoric and short on reliability, and provides no clear conclusion: 'the evidence is mixed regarding the relative advantage of either non-profit or proprietory nursing homes to provide high quality of care or low costs' (O'Brien *et al.*, 1983, p. 342).

Against this background, a study has been undertaken comparing the costs of local authority provision with charges in the private sector.[12] The comparative study is based on data collected from 218 local authority homes and 140 private homes in a stratified sample of twelve authorities. The cost function technique cannot *immediately* be employed in this comparison in the way it was used in the study of day care services. This is partly because the 'technologies' of care differ markedly between the private and public sectors so that the cost functions will be different, and partly because the dependent variables (average cost for public homes and average charge for private homes) are best modelled separately. Local authority operating costs do not include a reliable capital cost element and an estimated amount had therefore to be added on. Private home charges include a capital element (although the available evidence suggests that proprietors underestimate the cost of capital in setting charges) and, of course, a price-cost mark-up. The local authority cost function was reported in the previous chapter (see Table 9.2). The estimated charges function is detailed in Table 10.4. It should be interpreted as the conflation of a private sector cost function (which is likely to be similar but not identical to the local authority cost function) and a 'mark-up' function. The principles of the former were discussed in the previous chapter. Space does not permit a description of 'mark-up functions' here (see Hay and Morris, 1979, for a detailed account), and it would anyway not be possible to specify or estimate them separately because the necessary data are not available.

TABLE 10.4 *The estimated average charges function for private homes*

Average charge per resident per week† is equal to:

64.380**		
+ 31.372*	×	proportion of pensioners in the area with cars
+ 14.283*	×	proportion of staff with nursing qualifications
− 0.056**	×	no. of months home owned by proprietor
+ 31.317	×	proportion of residents with depression
+ 5.370*		if a home has a lift or all bedrooms on the ground floor
+ 12.865**	×	proportion of single rooms
+ 0.256*	×	no. of beds normally in use
− 51.857**	×	proportion of pensioners in the area in owner occupied households
+ 0.090**	×	average domestic rateable value in the area

Significance Levels: *0.01 ⩽ p ⩽ 0.05   **p ⩽ 0.01

F-value for equation: F = 15.88   p < 0.0001

$R^2 = 0.52$ Adjusted $R^2 = 0.49$

n = 140

† The dependent variable is a weighted average based on data about minimum and maximum charges for single and shared rooms.
SOURCE: Judge K., Knapp M. R. J. and Smith J., 'The comparative costs of public and private residential homes for the elderly', Discussion Paper 289, (PSSRU University of Kent, 1983).

It is unnecessary to describe the private sector charges function in detail, for many of the factors listed in Table 10.4 have readily interpretable effects (and see Judge, Knapp and Smith, 1983 for more details). The only resident characteristic to exert a significant influence was an indicator of depression. Private homes apparently did not alter their charges to reflect different dependency distributions in the same way as public homes. Secondly, there is a scale effect: larger homes have higher charges, probably reflecting a higher proportion of paid staff. The 'free' proprietorial input may be no smaller, but *proportionately* is less important. The higher charges may also reflect a broader range of facilities on offer in larger homes. Private homes with a high proportion of single rooms and with a lift had higher charges. This reflects both a *cost* difference, for both features are likely to raise operating and capital expenses, and a *demand* effect, since both features are attractive to residents. A similar dual interpretation can be placed on the positive effect of the proportion of staff with nursing qualifications on charges. Such staff are more expensive to employ, but may also suggest an attractive 'care environment' to prospective residents and their relatives. The longer the proprietor has owned the home, the lower the charge. This undoubtedly reflects the declining importance of capital (mortgage) costs over time, but obviously suggests that proprietors ignore the *opportunity cost* of capital. The other factors listed in Table 10.4 reflect area characteristics, and particularly 'wealth effects'.

The estimated public sector cost function and private sector charges function can now be compared. An immediate indication of the differences between sectors is provided by Figure 10.3. Both estimated functions have been standardised to remove the effects of all variables except scale, in much the same way as in the day care study. After accounting for differences in resident characteristics (which were few anyway), home design, occupancy, area factors and so on, private home charges are clearly lower than local authority costs.[13] These analyses, and the interviews conducted with proprietors of fifty homes by my colleagues,[14] suggest that this cost difference can be attributed to the long hours worked by proprietors, the low rate of return on capital, the lower wage rates (often in return for more flexible working hours), and the management of dependency in a way which is less costly. This conclusion that the private sector has a cost advantage accords with some of the North American evidence: 'facilities operated by non-profit voluntary and government organisations have higher costs than for-profit nursing homes', after allowing for 'patient mix and services offered' (Birnbaum *et al.*, 1981, p. 1097). However, both the British and North American conclusions might be hedged with caveats.

Principal among these caveats is obviously the absence of final

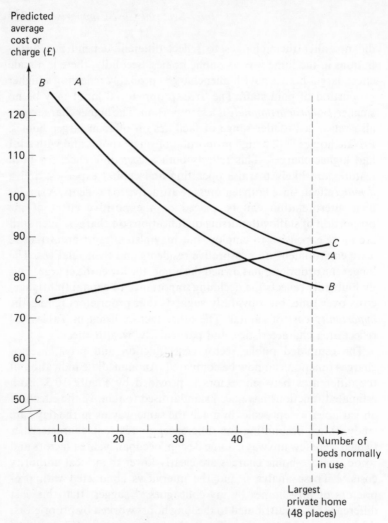

A-A: Predicted average aggregate (operating plus capital) cost per resident week in local authority homes.

B-B: Predicted average operating cost per resident week in local authority homes.

C-C Predicted average charge per resident week in private homes.

FIGURE 10.3 *Predicted average operating and aggregate costs (for local authority homes) and predicted average charges (for private homes)*

SOURCE: K. Judge, M. R. J. Knapp and J. Smith (1983) 'The comparative costs of public and private residential homes for the elderly', Discussion Paper 289, PSSRU, University of Kent, 1983.

output data. Whilst private homes may have a cost advantage, it is not yet clear whether this is at the expense of client well-being. There is a lot of anecdotal evidence from both sides of the Atlantic which suggests that quality of care is lower in profit-oriented than non-profit homes, but until quality of *life* measures are employed within a final output framework it may not be possible to reach any clear conclusion.[15] A second caveat must be that the charges currently set by private homes, many of which will have been established in just the last few years, may seriously underestimate the *long-run* charges. As homes become established it may no longer be possible for proprietors to pay low wages to care staff, nor for the proprietors themselves to contribute so much 'free' labour. Homes run by 'absentee proprietors' and chain organisations are likely to be more costly and to provide lower quality of care (Koetting, 1980; O'Brien *et al.*, 1983). This may explain why, in the face of very marked increases in resident dependency (Table 10.3), private homes hardly raised their real charges between 1971 and 1981. Average charge per week increased (in real terms) by less than 10 per cent. In local authority homes average costs rose by almost 30 per cent and yet resident dependency changed much less than in the private sector (Bebbington and Tong, 1983).

For all their blemishes, these results are the best that are currently available. One study suggests that voluntary care is cheaper than statutory care when the scale of provision is small, but that the cost advantage certainly disappears (and, in fact, may reverse) at larger levels of operation. The other study has found that private sector charges are generally lower than public sector costs. In both cases the comparisons have been made after standardising for as many inter-sectoral differences in clientele, style of operation and activities as could be measured. Together, these results (and their blemishes) suggest an urgent need for further investigation of inter-sectoral differences in the efficiency with which care is delivered.

Epilogue

Increasing fiscal pressures since the mid-1970s have forced economies on social care providers. These *economies in* social care signalled the greater acceptance of the *economics of* social care. Economic analysis will always be needed so long as there is an excess of needs over resources.

The discipline of economics, if it is applied sensibly and sensitively, can contribute to both policy-making and practice in social care. It will make its biggest and most pervasive contribution if it is integrated with other perspectives and disciplines. The *production of welfare* model, which is isomorphic to so many other approaches, appears to offer the best chance of mutually beneficial integration. However, its similarity to other approaches must not mask its particular contributions. It focuses attention on a number of fundamental issues that would otherwise be neglected. The production of welfare approach starts from a statement of objectives as a basis for defining welfare shortfalls and needs. The extent to which needs are met is the achievement of effectiveness or the production of output. Production is achieved by the suitable combination of resource inputs (staff, capital and consumables) and non-resource inputs (such as personal characteristics of clients, the social environment, and so on). Production will of course be constrained by the fixity – in the short or long run – of some of these inputs. Associated with the resource inputs are *costs*.

Because resources are scarce (and almost *always* scarce) their use in one activity necessarily means they cannot be used in any other. Their use entails an opportunity cost, defined as the benefit forgone by not using them in their best alternative uses. The production of welfare perspective is thus based on three premises:

(1) Objectives, needs and outputs are interrelated.

(2) Resource and non-resource inputs are combined to meet need, that is to produce outputs.

(3) Resources are scarce and their use therefore entails a cost.

Virtually all of the techniques of applied microeconomics could be employed in the study of social care, although only a small number have been explored to date. I have concentrated my attention on those techniques which have proved most productive (such as cost benefit, cost effectiveness, and cost function analysis) and I have focused on those social care questions which are either most amenable to economic analysis or most in need of an economic perspective. In none of these areas can economics alone provide a fully satisfactory answer, although there are clearly policy questions which require answers with an especial economic emphasis. In this category I would include questions about consumer charges and rationing, inter-authority and intra-authority cost variations, the privatisation of welfare, the responsivenes of supplies of resources to changes in price, the role of private insurance, and the pursuit of 'value for money' or efficiency. Well-researched but generally partial answers to some of these questions for some of the constituent services of the social care sector have been offered. It is clear, however, that the ratio of unanswered to answered questions is of a high order. The study of the economics of social care has barely begun.

Notes and References

Chapter 1 Introduction: Social Care and the Economist

1. This indiscerptibility of economic and social policy (and hence economic and social *well-being*) has been stressed by a great many writers. See, for example, Pinker (1979), Taylor-Gooby and Dale (1981), Walker (1982), Weale (1983, Ch. 1).
2. This series of hypotheses was subsequently published in a slightly different form in Judge, Knapp, Williams and Wright (1983, p. 188).

Chapter 2 The Production of Welfare

1. See Challis (1981), Davies and Knapp (1981), Knapp (1980a, Chapters 2 and 3), K. G. Wright (1974, 1978) for reviews of the policy and academic literatures.
2. Need is a rather slippery concept and I have not found any one discussion of it which *alone* is adequate or fully satisfactory. My colleague Bleddyn Davies has discussed need on a number of occasions (see, for example, Davies, 1976, 1977, 1982) and has developed sets of need indicators for local authority personal social services (see Bebbington and Davies, 1980, 1981, 1983a). The discussion of need in this book has benefited considerably from his work and (particularly) from his comments.
3. Strictly, it also exists when there is the potential for reducing the extent of deterioration in well-being. Need, therefore, has both a curative and preventive interpretation.
4. A slightly more complicated diagrammatic exposition of the production of welfare perspective for the special case of residential care for the elderly is given on p. 136 of Davies and Knapp (1981).

Chapter 3 Outputs

1. This also leads eventually to the issue of service sector productivity and the measurement of output for national accounts. This and other

broader issues of output measurement are discussed in Knapp (1983a). An examination of post-war trends in the 'outputs' of old people's homes is presented in Knapp (1983c).

2. Defining final output as the change in well-being is exactly the same as defining it as the change in the *shortfall* of well-being, that is the change in (reduction of) need, provided that the target level of well-being remains the same. This is discussed later in this chapter.

3. How, for example, can we compare, on the one hand, one thousand places (or residents) in children's homes and an annual turnover of 50 per cent with, on the other hand, five hundred places and a turnover of 100 per cent? How can we decide that a high level of throughput is actually desirable? What is 'good quality care' if it is not highly correlated with success in the achievement of resident-level objectives? The measurement of intermediate output is the measurement of a 'certain' number of places, a 'certain' proportion of which need to be occupied for a 'certain' length of time during which a 'certain' quality of care is to be rendered. The problem is that these numbers, proportions, lengths and qualities are neither certain nor unequivocal.

4. This is a narrow definition of externalities. I will broaden the definition and discuss them further in Chapter 6.

5. There are perhaps two situations in which trade-offs do not have to be made. The first is when there is a clear lexicographic ordering of client characteristics. For example, in the scaling of 'capacity for self care', K. G. Wright *et al.*, (1981) argued that an individual who cannot dress without help will also be unlikely to be able to walk outdoors without help or bathe without help. This will not always be true, but if it is a correct assumption for 'enough' people then it is possible to ignore the weighting of different dimensions and instead to construct a unidimensional, 'cumulative' scale of the Guttman type (see Moser and Kalton, 1971, pp. 366–73). The second situation in which trade-offs can be avoided is when two outputs are very highly correlated because they are jointly produced. In some circumstances it might be possible to make *empirical* trade-offs between the scales using, say, the techniques of multiple output production functions (Christensen *et al.*, 1973).

6. See any social statistics book for discussions of both the levels of measurement (nominal, ordinal, interval and ratio) and the concepts of validity and reliability. See, for example, Moser and Kalton (1971).

7. See also Cullis and West (1979), Culyer *et al.*, (1971), Knapp (1983a).

8. The argument that future levels of well-being are valued less highly than present levels is ultimately a testable proposition. Most of the 'tests' carried out in economic studies support it. Discounting is discussed in more detail in Chapter 7.

9. For example, reanalysis of the data collected by Goldberg (1970) demonstrated that a 35 per cent saving could have been achieved in the required sample sizes as compared with randomisation alone for some of the outcome dimensions and, on average, a 10 per cent saving (Bebbington, 1978; Bebbington, Davies and Edey, 1977).

10. See note 5 above.

11. See also Goldberg and Warburton (1979), Macdonald *et al.* (1982), the review by Goldberg and Connelly (1982) and the review of experimental studies of direct social work evaluations in the United States and Canada by Reid and Hanrahan (1981).

12. For example, see the studies by Cheyne and Jahoda (1971), Ferri (1981), Francis (1971), Tizard (1981) and Tizard and Joseph (1970). See Dinnage and Kelimer Pringle (1967a, 1967b), Prosser (1976, 1978) and Parker (1983) for partial reviews of the literature. Contrast the British experience with the North American work reviewed by Durkin and Durkin (1975).

13. See, for example, the study of illegitimacy and adoption reported by Lambert and Streather (1980) and the references therein.

Chapter 4 Costs and Inputs

1. 'All in all, cost matters are not in a happy state, so that every costing exercise tends to be a major piece of analysis, cutting against the grain of the system. Small wonder, then, that those concerned primarily with "effectiveness" rely uncritically on the "cost" data given to them by the accountants, for to do anything else would require a large intellectual endeavour for which very few of them have either the training or the inclination. Better to get on with helping the old folks as best one can' (Williams, 1977, pp. 286–7).

2. There are, in fact, no such guides published in Britain, but two fairly recent North American papers are useful in this regard (Elkin, 1980; Gross, 1980).

3. The discussion of *whose* opportunity costs by Challis and Davies (in press, chapter 10) is valuable here.

4. Alan Williams commented on this cash-consciousness thus:

    As a tribute to the probity and public responsibility of the administration it is commendable, but as a stumbling block to the perception of real resource costs it is execrable. On balance, I therefore execrate it! I do so because I believe that our cash-based, input-oriented budgetary systems have now become major obstacles to greater efficiency, instead of the vehicles by which efficiency is promoted, and this will not change until the economist's notion of opportunity cost (in real resource terms) becomes dominant in everyone's thinking, and a major source of control over their performance (Williams, 1977, p. 286).

    See also Williams (1978) for a discussion of the drawbacks of conventional accounting.

5. There are two complications here. There may be 'multiplier effects' – creating additional real incomes elsewhere in the local and national economy – and there may be an equilibrium level of unemployment. If the present level of unemployment is that which is necessary for 'policy optimisation', then employing an otherwise unemployed person may

create unemployment elsewhere, so that the shadow price is actually the salary that is paid.

6. For more details of these costs see Anderson (1976), Gray (1979) and Knapp (1983a).

7. Costs per *sentence* are obviously crucially dependent on the lengths of sentences and raise questions about the relative *outputs* of alternative treatment programmes. In the study reported here, opportunity cost per sentence was higher in the intermediate treatment programme than in a detention centre.

8. An example of the practical differences between long-run and short-run costs in the case of residential care of the elderly is provided by Davies and Knapp (1978, especially pp. 13–17).

9. See any microeconomics textbook for details; for example, Laidler (1981, pp. 141–5).

10. See, for example, Booth (1979), Ferlie and Judge (1981), Glenne.ster (1980), Judge (1978), M. Wright (1980).

Chapter 5   Efficiency in Social Care

1. Equity can either be justified as a moral imperative (e.g., Tawney, 1931) or deduced as the outcome of a process of rational thought (e.g., Rawls 1972).

2. Three years earlier, Culyer (1977, p. 148) had argued that *today*, 'as far as the economist is concerned, the arrangements chosen may be efficient and just, or inefficient and just, or efficient but unjust, or both inefficient and unjust, but they cannot be merely efficient or inefficient'.

3. Clearly these alternatives have important implications for 'territorial justice'. See Chapter 2 n. 2 for references.

4. Space does not allow me to say very much about these principles. See Davies (1968), Harvey (1973), Runciman (1972) and Weale (1978, 1983).

5. For some reservations on Rawlsian and other contractarian principles see Culyer (1976, pp. 82–3). Jones *et al.*, (1983, Chapter 1) McPherson (1977) and Weale (1983).

6. This number is doubled if we make the distinction between those efficiency measures which focus on *intermediate* outputs (the production, for example, of as much service from given resources) and those which focus on *final* outputs (the maximisation of the benefit to clients and other affected parties in given (resource) circumstances).

7. Effectiveness therefore is the same as a 'positive marginal product', in the economist's terminology, and productivity could alternatively be termed the 'average product'.

8. For further descriptions of total and marginal benefit or value schedules, see Culyer (1980, Chapter 1), Gordon (1982, Chapter 8). Williams and Anderson (1975, Chapter 5).

9. In this respect they correspond, respectively, to the preoccupations of the 'selectivists' and the 'universalists'. See Bebbington and Davies

(1983a, pp. 311–12) and Davies (1978, Chapters 1 and 6). These concepts are, of course, not the same as vertical and horizontal *equity*.

Chapter 6   Social Care and the Market

1. Useful discussions of rationing are provided by Foster (1983), Hall (1974), Judge (1978), Parker (1976, 1980), Prottas (1981), Rees (1972).
2. Some authors have argued that time prices provide a more equitable basis for allocation than do money prices (Nichols *et al.*, 1971). However, the validity of this argument rests on the validity of the assumption that equity should be defined in terms of earned income, to the apparent neglect of unearned income and, more importantly, of need, and on a particular set of assumptions about inter-personal differences in the marginal utility of income. See Culyer (1976, pp. 84–5) for a brief statement of the counter-arguments.
3. Risk-aversion is equivalent to a decreasing marginal utility of wealth (Cullis and West, 1979, pp. 61–2). For a more detailed account of risk-aversion, insurance and consumer choice see Green (1971, Chapters 13 to 15).
4. For more detailed discussions of insurance markets and their problems (mainly in the context of *health* care) see Cullis and West (1979, Chapter 3), Culyer (1980, Chapter 2; 1982), Maynard (1979).
5. This is quite different from subsidising *production* in order to cover the losses which may arise from marginal cost pricing. All public social care services receive production subsidies of this kind, since for none of them do consumer charges come anywhere near covering total costs. They are financed out of central or local taxation. Voluntary care organisations often subsidise services out of charitable donations, their charges generally being made to local authorities and not to individual clients. Private care agencies cannot afford to make sizeable losses unless they are prepared to cross-subsidise loss-making activities from profits obtained elsewhere. Judge and Matthews (1980a, Chapter 4) briefly describe production and consumption subsidies.
6. Judge and Matthews (1980a, Chapter 3) discuss the purposes and origin of charges in social care using Parker's fivefold classification. The discussion below draws heavily on their research.
7. I know of no empirical estimates of the price elasticity of demand for British social care services. If the price elasticity of demand were greater than unity, a rise in price would reduce total revenue from consumer charges.
8. House of Commons Debate, *Committee Stage of the Children and Young Persons Bill*, 13 May 1969, Column 597. Quote provided by Judge and Matthews (1980a, p. 62).
9. See, for example, Kushman (1979) and Robins and Spiegelman (1978) on the demand for day nursery places, Judge *et al.* (1981) on the responsiveness of home help demands to changes in charging practices,

and Chiswick (1976) and Scanlon (1980) on the demand for nursing home care. All but the Judge *et al.* evidence relate to the USA.

10. This is the case in a great many authorities, including Birmingham (Baba, 1976), Hackney (Harbert, 1972), Wandsworth (Tilley, 1974) and Lewisham (*Social Work Today*, 22 March, 1977, p. 3).

11. The literature generated by Titmuss's proposition is large. *Inter alia*, see Collard (1978, Chapter 13) Cooper and Culyer (1968), Pinker (1979), Pruger (1973) and Uttley (1980).

12. Simon's study suggests 'a positive relationship between the level of foster-child payments and the number of foster homes offered, and that the size of the relationship is fairly substantial – an elasticity of perhaps 0.50 to 1.0. This suggests that doubling the foster-child payment level would increase the number of foster homes offered by 50 to 100 per cent' (Simon, 1975, p. 408).

13. My colleague Ewan Ferlie is currently studying the innovative potential of social care organisations. Some preliminary findings are available (see Davies and Ferlie, 1982; Ferlie, 1982). I am grateful to him for his comments and suggestions on this topic.

14. Note, however, that these various 'efficiency analyses' are not straight alternatives. They each have their own areas of optimal application, their own data requirements (spread and depth), their own statistical back-up requirements and so on.

15. See, for example Fanshel (1975) Jackson and Himatsingani (1973), McDonald *et al.* (1974) and Duncan and Curnow (1978).

Chapter 7   Cost Benefit Analysis: The Principles

1. I do not intend to discuss consumer surpluses in this book. The concept of surplus is covered in any microeconomics textbook and was usefully reviewed by Currie *et al.* (1971). The *compensating variation* measure of consumer surplus is used by Cullis and West (1979, pp. 168–70) to illustrate how this fits into the CBA framework.

2. See, for example, Mishan (1971). This and the other main school of thought (espoused particularly by Dasgupta *et al.* 1972, Little and Mirrlees, 1974, and Sugden and Williams, 1978) are clearly described by Sugden and Williams (1978, Chapter 7) and Drummond (1981, pp. 125–8).

3. The efficiency concept used here is what I previously called *Pareto optimality* (see Chapter 5). I have not used this term here so as to avoid a multiplicity of 'Pareto' terms!

4. Note that whilst market prices established under these stringent conditions will equal the social opportunity costs of the goods and services concerned, they are not value-free. They are derived from a particular distribution of resources and within a particular institutional and legal framework (Drummond, 1980).

5. In fact, strict adherence to the human capital approach would mean, among other things, support for euthanasia.

6. There are many very readable accounts of these three methods. The ones that I find particularly useful are by Cullis and West (1978, pp. 198–209), Drummond (1981, pp. 134–40), Mooney (1978a, pp. 126–35), and Mooney (1979, pp. 33–42).

7. Because the benefits of one service could be seen as the costs of another (for example, the burden of caring for an aged parent in the community), the benefit-cost ratio could alter dramatically if the particular definition selected is altered. Any ratio can be substantially (and arbitrarily) raised by reclassifying a 'cost' as a 'reduction in benefit'.

8. In addition to the criteria discussed here there are others that have been used, though more commonly in financial appraisal than in evaluations. These include the pay-back period and annual return methods. The latter produces exactly the same result as the NPV criterion, but the former is inappropriate and can lead to some inconsistent recommendations (see Pearce and Nash, 1981, Chapter 4).

9. Under the Paretian approach CBA is a technique designed to ensure economic efficiency in the allocation of resources. The simple distributional assumption that an extra one pound of income has the same value from a social welfare point of view no matter to whom it accrues has led some economists to argue that the distribution of income or wealth (or whatever), either at the start or the end of the project, is not a concern of the cost benefit analyst. It is assumed that so long as the gainers from a project *can*, in principle, compensate the losers and still be better off than before then the project will raise social welfare; there is no obligation for the gainers to compensate the losers in practice. Adherents to the decision making approach cannot really afford the luxury of such an assumption. The decision maker does not reach decisions on the basis of *potential* compensation or improvement but has to deal with *actual* compensation and improvement.

10. The discounting of output will only be possible if *cardinal* measures of output have been constructed.

11. Sugden and Williams (1978) discuss the relative merits of explicit and hidden valuations in their final chapter.

Chapter 8 Residential and Community Care of the Elderly: An Application of Cost Benefit Analysis

1. These diagrams are similar to those drawn by, for example, Mooney (1978b) and K. G. Wright *et al.* (1981), but with certain important differences described below.

2. These costs are all marginal with respect to client numbers (as conventionally defined), and not marginal with respect to changes in dependency.

3. In the North American literature see, for example, George and Bearon (1980), Kane and Kane (1981) and – in a slightly, different vein – the classic study of Tobin and Lieberman (1976).

4. In addition to these cost elements, Challis and Davies (in press) consider

a range of macro effects, including the multiplier effects of additional social security payments (and presumably other additional expenditures) on local incomes, and the impact on the Rate Support Grant. From one point of view, these are too wide-ranging to be consistent with the microeconomic principles of cost benefit analysis. Once CBA is extended in this way one also needs to take into account the impact of service development on relative prices, on the behaviour of relevant actors, and so on, and in such circumstances the usefulness of the technique is much more limited. Alternatively, these multiplier effects can be seen to be of relevance to local authorities.

5. For example, Opit (1974, p. 32) commented: 'Superficially . . .one might be tempted to assume that the cost of this service [social worker time] for patients was negligible . . . The files, however, are a testimony to time spent writing, travelling, telephoning, and talking even if little visiting is identified. Any field social workers cost a lot even if the care of the elderly has a relatively low priority in their work, so that the inability to cost satisfactorily the work of social workers is a serious deficiency.'

6. Even with an excess demand for housing there will be delays in reoccupying accommodation vacated by elderly clients who move into hospital or residential establishments, but the overall effect on costs of such discontinuities will be minimal.

7. See Challis and Davies (in press, Chapter 4), Equal Opportunities Commission (1982a, 1982b), Finch and Groves (1980), Nissel and Bonnerjea (1982, appendix 2), and Ungerson (1983).

8. See also Audit Inspectorate (1983b) on services for the mentally handicapped and District Auditors (1981) on services for children.

Chapter 9   Variations in the Costs of Care

1. Average cost per *place* would be lower than usual by virtue of the definition of occupancy as (*no. of residents*) ÷ (*no. of places*); or, equivalently, because there are lower variable costs to allocate between the fixed number of places.

2. But see the silting-up studies of Davies *et al.* (1973) and Harris (1978).

3. Preliminary findings from this survey are given in Knapp and Smith (1984).

4. Gianfrancesco (1980) looked at hospital specialisation in Maryland and its effects on occupancy rates and costs, concluding that 'potential cost savings from reducing specialisation would be significant' (p. 266).

5. The studies of nursing homes in the USA by Meiners (1982) and Danzon (1982) found that the method of reimbursement of homes from Medicare, Medicaid and so on had a significant influence on costs.

6. Simple examples of the derivation of a cost function from a production function, a cost equation and an assumption regarding optimising behaviour are provided by Wallis (1973) and by Koutsoyiannis (1979). McFadden (1978) provides a more general, rigorous and demanding proof.

7. Exclusion is easily demonstrated if the cost function is derived properly from the production function and cost equation (see note 6).
8. In fact, a later reanalysis of his data suggested that a nonlinear form fitted much better. See Davies and Knapp (1978, p. 7).
9. This research is reported in more detail in Darton and Knapp (1984). I am grateful to my colleague Robin Darton for permission to describe our joint study here.
10. If such interpretations are felt to be insufficient, frontier cost functions may be fitted. These represent a relatively new development in econometrics. The techniques are not always easy to apply, and can be computationally expensive, but have the distinct advantage of producing meaningful measures of the cost-efficiency or price-efficiency of individual producing units. Residuals from estimated frontier functions are interpreted as measures of efficiency relative to the 'best possible' cost-output relationship, with 'pure' stochastic variations included as and when desired. An excellent review of the current state of play of these frontier techniques for cost and production functions (and others) is given in the whole issue of the *Journal of Econometrics*, 12, 1980.
11. Homes were categorised as group-living homes if residents ate, slept and mainly sat separately from other groups or residents and as semi-group homes if only the bedrooms and some or all of the sitting space were arranged for groups of residents. Group-living homes were found to have a significantly different cost-scale relationship from non-group homes. We tested the hypothesis that semi-group homes also had a different such relationship but this was not supported by the data. Semi-group design homes are included among the 'others'.
12. Rowntree (1947) wrote: 'Experience has shown that quite small homes can be run at costs not appreciably higher per resident that those of well-conducted large institutions' (p. 75). However, plotting (approximate) cost per head per week against the average number of residents, using his data tabulated on p. 144, reveals that small homes *are* appreciably more expensive. Re-estimation of Wager's cost function, adding back in the three homes considered by Wager to be 'too large' for inclusion, revealed that a U-shaped average cost function fitted the data much better than his simple monotonicaly decreasing linear function. The data collected and reported by Thomas and his colleagues were also reanalysed and again average cost did *not* appear to decline continually as home size increased, the cost-minimising size of home appearing to be one with approximately 55 places.

Chapter 10   Inter-Sectoral Cost Comparisons: An Application of the Cost Function Technique

1. 'The control framework which is most successful in minimising costs and maximising profitability is that designed and exercised by people with direct economic interest in such items. Whatever are the political objectives of government, the associated control framework on public

enterprises will have been designed and will be monitored by politicians and civil servants whose major interests are unlikely to be equivalent to a direct vested economic interest in minimising costs or maximising profits' (Millward, 1982, p. 61).

2. This cost advantage does not arise, of course, with 'multiple plant', private care organisations.

3. For example, the arrangements agreed between voluntary child care organisations, the Association of Metropolitan Authorities and the Association of County Councils allow charges to cover operating costs (including some of the overheads) but not capital costs. As the average vintage of local authority children's homes has gradually increased (because of the closure of old homes and the cessation of new investment) so the relative importance of the capital (depreciation) element in local authority costs has decreased, and so voluntary provision appears to be less cheap relatively to statutory provision. This reimbursement policy is less punitive than some earlier arrangements, whereby the Home Office advised local authorities to seek a 25 per cent subsidy for each child placed in a voluntary home (Judge, 1982b).

4. The Scottish census is reported by Carstairs and Morrison (1971) and the English and Welsh public and voluntary homes' census is reported by the Department of Health and Social Security (1975). The private homes' census, conducted by the DHSS in 1971, was never reported, but a few results are given by Bebbington and Tong (1983) and Darton (1984).

5. The analyses reported below use simple regression techniques, but in some cases it might be more suitable to explore the possibility of fitting *frontier* cost-output relationships.

6. This study is reported in more detail in Knapp and Missiakoulis (1982).

7. Operating costs cover both staff costs (wages, national insurance, superannuation, training, etc.) and running expenses (maintenance, rents, provisions, laundry, medical requisites, domestic supplies and equipment, fuel, lighting, cleaning, telephone, etc.). These operating costs also included transport costs, where these were available, but the accuracy of the accounting procedures whereby, for example, the costs of running a local authority minibus are shared between day units, lunch clubs, centres for the mentally handicapped, etc., is not known.

8. We also examined the effects on costs of the occupancy rate, the proportion of long stay or permanent attenders among the users, the modes of transport employed to get users to and from the units, the extent of the use of unpaid volunteer staff, a whole host of activities provided in each unit, and some aspects of physical design. None of these effects was statistically significant.

9. The 80 per cent confidence regions overlap much less, of course, but we choose to present the 95 per cent regions out of convention and consistency. The point is simply that one must have regard for prediction errors in the estimation of causal relationships.

10. This appears to be confirmed by the data. The average weekly attendance for voluntary day units with no unpaid staff was 65 whereas

the average was 38 for units with *some* paid staff. We also found that for the full sample of day units, the correlation between the attendance and the proportion of staff unpaid was 0.063 for local authority centres (not significant, 34 centres) and −0.395 for voluntary centres (significant at 95 per cent level, 19 centres). That is, larger voluntary units have a lower proportion of unpaid staff. We also found that those voluntary day units expressing a desire for more volunteer staff (but finding themselves constrained by supply) had an average attendance level of 57 per day. Those unit heads satisfied with the amount of voluntary help were based in units with an average daily attendance of 27.

11. Judge and Smith (1983) calculated that English local authorities spent about £21 million on contracted-out residential services for the elderly in 1978–79. This is about 7 per cent of their total expenditure on this service, and about 20 per cent of total spending on all contracted-out services.

12. I undertook this study with two of my colleagues, Ken Judge and Jillian Smith. They are conducting a number of further studies of the private residential care sector. This comparative costs research is reported in more detail in Judge, Knapp and Smith (1983). Parts of this section are based on that jointly written paper and I am grateful to my colleagues for permission to use our joint work here. The voluntary sector has been neglected because of major differences between voluntary homes, on the one hand, and public and private homes, on the other. The quality of the financial information that we were able to collect in our survey was also poor for the voluntary sector.

13. Other forms of comparison were also used in the study. The local authority cost function was used to predict average costs in private homes, and the private charges function was used to predict charges in local authority homes. Both comparisons of observed with predicted dependent variables confirmed the existence of a private sector cost advantage. See Judge, Knapp and Smith (1983).

14. Their more detailed findings are reported elsewhere. See Judge (1984).

15. I argued in Chapter 3 that quality of care indicators are only really of value if they correlate with final outputs. O'Brien and his colleagues (1983) are particularly critical of the *ad hoc* quality of care variables used in much of the work on inter-sectoral differences.

Bibliography

Alchian, A. (1959) Costs and outputs, in M. Abramovitz (ed.), *The Allocation of Economic Resources* (Stanford University Press).

Anderson, R. (1976) *The Economics of Crime* (Macmillan).

Armitage, M. (1979) 'The cost of caring for the elderly', *Social Work Today*, 5 June, pp. 15–16.

Audit Inspectorate (1983a) *Social Services: Provision of Care to the Elderly* (HMSO for the Department of the Environment).

Audit Inspectorate (1983b) *Social Services: Care of Mentally Handicapped People* (HMSO for the Department of the Environment).

Avon County Council (1980) 'Admissions to homes for the elderly', mimeograph, (County of Avon Social Services Department, Bristol).

Baba, A. (1976) 'Determining an appropriate charging structure for the home help service in Birmingham', *Clearing House for Local Authority Social Services Research*, no. 2, pp. 79–104.

Baldwin, S. (1977) *Disabled Children – Counting the Costs*, Pamphlet No. 8, (The Disability Alliance).

Baldwin, S. (1981) 'The financial consequences of disablement in children', Working Paper 76.6/81, (Social Policy Research Unit, University of York).

Banks, G. T. (1979) 'Programme budgeting in the DHSS', in T. A. Booth (ed.) *Planning for Welfare* (Blackwell; also Martin Robertson).

Barclay, P. M. (Chairman, Barclay Committee) (1982) *Social Workers: Their Role and Tasks*, (Bedford Square Press).

Baumol, W. J. (1982) 'Applied fairness theory and rationing policy', *American Economic Review*, 72, pp. 639–51.

Bebbington, A. C. (1978) 'The experimental evaluation of social intervention', Discussion Paper 93, (PSSRU, University of Kent).

Bebbington, A. C. and O. B. Coles (1978) 'Priorities in job choice: a preliminary analysis of the social work trainees survey', Discussion Paper 97 (University of Kent).

Bebbington, A. C. and B. P. Davies (1980) 'Territorial need indicators: a new approach (part II)', *Journal of Social Policy*, 9, pp. 433–62.

Bebbington, A. C. and B. P. Davies (1981) 'Patterns of social service provision for the elderly', in A. M. Warnes (ed.) *Geographical Perspectives on the Elderly* (Wiley).

Bebbington, A. C. and B. P. Davies (1983a) 'Territorial need indicators: a reply', *Journal of Social Policy*, 12, pp. 246–50.

Bebbington, A. C. and B. P. Davies (1983b) 'Equity and efficiency in the allocation of the personal social services', *Journal of Social Policy*, 12, pp. 309–30.

Bebbington, A. C., B. P. Davies and O. B. Coles (1979) 'Social workers and client numbers: a research note', *British Journal of Social Work*, 9, pp. 93–100.

Bebbington, A. C., B. P. Davies and R. Edey, (1977) 'Sample size, matching and the balance of clients in the target groups of the Kent Community Care Project evaluation' (PSSRU, University of Kent).

Bebbington, A. C. and M. S. Tong (1983) 'Residential survey – preliminary needs indicator report', Discussion Paper 265 (PSSRU, University of Kent).

Birnbaum, H., C. Bishop, A. J. Lee and G. Jensen (1981) Why do nursing home costs vary? *Medical Care*, 19, pp. 1095–1107.

Black, S. and D. Gray (1983) 'Value for money in the public sector', *Arthur Young Business View*, pp. 4–9.

Blau, P. M. (1964) *Exchange and Power in Social Life* (Wiley).

Booth, T. A. (1978) 'Finding alternatives to residential care – the problem of innovation in the personal social services', *Local Government Studies*, 4, pp. 3–14.

Booth, T. A. (1979) *Planning for Welfare* (Blackwell; also Martin Robertson).

Booth, T. A. (1981) 'Some American lessons for social services researchers', *Social Services Research Group Journal*, 11, pp. 12–24.

Bradshaw, J. (1972) 'The concept of need', *New Society*, 496, pp. 640–3.

Buxbaum, C. B. (1981) 'Cost-benefit analysis: the mystique versus reality', *Social Services Review*, 55, pp. 453–71.

Carstairs, V. and N. Morrison (1971) *The Elderly in Residential Care*, (Scottish Home and Health Department, Edinburgh).

Carter, J. (1981) *Day Services for Adults* (Allen and Unwin).

Casmas, S. T. (1976) 'Inter-hospital and inter-local authority variation in patterns of provision for the mentally disordered', unpublished Ph.D. thesis, (University of Manchester Institute of Science and Technology).

Casson, M. C. (1973) 'Linear regression with error in the deflating variable', *Econometrica*, 41, pp. 751–9.

Central Policy Review Staff (1975) *A Joint Framework for Social Policies*, (HMSO).

Challis, D. J. (1981) 'The measurement of outcome in social care of the elderly', *Journal of Social Policy*, 10, pp. 179–208.

Challis, D. J. and B. P. Davies (In Press) *Matching Resources to Needs in Long Term Care*, forthcoming.

Cheyne, W. M. and G. Jahoda (1971) 'Emotional sensitivity and intelligence in children from orphanages and normal homes', *Journal of Child Psychology and Psychiatry*, 12.

Chiswick, B. (1976) 'The demand for nursing home care: an analysis of the substitution between institutional and non-institutional care', *Journal of Human Resources*, 11, pp. 295–316.

Christensen, L. R., D. W. Jorgensen and L. J. Lau (1973) 'Transcendental logarithmic production frontiers', *Review of Economics and Statistics*, 55, pp. 28–45.

Clough R. (1983) 'Staffing of residential homes', paper presented at DHSS Seminar on Residential Care, October.

Collard, D. (1978) *Altruism and Economy* (Martin Robertson).

Collison, P. and J. Kennedy (1977) 'Graduate recruits to social work – a profile', *Social and Economic Administration*, 11, pp. 117–36.

Conley, R. W. (1973) *The Economics of Mental Retardation* (John Hopkins University Press).

Cooper, M. H. and A. J. Culyer (1968) *The Price of Blood* (Institute of Economic Affairs).

Crine, A. (1983) 'Not called in to make cuts?', *Community Care*, 7 July, pp. 12–14.

Cullis, J. G. and P. A. West (1979) *The Economics of Health* (Martin Robertson).

Culyer, A. J. (1976) *Need and the National Health Service* (Martin Robertson).

Culyer, A. J. (1977) 'The quality of life and the limits of cost-benefit analysis', in L. Wingo and A. Evans (eds) *Public Economics and the Quality of Life* (John Hopkins University Press).

Culyer, A. J. (1978) 'Need, values and health status measurement', in A. J. Culyer and K. G. Wright (eds) *Economic Aspects of Health Services* (Martin Robertson).

Culyer, A. J. (1980) *The Political Economy of Social Policy* (Martin Robertson).

Culyer, A. J. (1981) 'Economics, social policy and social administration: the interplay between topics and disciplines', *Journal of Social Policy*, 10, pp. 311–29.

Culyer, A. J. (1982) 'Health services in the mixed economy', in Lord Roll (ed.) *The Mixed Economy* (Macmillan).

Culyer, A. J., R. Lavers and A. Williams (1971) 'Social indicators: health', *Social Trends*, 2, pp. 31–42.

Cumming, E. and W. E. Henry (1961) *Growing Old: The Process of Disengagement* (Basic Books, New York).

Currie, J. M., J. A. Murphy and A. Schmitz (1971) 'The concept of economic surplus and its use in economic analysis', *Economic Journal*, 81, pp. 741–99.

Cyert, R. M. and J. G. March (1963) *A Behavioural Theory of the Firm* (Prentice-Hall).

Danzon, P. M. (1982) 'Hospital 'profits': the effects of reimbursement policies', *Journal of Health Economics*, 1, pp. 29–52.

Darton, R. A. (1984) *The PSSRU Survey of Old People's Homes* (PSSRU) forthcoming.

Darton, R. A. and M. R. J. Knapp (1984) 'The cost of residential care for the elderly: the effects of dependency, design and social environment', *Ageing and Society*, 4.

Darton, R. A. and P. V. McCoy (1981) 'Survey of residential accommodation for the elderly', *Clearing House for Local Authority Social Services Research*, pp. 23–41.

Dasgupta, P., S. Marglin and A. K. Sen (1972) *Guidelines for Project Evaluation* (United Nations Industrial Development Organisation).

Davies, B. P. (1968) *Social Needs and Resources in Local Services* (Michael Joseph).

Davies, B. P. (1976) 'The measurement of needs and the allocation of grants', in Appendix 10 to *Local Government Finance* (Report of the Layfield Committee), Cmnd 6453, (HMSO).

Davies, B. P. (1977) 'Needs and outputs', in H. Heisler (ed.) *Fundamentals of Social Administration* (Macmillan).

Davies, B. P. (1978) *Universality, Selectivity and Effectiveness in Social Policy* (Heinemann).

Davies, B. P. (1982) 'Assessing the spending needs of British local authorities for social care services: a new approach and its implementation', Discussion Paper 238, PSSRU (University of Kent).

Davies, B. P., A. Barton and I. McMillan (1973) 'The silting-up of unadjustable resources and the planning of the personal social services', *Policy and Politics*, 1, pp. 341–55.

Davies, B. P. and O. B. Coles (1981) 'Towards a territorial cost function for the home help service', *Social Policy and Administration*, 15, pp. 30–40.

Davies, B. P. and E. B. Ferlie (1982) 'Efficiency promoting innovation in social care: social services departments and the elderly', *Policy and Politics*, 10, pp. 181–203.

Davies, B. P. and M. R. J. Knapp (1978) 'Hotel and dependency costs of residents in old people's homes', *Journal of Social Policy*, 7, pp. 1–22.

Davies, B. P. and M. R. J. Knapp (1981) *Old People's Homes and the Production of Welfare* (Routledge and Kegan Paul).

Dean, J. (1976) *Statistical Cost Estimation* (Indiana University Press).

DHSS (1975) *The Census of Residential Accommodation 1970* (HMSO).

DHSS (1976) *Priorities for Health and Personal Social Services in England* (HMSO).

DHSS (1981) *Growing Older*, Cmnd 8173 (HMSO).

Dinnage, R. and M. Kellmer Pringle (1967a) *Foster Home Care: Facts and Fallacies* (Longman).

Dinnage, R. and M. Kellmer Pringle (1967b) *Residential Child Care: Facts and Fallacies* (Longman).

District Auditors (1981) 'The provision of child care: a study at eight local authorities in England and Wales, Final Report' (District Auditors, Bristol).

Doherty, N. J. G. and B. C. Hicks (1977) 'Cost-effectiveness analysis and alternative health care programmes for the elderly', *Health Services Research*, 12, pp. 190–203.

Dowd, J. J. (1975) 'Ageing as exchange: a preface to theory', *Journal of Gerontology*, 30, pp. 584–94.

Drummond, M. F. (1980) *Principles of Economic Appraisal in Health Care* (Oxford University Press).

Drummond, M. F. (1981) 'Welfare economics and cost benefit analysis in health care', *Scottish Journal of Political Economy*, 28, pp. 125–45.

Duncan, I. B. and R. N. Curnow, (1978) 'Operational research in the health and social services', *Journal of the Royal Statistical Society*, 141, pp. 153–94.

Durkin, R. P. and A. B. Durkin (1975) 'Evaluating residential treatment programs for disturbed children', in M. Guttentag and F. L. Struening (eds) *Handbook of Evaluation Research*, Volume 2 (Sage).

Edwards, C. and J. Carter (1980) *The Data of Day Care*, 3 vols (National Institute for Social Work).

Edwards, C., P. Gorbach and I. Sinclair (1980) 'Day centres for the elderly: variations in type, provision and user response', *British Journal of Social Work*, 10, pp. 419–30.

Elkin, R. (1980) *A Human Services Manager's Guide to Developing Unit Costs* (Institute for Information Studies, Falls Church, Virginia).

Equal Opportunities Commission (1982a) *Who Cares for the Carers?* (EOC).

Equal Opportunities Commission (1982b) *Caring for the Elderly and Handicapped* (EOC).

Fanshel, S. (1975) 'The Welfare of the elderly: a systems analysis viewpoint', *Policy Sciences*, 6, pp. 343–57.

Feldstein, M. S. (1967) *Economic Analysis for Health Services Efficiency* (North Holland, Amsterdam).

Feldstein, M. S. (1976) 'On the theory of tax reform', *Journal of Public Economics*, 6, pp. 77–104.

Ferlie, E. B. (1982) 'A sourcebook of initiatives in the community care of the elderly', Discussion Paper 261 (PSSRU, University of Kent).

Ferlie, E. and K. Judge (1981) 'Retrenchment and Rationality in the personal social services', *Policy and Politics*, 9, pp. 311–30.

Ferri, E. (1981) 'Evaluating combined nursery centres', in E. M. Goldberg and N. Connelly (eds) *Evaluative Research in Social Care* (Heinemann).

Finch, J. and D. Groves (1980) 'Community care and the family: a case for equal opportunities?' *Journal of Social Policy*, 9, pp. 487–511.

Foster, P. (1983) *Access to Welfare* (Macmillan).

Francis, S. H. (1971) 'The effects of own-home and institution-rearing on the behavioural development of normal and mongol children', *Journal of Child Psychology and Psychiatry*, 12.

Friedman, M. and R. Friedman (1980) *Free to Choose* (Penguin).

Fry, A. (1983) 'Huge variations in cost of same services', *Community Care*, 7 July, pp. 4–5.

Fuller, M. and A. C. Bebbington (1984) 'A test of equity, based on ratios from contingency tables', Discussion Paper 278 (University of Kent).

George, L. K. and L. B. Bearon (1980) *Quality of Life in Older Persons* (Human Sciences Press, New York).

George, V. (1970) *Foster Care* (Routledge and Kegan Paul).

Gianfrancesco, F. D. (1980) 'Hospital specialisation and bed occupancy ratios', *Inquiry*, 17, pp. 260–7.

Gilbert, N. (1983) *Capitalism and the Welfare State* (Yale University Press).

Gilbert, N. (1984) 'Welfare for profit: moral, empirical and theoretical perspectives', *Journal of Social Policy*, 13, pp. 63–74.

Gillingham, R. (1980) 'Estimating the user cost of owner-occupied housing', *Monthly Labour Review*, pp. 31–5.

Gladstone, F. J. (1979) *Voluntary Action in a Changing World* (National Council for Social Service).

Glass, N. J. and D. Goldberg (1977) 'Cost-benefit analysis and the evaluation of psychiatric services', *Psychological Medicine*, 7, pp. 701–7.

Glennerster, H. (1975) *Social Services Budgets and Social Policy* (Allen and Unwin).

Glennerster, H. (1980) 'Prime cuts: public expenditure and social service planning in a hostile environment', *Policy and Politics*, 8, pp. 367–83.

Goldberg, E. M. (1970) *Helping the Aged* (Allen and Unwin).

Goldberg, E. M., J. Barnes, K. Corcoran, B. Davies, M. Davies, D. Fruin, P. Hardwood, D. Plank and N. Timms (1980) 'Directions for research in social work and the social services', *British Journal of Social Work*, 10, pp. 207–17.

Goldberg, E. M. and N. Connelly (1982) *The Effectiveness of Social Care for the Elderly* (Heinemann).

Goldberg, E. M. and R. W. Warburton (1979) *Ends and Means in Social Work* (Allen and Unwin).

Gordon, A. (1982) *Economics and Social Policy* (Martin Robertson).

Gould, F. and B. Roweth (1980) 'Public spending and social policy: the United Kingdom, 1950–77', *Journal of Social Policy*, 9, pp. 337–57.

Gray, C. M. (ed.) (1979) *The Costs of Crime* (Sage).

Green, H. A. J. (1971) *Consumer Theory* (Penguin).

Griliches, Z. (1972) 'Cost allocation in railroad regulation', *Bell Journal of Economics and Management Science*, 3, pp. 26–41.

Gross, A. M. (1980) 'Appropriate cost reporting: an indispensable link to accountability', *Administration in Social Work*, 4, pp. 31–41.

Guilleband Committee (1956) *Report of the Committee of Enquiry into the Cost of the National Health Service*, Cmd 9663 (HMSO).

Hall, A. S. (1974) *The Point of Entry* (Allen and Unwin).

Hampson, R. (1979) 'X-inefficiency, bureaucracy and social policy', mimeograph (University of Bristol).

Hanushek, E. A. (1979) 'Conceptual and empirical issues in the estimation of educational production functions', *Journal of Human Resources*, 14, pp. 351–88.

Harbert, W. B. (1972) 'A free home help service', *British Hospital Journal and Social Service Review*, 9 December, pp. 2759.

Harris, A. I. (1968) *Social Welfare for the Elderly* (HMSO).

Harris, J. M. (1978) 'Child observation and assessment centres: psychiatrists' and social workers' difficulties', *British Journal of Psychiatry*, 132, pp. 195–9.

Harvey, D. W. (1973) *Social Justice and the City* (Edward Arnold).

Hatch, S. (ed.) (1983) *Volunteers: Patterns, Meanings and Motives* (Policy Studies Institute).

Hatch, S. and I. Mocroft (1979) 'The relative costs of services provided by voluntary and statutory organisations', *Public Administration*, 57, pp. 397–405.

Havighurst, R. J. and R. Albrecht (1953) *Older People* (Longman).

Hay, D. A. and D. J. Morris (1979) *Industrial Economics: Theory and Evidence* (Oxford University Press).

Hayek, F. A. (1960) *The Constitution of Liberty* (Routledge and Kegan Paul).

Hedley, R. and A. Norman (1982) *Home Help: Key Issues in Service Provision* (Centre for Policy on Ageing).

Hellinger, F. J. (1980) 'Cost benefit analysis of health care: past applications and future prospects', *Inquiry*, 17, pp. 204–15.

Hirsch, W. Z. (1968) 'The supply of urban public services', in H. S. Perloff and L. Wingo (eds) *Issues in Urban Economics* (John Hopkins University Press).

Hirschman, A. O. (1970) *Exit, Voice and Loyalty* (Harvard University Press).

H M Treasury, *Public Expenditure to 1977–78*, Cmnd 5519 (HMSO).

Holman, B. (1981) 'The place of voluntary societies', *Community Care*, 12 November, pp. 16–18.

House of Commons Expenditure Committee (1972) *Eighth Report: Relationship of Expenditure to Needs*, HC 515 (HMSO).

Hyman, M. (1977) *The Extra Costs of Disabled Living* (The National Fund for Research into Crippling Diseases).

Hyman, M. (1980) 'The home help service: a case study in the London Borough of Redbridge', mimeograph (Redbridge Social Services Department).

Jackson, R. R. P. and C. Himatsingani (1973) 'Measurement and evaluation of health and personal social services for the elderly', in R. W. Canvin and N. G. Pearson (eds) *Needs of the Elderly for Health and Welfare Services* (University of Exeter).

Johnston, J. (1960) *Statistical Cost Analysis* (McGraw-Hill).

Jones, K., J. Brown and J. Bradshaw (1983) *Issues in Social Policy*, 2nd edn (Routledge and Kegan Paul).

Judge, K. (1978) *Rationing Social Services* (Heinemann).

Judge, K. (1979) 'Resource allocation in the welfare state: bureaucrats or prices', *Journal of Social Policy*, 8, pp. 371–82.

Judge, K. (1982a) 'Is there a crisis in the welfare state?' *International Journal of Sociology and Social Policy*, 2, pp. 1–21.

Judge, K. (1982b) 'The public purchase of social care: British confirmation of the American experience', *Policy and Politics*, 10, pp. 397–416.

Judge, K. (1983a) 'New social policies for the elderly: the role of insurance in the mixed economy of welfare', Discussion Paper 269 (PSSRU, University of Kent).

Judge, K. (1983b) 'Residential care for the elderly: purposes and resources', Discussion Paper 298 (PSSRU, University of Kent). Paper prepared for DHSS seminar on residential care, October.

Judge, K. (1984) *Caring for Profit*, forthcoming.

Judge, K., E. Ferlie and J. Smith (1981) 'Home help charges', Discussion Paper 201, PSSRU, University of Kent, (Policy Studies Institute).

Judge, K., M. Knapp and J. Smith (1983) 'The comparative costs of public and private residential homes for the elderly', Discussion Paper 289 (PSSRU, University of Kent). Paper prepared for DHSS seminar on residential care, October.

Judge, K., M. R. J. Knapp, A. Williams and K. G. Wright (1983) 'Resource implications of community care options', in DHSS, *Services for Elderly People Living in the Community* (HMSO).

Judge, K. and J. Matthews (1980a) *Charging for Social Care* (Allen and Unwin).

Judge, K. and J. Matthews (1980b) 'Pricing personal social services', in K. Judge (ed.) *Pricing the Social Services* (Macmillan).

Judge, K. and J. Smith (1983) 'Purchase of service in England', *Social Service Review*, 57, pp. 209–33.

Kakabadse, A. P. and R. Worrall (1978) 'Job satisfaction and organisational structure: a comparative study of nine social services departments', *British Journal of Social Work*, 8, pp. 51–70.

Kane, P. L. and R. A. Kane (1981) *Assessing the Elderly: A Practical Guide to Measurement* (Heath, Lexington).

Key, M., P. Hudson and J. Armstrong (1976) *Evaluation Theory and Community Work* (Young Volunteer Force, London).

Klein, R. and P. Hall (1974) *Caring for Quality in the Caring Services*, Doughty Street Paper 2 (Centre for Studies in Social Policy).

Knapp, M. R. J. (1976) 'Predicting the dimensions of life satisfaction', *Journal of Gerontology*, 31, pp. 595–604.

Knapp, M. R. J. (1977) 'The activity theory of ageing: an examination in the English context', *Gerontologist*, 17, pp. 553–9.

Knapp, M. R. J. (1978) 'Economies of scale in residential care', *International Journal of Social Economics*, 5, pp. 81–92.

Knapp, M. R. J. (1980a) 'Production relations for old people's homes', unpublished Ph.D. thesis (University of Kent).

Knapp, M. R. J. (1980b) 'Planning for balance of care of the elderly: a comment', *Scottish Journal of Political Economy*, 27, pp. 288–94.

Knapp, M. R. J. (1981) 'Cost information and residential care of the elderly', *Ageing and Society*, 1, pp. 199–228.

Knapp, M. R. J. (1983a) 'The outputs of the personal social services', Discussion Paper (PSSRU, University of Kent).

Knapp, M. R. J. (1983b) 'The resource consequences of changes in child care policy: foster care and intermediate treatment', in J. Lishman (ed.), *Research Highlights: Working with Children* (University of Aberdeen).

Knapp, M. R. J. (1983c) 'The outputs of old people's homes in the post-war period, *International Journal of Sociology and Social Policy*, 3, pp. 55–85.

Knapp, M. R. J. (1984a) 'In pursuit of the three Es', *Community Care*, June.

Knapp, M. R. J. (1984b) Review of Audit Inspectorate (1983a), *op. cit.*, in *Ageing and Society*, 4(4).

Knapp, M. R. J., D. Bryson, and J. Matthews (1982) 'Child care costs and policies', *Social Work Service*, 32, pp. 33–7.

Knapp, M. R. J., S. E. Curtis and E. Giziakis (1979) 'Observation and assessment centres for children: a national study of the costs of care', *International Journal of Social Economics*, 6, pp. 128–50.

Knapp, M. R. J., D. Goda and S. Missiakoulis (1983) 'Cost variations in Scottish adult training centres', *Local Government Studies*, 9, pp. 17–30.

Knapp, M. R. J., K. Harissis and S. Missiakoulis (1981) 'Who leaves social work? A statistical analysis', *British Journal of Social Work*, 11, pp. 421–44.

Knapp, M. R. J., K. Harissis and S. Missiakoulis (1982) 'Investigating labour turnover and wastage using the logit technique', *Journal of Occupational Psychology*, 55, pp. 129–38.

Knapp, M. R. J. and S. Missiakoulis (1982) 'Inter-sectoral cost comparisons: day care for the elderly', *Journal of Social Policy*, 11, pp. 335–54.

Knapp, M. R. J. and J. Smith (1984) 'The PSSRU national survey of children's homes: report number 2', Discussion Paper 322 (PSSRU, University of Kent).

Koetting, M. (1980) *Nursing Home Organisation and Efficiency* (Lexington).

Koutsoyiannis, A. (1979) *Modern Microeconomics*, 2nd edn (Macmillan).

Kushman, J. E. (1979) 'A three-sector model of day care center services', *Journal of Human Resources*, 14, pp. 543–62.

Laidler, D. E. W. (1981) *Introduction to Microeconomics*, 2nd edn (Philip Allan).

Lambert, L. and J. Streather (1980) *Children in Changing Families* (Macmillan).

Latto, S. (1982) 'The Coventry home help project – short report', mimeograph, (Coventry Social Services Department).

Lawton, M. P. (1972) 'The dimensions of morale', in D. Kent, R. Kastenbuam and S. Sherwood (eds) *Research, Planning and Action for the Elderly* (Behavioural Publications, New York).

Layard, R., D. Piachaud and M. Stewart (1978) *The Causes of Poverty*, Background Paper 5 to Royal Commission on the Distribution of Income and Wealth, *Lower Incomes* (HMSO).

Layfield Committee (1976) *Report of the Committee of Enquiry into Local Government Finance*, Cmnd 6453 (HMSO).

Leat, D. (1978) *Why Volunteers?* (The Volunteer Centre, London).

Lee, K. and S. Martin (1979) 'An economic analysis of the meals-on-wheels service', mimeograph (Nuffield Centre for Health Service Studies, University of Leeds).

Le Grand, J. (1982) *The Strategy of Equality* (Allen and Unwin).

Leibenstein, H. (1978) *General X-Efficiency Theory and Economic Development* (Oxford University Press).

Leibenstein, H. (1979) 'A branch of economics is missing: micro-micro theory', *Journal of Economic Literature*, 17, pp. 477–502.

Levine, A. S. (1968) 'Cost benefit analysis and social welfare program evaluation', *Social Service Review*, 42, pp. 173–83.

Lindblom, C. (1963) *The Intelligence of Democracy* (Free Press, New York).

Little, I. M. D. and J. A. Mirrlees (1974) *Project Appraisal and Planning for Developing Countries* (Heinemann).

Lutz, M. A. and K. Lux (1979) *The Challenge of Humanistic Economics* (Benjamin Cummings, Mento Park, California).

Macdonald, A. J. D., A. H. Mann, R. Jenkins, L. Richard, C. Godlove and G. Rodwell (1982) 'An attempt to determine the impact of four types of care upon the elderly in London by the study of matched pairs', *Psychological Medicine*, 12, pp. 193–200.

McDonald, A. G., G. C. Cuddeford and E. M. L. Beale (1974) 'Balance of care: some mathematical models of the National Health Service', *British Medical Bulletin*, 30, pp. 262–70.

McFadden, D. (1978) 'Cost, revenue, and profit functions', in M. Fuss and D. McFadden (eds) *Production Economics: A Dual Approach to Theory and Applications* (North-Holland, Amsterdam).

McGuire, T. G. (1981) 'Financing and demand for mental health services', *Journal of Human Resources*, 16, pp. 501–22.

McGuire, T. G. and B. A. Weisbrod (1981) 'Perspectives on the economics of mental health', *Journal of Human Resources*, 16, pp. 494–500.

McPherson, T. (1977) 'Responsibility and justice' in H. Heisler (ed.) *Foundations of Social Administration* (Macmillan).

Maslow, A. H. (1943) 'A theory of human motivation', *Psychological Review*, 50, pp. 370–96.

Maynard, A. (1979) 'Pricing, insurance and the National Health Service', *Journal of Social Policy*, 8, pp. 157–76.

Maynard, A. (1980) 'Medical care and the price mechanism', in K. Judge (ed.) *Pricing the Social Services* (Macmillan).

Meiners, M. R. (1982) 'An econometric analysis of the major determinants of nursing home costs in the United States', *Social Science and Medicine*, 16, pp. 887–98.

Millward, R. (1982) 'The comparative performance of public and private ownership', in Lord Roll (ed.) *The Mixed Economy* (Macmillan).

Ministry of Health (1949) *Annual Report for 1948–9*, Cmd 7910 (HMSO).

Ministry of Health (1954) *Annual Report for 1953*, Cmd 9321 (HMSO).

Ministry of Health (1961) *Annual Report for 1960*, Cmd 1418 (HMSO).

Mishan, E. J. (1967) 'A proposed normalisation procedure for public investment criteria', *Economic Journal*, 77, pp. 777–96.

Mishan, E. J. (1971) *Cost Benefit Analysis* (Unwin).

Mooney, G. H. (1978a) 'Human life and suffering', in D. W. Pearce (ed.) *The Valuation of Social Cost* (Allen and Unwin).

Mooney, G. H. (1978b) 'Planning for balance of care of the elderly', *Scottish Journal of Political Economy*, 25, pp. 149–64.

Mooney, G. H. (1979) 'Values in health care', in K. Lee (ed.) *Economics and Health Planning*, (Croom Helm).

Mooney, G. H., E. M. Russell and R. D. Weir (1980) *Choices for Health Care* (Macmillan).

Moroney, R. M. (1976) *The Family and the State* (Longman).

Morris, R. (1982) 'Government and voluntary agency relationships', *Social Service Review*, 56, pp. 333–45.

Moser, C. A. and G. Kalton (1971) *Survey Methods in Social Investigation* (Heinemann).

Musgrave, R. A. (1959) *The Theory of Public Finance* (McGraw Hill).

Nath, S. K. (1969) *A Reappraisal of Welfare Economics* (Routledge and Kegan Paul).

NCCOP and Age Concern (1977) *Extra Care?* (NCCOP and Age Concern).

Newhouse, J. P. (1970) 'Towards a theory of nonprofit institutions: an economic model of a hospital', *American Economic Review*, 60, pp. 64–74.

Ng, Y.–K. (1979) *Welfare Economics* (Macmillan).

Nichols, D., E. Smolensky and T. N. Tideman (1971) 'Discrimination by waiting time in merit goods', *American Economic Review*, 63, pp. 312.

Niskanen, W. A. (1971) *Bureaucracy and Representative Government* (Aldine-Athurton, Chicago).

Nissel, M. and L. Bonnerjea (1982) *Family Care of the Handicapped Elderly: Who Pays?* (Policy Studies Institute).

O'Brien, J., B. O. Saxberg and H. L. Smith (1983) 'For-profit or not-for-profit nursing homes: does it matter?', *Gerontologist*, 23, pp. 341–8.

Opit, L. J. (1974) 'Domiciliary care for the elderly sick: an assessment of the use of health and social service resources and its cost in a sample of patients from a single nursing area', mimeograph (University of Birmingham).

PA International Management Consultants (1972) 'Cost benefit analysis in social services for the City of Leicester', mimeograph.

Parker, R. A. (1966) *Decision in Child Care* (Allen and Unwin).

Parker, R. A. (1976) 'Charging for the social services', *Journal of Social Policy*, 5, pp. 359–73.

Parker, R. A. (1980) 'Policies, presumptions and prospects in charging for the social services', in K. Judge (ed.) *Pricing the Social Services* (Macmillan).

Parker, R. A. (1983) *A Forward Look at Research and the Child in Care* (SSRC).

Payne, C. (1981) 'Research and evaluation in group care', in F. Ainsworth and L. C. Fulcher (eds) *Group Care for children* (Tavistock).

Pearce, D. W. and C. A. Nash (1981) *The Social Appraisal of Projects* (Macmillan).

Personal Social Services Council (1977) *Residential Care Reviewed* (PSSC).

Philips, T. J. (1981) 'A comparative cost evaluation of alternative modes of long-term care for the aged', mimeograph report (School of Health Administration, University of New South Wales).

Pinker, R. (1979) *The Idea of Welfare* (Heinemann).

Pinniger, R. (1981) 'The estimated opportunity costs of preventive social work with children and families', *Clearing House for Local Authority Social Services Research*, pp. 55–73.

Plank, D. (1977) 'Caring for the elderly', Research Memorandum 512, GLC.

Plotnick, R. (1982) 'The concept and measurement of horizontal inequity', *Journal of Public Economics*, 17, pp. 373–91.

Pollak, W. (1976) 'Costs of alternative care settings for the elderly', in M. P. Lawton, R. J. Newcomer and T. O. Byerts (eds) *Community Planning for an Ageing Society* (McGraw Hill).

Power, M., R. Clough, P. Gibson and S. Kelly (1983) *Helping Lively Minds* (University of Bristol).

Prosser, H. (1976) *Perspectives on Residential Child Care: An Annotated Bibliography* (NFER, London).

Prosser, H. (1978) *Perspectives on Foster Care* (NFER, London).

Prottas, J. M. (1981) 'The cost of free services: organisational impediments to access to public services', *Public Administration Review*, pp. 526–34.

Pruger, R. (1973) 'Social policy: unilateral transfer or reciprocal exchange', *Journal of Social Policy*, 2, pp. 289–302.

Qureshi, H., D. Challis and B. Davies (1983) 'Motivations and rewards of helpers in the Kent Community Care Scheme', in S. Hatch (ed.) *Volunteers: Patterns, Meanings and Motives* (Policy Studies Institute).

Rawls, J. (1972) *A Theory of Justice*, (Clarendon Press).

Rees, A. M. (1972) 'Access to the personal health and welfare services', *Social and Economic Administration*, 6.

Reid, P. N. (1972) 'Reforming the social services monopoly', *Social Work*, 17, pp. 44–54.

Reid, W. J. and P. Hanrahan (1981) 'The effectiveness of social work: recent evidence', in E. M. Goldberg and N. Connelly (eds) *Evaluative Research in Social Care* (Heinemann).

Reisman, D. A (1977) *Richard Titmuss: Welfare and Society* (Heinemann).

Rivera-Batiz, F. (1981) 'The price system vs. rationing: an extension', *Bell Journal of Economics*, 12, pp. 245–8.

Robins, P. K. and R. G. Spiegelman (1978) 'An econometric model of the demand for child care', *Economic Inquiry*, 16, pp. 83–94.

Rosser, R. (1983) 'Issues of measurement in the design of health indicators: a review', in A. J. Culyer (ed.) *Health Indicators* (Martin Robertson).

Rossi, P. H. and H. E. Freeman (1982) *Evaluation: A Systematic Approach*, 2nd edn (Sage).

Rowntree, B. S. (1947) *The Nuffield Foundation Survey Committee on the Problems of Ageing and the Care of Old People* (Oxford University Press).

Runciman, W. G. (1972) *Relative Deprivation and Social Justice* (Routledge and Kegan Paul).

Savas, E. S. (1977) *Alternatives for Delivering Public Services* (Westview Press, Boulder, Colorado).

Scanlon, W. J. (1980) 'A theory of the nursing home market', *Inquiry*, 17, pp. 25-41.

Schofield, J. A. (1976) 'The economic return to preventive social work', *International Journal of Social Economics*, 3, pp. 167–78.

Seldon, A. (1977) *Charge* (Temple Smith).

Sheldon, J. H. (1948) *The Social Medicine of Old Age* (Oxford University Press).

Shenfield, B. E. (1957) *Social Policies for Old Age* (Routledge and Kegan Paul).

Shepherd, R. W. (1953) *Cost and Production Functions* (Princeton University Press).

Shyne, A. W. (1976) 'Evaluation in child welfare', *Child Welfare*, 55, pp. 5–18.

Simon, J. L. (1975) 'The effect of foster care payment levels on the number of foster children given homes', *Social Service Review*, 49, pp. 405–11.

Smith, G. (1980) *Social Need* (Routledge and Kegan Paul).

Stewart, M. (1980) 'Issues in pricing policy', in K. Judge (ed.), *Pricing the Social Services* (Macmillan).

Stigler, G. J. (1975) *The Citizen and the State* (Chicago University Press).

Stillwell, J. (1981) 'Mental health: shifting the balance of care', *Public Money*, September, pp. 31–4.

Sugden, R. (1980) 'Altruism, duty and the welfare state', in N. Timms (ed.) *Social Welfare: Why and How?* (Routledge and Kegan Paul).

Sugden, R. and A. Williams (1978) *The Principles of Practical Cost Benefit Analysis* (Oxford University Press).

Sumner, G. and R. Smith (1969) *Planning Local Authority Services for the Elderly* (Allen and Unwin).

Tawney, R. H. (1931) *Equality* (Allen and Unwin).

Taylor-Gooby, P. and J. Dale (1981) *Social Theory and Social Welfare* (Edward Arnold).

Terrell, P. (1976) *The Social Impact of Revenue Sharing* (Praeger, New York).

Thomas, N., J. Gough and H. Spencely (1979) 'An evaluation of the group unit design for old people's homes', mimeograph (Wyvern Partnership and Social Services Unit, University of Birmingham).

Tilley. T. (1974) 'Charges and means tests', *Social Work Today*, 25 July.

Titmuss, R. H. (1968) *Commitment to Welfare* (Allen and Unwin).

Titmuss, R. H. (1970) *The Gift Relationship* (Allen and Unwin).

Tizard, B. (1981) 'Relating outcome to institutional setting for young children taken into care', in E. M. Goldberg and N. Connelly (eds) *Evaluative Research in Social Care* (Heinemann).

Tizard, B. and A. Joseph (1970) 'Cognitive development of young children in residential care. A study of children aged 24 months', *Journal of Child Psychology and Psychiatry*, 11.

Tobin, S. S. and M. A. Lieberman (1976) *Last Home for the Aged* (Jossey-Bass, San Francisco).

Townsend, P. (1962) *The Last Refuge* (Routledge and Kegan Paul).

Turvey, R. (1963) 'Present value versus internal rate of return: an essay in the theory of third best', *Economic Journal*, 73, pp. 93–8.

Ungerson, C. (1983) 'Why do women care?' in J. Finch and D. Groves (eds) *A Labour of Love: Women, Work and Caring* (Routledge and Kegan Paul).

Usher, D. (1977) 'The welfare economics of the socialisation of commodities', *Journal of Public Economics*, 8, pp. 151–68.

Uttley, S. (1980) 'The welfare exchange reconsidered', *Journal of Social Policy*, pp. 187–205.

Verry, D. M. and B. P. Davies (1975) *University Costs and Outputs* (Elsevier).

Wager, R. A. (1972) *Care of the Elderly* (IMTA)

Walker, A. (1982) 'Introduction: Public expenditure, social policy and social planning', in A. Walker (ed.) *Public Expenditure and Social Policy* (Heinemann).

Wallis, K. F. (1973) *Topics in Applied Econometrics* (Gray-Mills).

Weale, A. (1978) *Equality and Social Policy* (Routledge and Kegan Paul).

Weale, A. (1983) *Political Theory and Social Policy* (Macmillan).

Webb, A. and Wistow, G. (1982a) 'The personal social services: incrementalism, expediency or systematic social planning?', in A. Walker (ed.) *Public Expenditure and Social Policy* (Heinemann).

Webb, A. and G. Wistow (1982b) 'The personal social services: trends in expenditure and provision', Working Paper in Social Administration No. 5 (Loughborough University).

Weihl, H. (1981) 'On the relationship between size of residential institutions and the well-being of residents', *Gerontologist*, 21, pp. 247–56.

Weisbrod, B. A. (1979) 'A guide to benefit cost analysis as seen through a controlled experiment in treating the mentally ill', Discussion Paper 559–79, (Institute for Research on Poverty, University of Wisconsin, Madison).

Weisbrod, B. A. (1981) 'Benefit cost analysis of a controlled experiment: treating the mentally ill', *Journal of Human Resources*, 16, pp. 523–50.

Weisbrod, B. A. and Helming, M. (1980) 'What benefit cost analysis can and cannot do: the case of treating the mentally ill', in E. W. Stromsdorfer and G. Farkas (eds), *Evaluation Studies Review Annual* (Sage).

Weiss, C. H. (1972) *Evaluation Research* (Englewood Cliffs, New Jersey).

Weitzman, M. L. (1977) 'Is the price system or rationing more effective in getting a commodity to those who need it most?', *Bell Journal of Economics*, 8, pp. 517–24.

West, P. A. (1981) 'Theoretical and practical equity in the National Health Service in England', *Social Science and Medicine*, 15C, pp. 117–22.

Westland, P. (1981) 'The year of the voluntary organisation', *Community Care*, 19 November, pp. 14–15.

Whittaker, J. K. (1979) *Caring for Troubled Children* (Jossey-Bass).

Willcocks, D. M., S. M. Peace, L. A. Kellaher with J. Ring (1982) *The residential life of old people: a study in 100 local authority old people's homes*, Vol I and II (Survey Research Unit, Polytechnic of North London).

Williams, A. (1974) 'The cost benefit approach', *British Medical Bulletin*, 30, pp. 252–6.

Williams, A. (1977) 'Measuring the quality of life of the elderly, in L. Wingo and A. Evans (eds) *Public Economics and the Quality of Life* (The John Hopkins University Press).

Williams, A. (1978) 'The budget as a (mis-) information system', in A. J. Culyer and K. G. Wright (eds) *Economic Aspects of Health Services* (Martin Robertson).

Williams, A. (1979) 'One economist's view of social medicine', *Epidemiology and Community Health*, 33, pp. 3–7.

Williams, A. and R. Anderson (1975) *Efficiency in the Social Services*, (Blackwell; also Martin Robertson).

Williamson, O. (1964) *The Economics of Discretionary Behaviour* (Prentice-Hall).

Wilson, T. and D. Wilson (1982) *The Political Economy of the Welfare State* (Allen and Unwin).

Wolfenden Committee (1978) *The Future of Voluntary Organisations* (Croom Helm).

Wright, K. G. (1974) 'Alternative measures of output of social programmes: the elderly', in A. J. Culyer (ed.) *Economic Policy and Social Goals* (Martin Robertson).

Wright, K. G. (1978) 'Output measurement in practice', in A. J. Culyer and K. G. Wright (eds) *Economic Aspects of Health Services* (Martin Robertson).

Wright, K. G., J. A. Cairns and M. C. Snell (1981) *Costing Care* (Joint Unit for Social Services Research, Sheffield).

Wright, M. (ed.) (1980) *Public Spending Decisions: Growth and Restraint in the 1970s* (Allen and Unwin).

Young, D. R. (1976) 'Provision of foster care services by voluntary agencies: toward a theory of non profit organisations', *Urban Analysis*, 3, pp. 29–59.

Index